Alleviating Poverty through
Business Strategy

Alleviating Poverty through Business Strategy

Global Case Studies in Social Entrepreneurship

Edited by

Charles Wankel

ALLEVIATING POVERTY THROUGH BUSINESS STRATEGY
Copyright © Charles Wankel, 2008.

All rights reserved.

First published in hardcover in 2008 by PALGRAVE MACMILLAN® in the United States—a division of St. Martin's Press LLC, 175 Fifth Avenue, New York, NY 10010.

Where this book is distributed in the UK, Europe and the rest of the world, this is by Palgrave Macmillan, a division of Macmillan Publishers Limited, registered in England, company number 785998, of Houndmills, Basingstoke, Hampshire RG21 6XS.

Palgrave Macmillan is the global academic imprint of the above companies and has companies and representatives throughout the world.

Palgrave® and Macmillan® are registered trademarks in the United States, the United Kingdom, Europe and other countries.

ISBN: 978–0–230–10404–4

Library of Congress Cataloging-in-Publication Data

Alleviating poverty through business strategy / edited by Charles Wankel.
    p. cm.
Includes bibliographical references and index.
ISBN 1–4039–8450–6
    1. Social entrepreneurship—Case studies. 2. Poverty—Developing countries—Case studies. 3. Poverty—Prevention. I. Wankel, Charles.

HD60.A396 2008
362.5_570684—dc22   2007030418

A catalogue record of the book is available from the British Library.

Design by Newgen Imaging Systems (P) Ltd., Chennai, India.

First PALGRAVE MACMILLAN paperback edition: April 2010

10 9 8 7 6 5 4 3 2 1

Printed in the United States of America.

Transferred to Digital Printing in 2010.

Table of Contents

Tables and Figures

Tables

Figures

Acknowledgments

I would like to acknowledge Laura, my wife, for her willingness to indulge my overextended focus on this and my other books, which enabled the success of this project. Charnsmorn "Lily" Hwang was extraordinary as the managing editor of the project with her ability to keep in contact with academics scurrying around the world and their many drafts and forms. Bret Wankel proved to be an adept editor and indexer of the volume.

Chapter One

Introduction: A Variety of Approaches to Alleviating Poverty through Business Strategy

Charles Wankel

This volume has been developed to communicate important developments in the lessening of poverty in the world's developing countries through initiatives by larger businesses and individual entrepreneurs. Expectations are currently ballooning as new possibilities are seen for using new technologies and collaborations to empower the very poor to participate in the global economy. We see surge of imagination around the world in the creation of new and successful approaches to using business strategy to alleviate poverty.

Scott Kelley, Patricia Werhane, and Laura Hartman's chapter "The End of Foreign Aid as We Know it: The Profitable Alleviation of Poverty in a Globalized Economy" defends the thesis that poverty can be alleviated, if not *eradicated*, both locally and globally, but only if we change our narratives about global free enterprise and only if we rethink our mindsets regarding how poverty issues are most effectively addressed. Their main attention is on creative, profitable practices of global corporations that reduce global poverty, identifying the ways in which commerce may contribute to poverty alleviation that can be both profitable and sustainable.

Emmanuel Raufflet, Alain Berranger, and Alam Aguilar-Platas' chapter "Innovative Business Approaches and Poverty: Toward a First Evaluation" aims to evaluate the potential contributions and shortcomings of emerging business approaches to alleviating poverty using Amartya Sen's definition and framework of development. Specifically, they evaluate: 1) the Bottom of Pyramid, 2) Social Entrepreneurship, and 3) Business and Nature Conservation approaches.

Nilay Yajnik's chapter "Information and Communication Technology for Poverty Alleviation through Education and Healthcare—The India Experience" sees poverty alleviation in developing and emerging countries is a very complex process. Parameters such as political, social, and technological are connected with economic and are also interlinked. Two of the most important issues that could help alleviate poverty in developing and emerging nations are healthcare and education. However one of the major challenges in these nations is to be able to make these affordable and accessible to people across the socioeconomic strata. Information and Communication Technology (ICT) can be used very effectively to reach out to a wide populace living in rural and semi-urban areas. Yajnik discusses various applications of information and communication technology in education and healthcare in India.

James Ritchie-Dunham's "A Collaborative-Systemic Strategy Addressing the Dynamics of Poverty in Guatemala: Converting Seeming Impossibilities into Strategic Probabilities" reports on a multiyear, ongoing project, sponsored by CARE and the Institute for Strategic Clarity, brought together Guatemalan leaders from 26 conflicting groups in business, civil society, and government, developing their first shared understanding of what causes their poverty and how to collectively address these causes. This strategy-level project incorporated collaborative appreciative inquiry and resource-based systems thinking processes. Project findings are now being implemented by Guatemalan leaders. This chapter shows the power of multi-stakeholder business strategy frameworks for developing and implementing collaborative strategy in complex societal settings.

Shelby McIntyre, Albert Bruno, and Patrick Guerra in their chapter "In Search of Sustainable Social Mission Ventures to Alleviate Poverty" discuss the Global Social Benefit Incubator (GSBI), a strategic initiative of the Center for Science Technology and Society at Santa Clara University (SCU). Its in-residence boot-camp provides an intense collaborative experience with mentoring by Silicon Valley experts in developing business models and presentation of the emerging concepts. They describe and critique its three phases: 1) pre-camp screening and selection (identifying a group of about 20 social entrepreneurs from around the world who have been coached and mentored), 2) a fortnight boot-camp at SCU that culminates in business plan presentation to a panel of Silicon Valley venture capitalists and business executives, and, 3) a follow up accelerator program via an online wiki coupled with on-the-ground support from a major consulting firm. The goal is to foster the expansion of emerging enterprises in alignment with the vision and long-term objectives of social entrepreneurs. The GSBI initiative seeks to develop a synergistic melding of the interests of NGOs, development banks, angel investors, and venture capitalists in the development cycle of social enterprises in novel stakeholder collaborations meant to be practical and sustainable with the purpose of eliminating poverty on a global basis.

Mine Eder and Özlem Öz's "Scrutinizing the Link between Poverty and Business Strategy: What Can We Learn from the Case of Shuttle Traders in Laleli, Istanbul?" examines the link between poverty and business strategy. They discuss how individual entrepreneurs can develop very new and creative business strategies spurred by their exclusion from the legally sanctioned economy. They investigate the interplay between Istanbul's garment producers and the so-called shuttle traders from Russia and other nations of the former Soviet Union. They explicate how business ties in informally organized parts of the economy are established and how trust develops there. The chapter tracks the journey of a typical textile item on its route to a shop in the informal economy in Istanbul and onward through transportation firms, government customs, and to its final destination abroad.

Lisa Jones Christensen's chapter "Alleviating Poverty Using Microfranchising Models: Case Studies and a Critque" grapples with the question of how best to alleviate poverty using "business" strategies (ACCION 2007; Yunus and Jolis, 2003). She finds the answer includes have come in the form of the concept of microfinancing, microcredit, and microfranchising, among other innovations. She focuses on microfranchising with comparative case study grounding.

Jan Hack Katz' "Using Business to Create a More Vibrant Craft Sector" discusses how globalization has created many problems for artisans, leading to displacement through a variety of mechanisms. Globalization has also created opportunities for some in the sector by providing access to new consumers. For the past five decades, governments and nongovernmental organizations (NGOs) have developed programs to maintain the sector and have had many successes. More recently, however, for-profit businesses have also entered the arena and because they face market pressures, they have innovated in ways that can significantly improve the vibrancy of the sector. Here, two case studies—one in South Africa and another in Colombia—show how that innovation has occurred.

Wolfgang Amann and Shiban Khan's chapter "Doing Well by Doing Good—Strategizing for the Bottom of the Pyramid in India" is a critical overview and analysis of the unique business strategy that Unilever India developed to increase its financial bottom line, along with the household income of the poorest nonurban Indians. It describes how Unilever mobilized women living below the poverty line to distribute its products, financed by microcredits, in remote areas. Unilever consequently gained market access in improbable areas, and the women received a rare opportunity for income generation and self-esteem. Thirteen thousand women have doubled their household income, serving 15 million people. A planned nationwide replication envisages 100,000 of such self-employed women by 2010, potentially reaching 500,000 households. This business strategy for poverty alleviation incorporates the latest strategic thinking on network strategies for growth in dynamic networks, has resulted in phenomenal success.

Madhu Viswanathan, Srinivas Sridharan, and Robin Ritchie's chapter "Marketing in Subsistence Marketplaces" discusses how management research has begun to highlight the potential for businesses to serve the Bottom of the Pyramid profitably while also alleviating poverty. Using a variety of sources including a six-year research program in subsistence marketplaces in South India, their chapter offers insight into ways that innovative marketing approaches can serve as a basis for business success in such markets. Such innovation can take place at the level of marketing strategy (e.g., marketing research, product design, pricing, and other marketing mix factors), marketing structure (decentralized, externalized), or marketing culture (values, norms, biases). They draw on their research and educational initiatives, as well as existing business examples, to illustrate the fundamental differences in approach needed for firms to succeed in subsistence marketplaces. Their findings emphasize the need to view individuals living in subsistence marketplaces as both producers and consumers and using an understanding of buyer and seller behavior to devise marketing strategies. This bottom-up approach complements existing economic and strategic perspectives, most of which are at a relatively macro-level.

Since this is a dynamic area, we see this volume as a bridge to the future. These proposals for new approaches to ambitiously reducing global poverty hopefully will inspire businesses and individuals in many nations to join in this growing movement.

References

ACCION International. 2007. Our History. http://www.accion.org/NET COMMUNITY/Page.aspx?pid=506&srcid=253 (accessed December 5, 2007).

Yunus, M. and A. Jolis. 2003. Banker to the Poor: Micro-lending and the Battle against World Poverty. New York: Perseus Books.

Chapter Two

The End of Foreign Aid as We Know It: The Profitable Alleviation of Poverty in a Globalized Economy

*Scott Kelley, Patricia H. Werhane, and
Laura P. Hartman*

The question I want to ask . . . . is, if you should want to die first of
starvation or pollution

—*(Langewiesche 2000, 48)*

How selfish soever man may be supposed, there are evidently some
principles in his nature, which interest him in the fortune of others, and
render their happiness necessary to him, though he derives nothing from
it except the pleasure of seeing it . . . . The greatest ruffian, the most
hardened violator of the laws of society, is not altogether without it

—*(Smith 1759; 1976, I.i.1.I)*

Introduction

This chapter will defend the following thesis: poverty can be alleviated,
if not *eradicated*, both locally and globally, but only if we change our
narratives about global free enterprise and only if we rethink our
mindsets regarding how poverty issues are most effectively addressed.

We will begin the chapter with an overview of the current state of
the economic landscape with particular focus on—and criticism of—
the failures of strategies employed since the middle of the last century.
There is significant fresh thinking about poverty in the post-2000
literature, yet also considerable challenging ideas. Some of these
support grand social engineering projects conducted by organizations
such as the World Bank and the International Monetary Fund; others
bring such projects into question. Many advocates defend microfinancing; others believe in the success of public-private partnerships.

We will focus on one innovative mindset of poverty-reducing initiatives: the transfer of one segment of the responsibility for global poverty from traditional international development practices to pioneering, private, for-profit organizations. Some of these are bottom-up microlending ventures; others involve public-private initiatives. Our main attention will be on creative, profitable practices of global corporations that reduce global poverty. This transfer, we will argue, can produce appropriate and effective incentives, stakeholder interest maximization, economic growth, and the potential for the reduction of both poverty and the unfulfilled needs of the abject poor.

The primary aim of this chapter is not to present a conceptual framework for *the* ideal way to alleviate poverty. Our concern is not to arrive at any single theory of economic development for poverty eradication or to assign particular roles or responsibilities to the various institutions that comprise the social whole. Our concern instead is to identify the ways in which commerce may contribute to poverty alleviation that can be both profitable and sustainable. The argument emerges from a basic assumption: commerce makes or is capable of making necessary and unique contributions to the alleviation of poverty. In fact, its sustainability derives in part from, and depends on, its profitability. While there are critiques of the Bottom of the Pyramid (BoP) arguments that we will address, it is our contention that alleviating poverty is a growth opportunity for the poor and for business.

We will exemplify the power of the for-profit model through case studies based on actual experiences. We conclude that, while for-profit sector initiatives are only one of several viable models for poverty reduction, it is one that challenges both traditional classical economic models and the view that *only* private charitable or governmental initiatives are capable of addressing poverty.

The Global Economic Pyramid

From a purely economic perspective, the world appears to form a pyramid: four of the world's 6.6 billion people live on less than $2 a day. Prahalad defines the economic pyramid in *The Fortune at the Bottom of the Pyramid: Eradicating Poverty through Profits* (2005). Following the definitions of the World Bank, Sachs uses the term "moderate poverty" to refer to those with incomes between $1 per day and $2 per day. He uses the term "extreme poverty" to refer to those with incomes of less than $1 per day (Sachs 2005, 20). We will use Prahalad's term "bottom of the pyramid" to encompass both moderate and extreme poverty. A mid-level is comprised of 1.5 to 2 billion people and, in relative terms, a small top tier of 75 million world inhabitants comprise a privileged group of elite decision makers. (See figure 2.1.) Astonishing is the imbalance when one considers that the top 1 percent of the world's population represents 40 percent of the world's total net worth while the entire bottom half of the world represents only 1.1 percent of the world's total net worth (Davies et al. 2006).

Despite the sharp economic disparity in the global economic pyramid, Tom Friedman argues that a full half of the world is experiencing economic development and extreme poverty is shrinking (Friedman 2005). Accordingly, there is strong evidence to suggest the pyramid is flattening into a diamond (*Economist* 2004). India and China are both excellent examples of this flattening, pyramid-to-diamond trend that Friedman describes (Friedman 2005). In fact, much of his evidence comes from these two countries.

Even though there is a flattening trend, one sixth of humanity is not on the economic ladder at all. In sub-Saharan Africa, extreme poverty is rising in absolute numbers and as a share of the population (Sachs 2005, 24). Beyond the $1 a day metric, extreme poverty means that households cannot meet the basic demands of survival; from hunger to

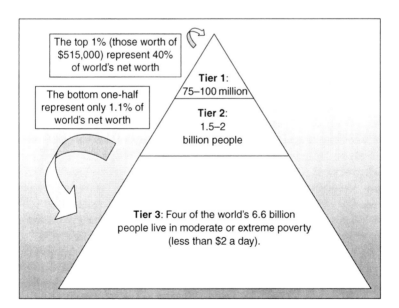

Figure 2.1 The new pyramid design change from Bottom of the Pyramid and a privileged group of elite decision makers.

education, healthcare to employment, savings to child care, one's existence is radically different at the bottom compared to the top. Malawi, for example, is a "perfect storm" of climactic disaster, impoverishment, and health concerns according to Carol Bellamy of UNICEF (Sachs 2005, 10). Malawi is not a part of the flattening trend that Friedman describes. A child born in Malawi is expected to live 39.8 years, which is a full 37 years shorter than a child born in the United States and less than half as long as a child born in Japan (United Nations Development Programme 2006). Whatever the metric, it is clear that there are regions of the world that do not enjoy the fruits of increased global prosperity.

A good deal of economic development, according to Friedman, has to do with the globalization as well as the expansion of commerce. Indeed, "[g]lobalization has now shifted into warp drive . . ." (Wright 2005). That is, free enterprise has not only infiltrated most of the corners of the earth, but jobs, ideas, goods, and services, like the Internet, are now global. If this well-documented conclusion is even partly accurate, there is no longer an "over there" there. Global organizations are embedded in a complex economic and changing set of global political, economic, and cultural networks. What we once called "externalities" are part of an interrelated, networked global system in which businesses operate. A company can no longer "outsource" environmental degradation or dumping in less developed countries (even with the permission of that country) without this action affecting the global environment and receiving media attention. This conclusion is widely understood and accepted today. But globalization also means that one cannot outsource underpaid labor, product or service quality, issues of diversity, disregard of cultural or religious differences, or even corporate social responsibilities. If, for example, the clothes we wear are made under subhuman labor conditions *as defined in the country of origin*, one cannot dismiss that as someone else's problem, even if the factory is locally owned and operated. It is ours. Moreover, cultural differences are not merely opportunity costs, even when one is operating in remote and poor regions. These differences have to do with human relationships, with cultural conflicts as well as consensus, and one cannot ignore them (Werhane 2007).

This globalization is dramatically illustrated by the ways in which regional phenomena of extreme poverty impact the rest of the pyramid. Because the world is increasingly interdependent, the problems caused by extreme poverty are no longer merely regional concerns. From Avian flu to global climate change, the world is not the static, boundless expanse it once appeared to be. There are several significant challenges that extreme poverty poses to the global economy: security, population growth, and environmental degradation. Regional economic failure often leads to state failure, which consequently poses a threat to national and economic security. The social problems emerging from failed states, such as ethnic war, genocide, terrorism, mass migration, refugee movements, drug trafficking, and disease are anything but regional. Second, the global population is expected to plateau at 9.1 billion around the year 2050 (Gore 2006, 217). Much of the population growth occurs at the base of the pyramid, since birth rates are inversely related to living standards and levels of education (Hart 2005, 32). Third, an increasingly urban population creates significant concerns regarding environmental degradation and the scarcity of resources. A sober assessment of today's interdependent global economy reveals an important lesson: extreme poverty anywhere is a threat to prosperity everywhere.

Given this bleak scenario and grounded in the *UN Universal Declaration of Human Rights*, the United Nations has proposed as one of its eight Millennium goals a 50 percent reduction in poverty by 2015 (United Nations 2007). The justification for the Declaration is that human beings have intrinsic dignity simply because they are human. Thus, as human beings we all have claims to basic rights, equal universal rights that also incur reciprocal responsibilities to respect the rights of others. So if, for example, we affirm a right to life, this claim has standing only if it is a universal declaration for which we have the responsibility to protect on behalf of others.

This Millennium goal is also grounded in utility. From a utilitarian perspective, improving well-being or, at a minimum, reducing suffering is the basic end of morality and moral action. Accordingly, it is morally wrong to refrain from undertaking projects to reduce poverty. Moreover, as we have just pointed out, poverty is no longer a regional problem. Poverty, and its accompanying disease and environmental degradation, affect the whole planet. Thus, poverty reduction is necessary to reduce suffering and harm globally as well as locally.

But how does one operationalize this Millennium ideal? Why haven't wealthy nations, nongovernment organizations and profitable global corporations done more to reduce poverty, given these strong moral arguments? There are myriad reasons, as we shall argue. Our mental models often wrongly construe the nature of poverty and the abilities of the poor. Our conceptual schemes conclude that poverty can be addressed only through elaborate and complicated social engineering projects without imagining other alternatives. Or, we sometimes too narrowly define roles and responsibilities for social evils, often putting the burden on local governments that then exclude innovative options for reducing poverty.

Poverty, Mental Models, and Bias

The Jesuit philosopher Bernard Lonergan spent much of his career examining what he termed "insight," a phenomenon of human understanding. Considering various historical descriptions of human understanding, he found that insight occurs in response to inquiry. It consists in "a grasp of intelligible unity or relation in the data," and is the "active ground whence proceed conception, definition, hypothesis, theory, system" (Lonergan 1971, 212–213). Insight only emerges from critical and sustained attention to the relevant data. The quest for insight is often dogged by various forms of bias that dismiss relevant data and subsequent inquiry. Like a malignant form of cancer, biases are not merely impediments to the individual, but can also become conditions leading to social decline or even collapse. Biases can be pervasive, destructive, and oppressive.

Individual bias can lead to group bias expressed in various socially constructed mental models. Although the term is not always clearly defined, the term "mental model" or "mindset" connotes the idea that human beings have mental representations, cognitive frames, or mental pictures of their experiences, representations that model the stimuli or data with which they are interacting, and these are frameworks that set up parameters through which experience or a certain set of experiences, is organized or filtered (Senge 1990, ch. 10; Gorman 1992; Gentner and Whitley 1997, 210–211; Werhane 1999). Mental models function as selective mechanisms and filters for dealing with experience. In focusing, framing, organizing, and ordering what we experience, mental models bracket and leave out data, and emotional and motivational foci taint or color experience. These points of view or mental models are socially learned; they are incomplete, and sometimes distorted, narrow, single-framed. Nevertheless, because schema we employ are socially learned and altered through religion, socialization, culture, educational upbringing, and other experiences, they are shared and often turn into culturally biased ways of perceiving, organizing, and learning (Johnson 1993; Werhane 1999).

Two particular kinds of mental models are helpful when examining the roots of extreme poverty: what Lonergan labels "the bias of conceptualism" and "the bias of common sense." One of the greatest dangers of addressing the problems of extreme poverty is the bias of conceptualism: the refusal to modify, adjust, or abandon abstract concepts in light of emerging insights or failures of policy. Conceptualism is "a strong affirmation of concepts, and a skeptical disregard of insights," which leads to "anti-historical immobilism" and "excessive abstractness" (Morelli and Morelli 1997, 425). For example, the concept that only large international organizations can solve poverty problems can lead to distortions in outcomes and exclude new possibilities. If William Easterly is correct (2006), since the 1950's industrial revolution, developed countries have spent approximately $2.3 trillion to aid less developed countries (LDCs). Yet, notwithstanding these historically unsurpassed expenditures, the results are mixed, at best. Foreign aid in the form of the Marshall Plan transformed Europe after World War II; and U.S. aid to Japan was equally successful. IMF and World Bank efforts have been effective in China, Japan, Korea, and in other parts of the world. But, in Africa, parts of the sub-continent of India, Pakistan, and Bangladesh, in particular, foreign aid has done little to change these economic landscapes and has accomplished virtually nothing in terms of poverty reduction in these countries. Why, if these results are so dubious can we not shake loose of our mental model that foreign aid or charity are the *only* answers to poverty reduction? It is perhaps because we are caught in believing in an abstract, conceptual framework that this single idea can solve all poverty problems, despite data to the contrary.

   Another expression of conceptualism is a fixed social theory that assigns exact roles and responsibilities to various institutions that, taken together, supposedly comprise the common good. Narrow or rigidly defined roles often dismiss the variety of ways that different cultures respond to the demands of a flourishing society. One of these is the failure to recognize the strengths and intelligence of the poor. This failure emerges from what Lonergan would call a bias of common sense, that is, the refusal to get beyond the familiar and exclusive world of the way things appear to us (Morelli and Morelli 1997, 97). C.K. Prahalad finds four pervasive and problematic "biases" or assumptions about poverty: 1) the poor lack resources, 2) aid from rich countries to the government of poor countries is the best way to reduce poverty, 3) aid skewed to social goods such as education and healthcare are best for economic development, and 4) business has little to offer poverty reduction (Prahalad 2005, 78). William Easterly makes a strong case that it was these assumptions coupled with a paternalistic residue of the colonial mentality—a contextually based bias—that is largely responsible for many of the failed, development-era social engineering projects (Easterly 2006, 23–26). These biased assumptions are rooted in the faulty view that the poor are not intelligent, that they need to be taken care of, and that they have little capacity for initiative, innovation, and self-development.

Insights for Poverty Alleviation

To shake loose from our learned and traditional mental models, there are at least four insights that are essential for new thinking about successful poverty alleviation: 1) the poor do not lack resources, 2) poverty alleviation is an evolving, dynamic process, 3) poverty is often the result of patterns of exclusion, and 4) there are many feasible approaches to poverty reduction that have been and can be created through commerce.

In support of the first insight, Albina Ruiz's project, Ciudad Saludable, demonstrates the profound creativity and initiative to be found among the poor. Using garbage to create jobs and to clean the local environment in Lima, Peru, Albina Ruiz is an entrepreneur in the truest sense of the term. Garbage has become an increasing problem in Lima, where 1.6 million people produce nearly 600 metric tons of garbage daily. Since the municipal authorities can process only half that much, garbage lines the streets, fills vacant lots, and clogs rivers, creating a significant health menace. Poor families scavenge through the trash to eek out a living. Trained in industrial engineering, Albina began to organize the community and to create a positive alternative, knowing that the municipal authorities were unable or unwilling to address the garbage problem. In collaboration with community members, she encouraged microentrepreneurs to collect and process the garbage. With a collection fee of around $1.50, a fee many were eager to pay for the service, Ciudad Saludable converts garbage into compost and other useful materials, creating jobs in the process. Her story was featured on a PBS documentary about social entrepreneurs titled "The New Heroes" (Cohen et al. 2007). Albina Ruiz's story illustrates two important messages in poverty alleviation: successful solutions can come from the poor themselves and government is not always the best institution for addressing public goods like garbage disposal (Ashoka 2007). Ruiz's success blurs the lines between public and private goods and challenges rigidly defined roles and responsibilities.

With regard to the second insight, poverty alleviation (or the economic development that leads to this consequence) can be an evolving, dynamic, bottom-up process that requires frequent evaluation, modification, and adjustment. An example of bottom-up thinking is demonstrated by KickStart's MoneyMaker Irrigation Pump that has helped many small farmers transition from subsistence farming into commercial enterprise (Kickstart 2007). The small, affordable pumps make impressive contributions to poverty alleviation. Felix Mururi, for example, is married with three children and lives in Kenya. He left his rural home to look for work in the slums of Nairobi to little avail, earning $40 month. He discovered in the city that he could make more money as a farmer and decided to rent a plot of land and save money for the $33 manually operated water pump. The increased yield from his single plot was so profitable that Felix and his family now rent six plots, making $580 profit on just two of them. They plan to rent and irrigate another acre and eventually buy a house (Fisher 2007). For Felix Mururi, increased access to water did not come from the public development of infrastructure but from a $33 pump.

Third, poverty is often the result of systematic patterns of exclusion. Hernando de Soto illustrates how pervasive and systematic is the nature of exclusion in *The Mystery of Capital* (2000). While the value of savings among the poor is 40 times greater than all foreign aid received worldwide since 1945, it is still unable to morph into living capital, the force that raises productivity and creates wealth. He contends that capital is dead in many regions of the world, in part, because of the patterns of exclusion buried deep within the formal systems of property rights. Lack of legal title and extensive bureaucracy prevent the vibrant informal sector from joining its formal, visible counterpart. The large, extralegal sectors of Brazilian cities called *favelas* are filled with "squatters" who participate in economies not recognized by the law. Purchasing land legally in a country like the Philippines, for example, can take 13 to 25 years. In the West, formal recognition of property title is a key condition for access to collateral. Without access to a timely, transparent, and structured system, the poor do not participate in the formal system that recognizes property rights. As a result, they are more vulnerable and more susceptible to exploitation.

Muhammad Yunus found the same problem with the poor women of Jobra, Bangladesh; they were systematically excluded from the formal banking sector and were unable to secure even the smallest loans to help with their microbusinesses (Yunus 2003). Hernando de Soto's and Muhammad Yunus's studies illustrate that poverty is often the result of systematic patterns of exclusion, not a lack of resources or creativity or initiative. Building on these insights concerning poverty alleviation, we now turn to the role of commerce.

A Fourth Insight: Profits and Poverty Reduction at the Base of the Pyramid

For some, profit is a suspicious partner in poverty alleviation efforts. The socially conscious are often skeptical of business interests, considering well-publicized patterns of exploitation. Even from a business perspective, poverty alleviation is often seen as tangential to core interests, which raises a perhaps counterintuitive question about the potential of the market to respond to these fundamental human needs.

Concerning the latter, Stuart Hart makes a strong argument that future economic growth will not come from the top of the pyramid but from the base, considering the demographic trend in population growth. Capitalism is at a crossroads, he believes, because the top of the market is saturated and current patterns of growth and resource exploitation are unsustainable (Hart 2005). The common bias that the bottom of the pyramid offers no commercial opportunities can result in missed opportunities, and can even have potentially devastating effects.

C.K. Prahalad believes there is growth opportunity at the bottom of the pyramid when the poor are seen as brand-conscious consumers. Seeing the poor as the consumers they actually are can be both profitable for a business and socially transformative. Both Prahalad and Hart are convinced that the bottom of the pyramid is the next wave of growth. However, viewing the poor as a new market for business raises concerns for some nonprofit organizations who see profitability as exploitation rather than a means for poverty alleviation, especially in BoP countries. Moreover, one might ask, why would a global corporation place any efforts on poverty alleviation if it is already providing jobs, goods and/or services to the global economy? What is the extent of its responsibilities? Might a preoccupation with poverty reduction distract companies from their main purposes?

In order to appropriately explore, evaluate, and balance a corporation's profit motive with its arguable obligations to a social contract, it is critical to understand the nature of the responsibilities it maintains. At its core, these obligations are rooted in the dichotomy between stockholder theory and stakeholder theory, dating to the 1960s when stakeholder theory was developed as a model of applied corporate responsibility and as a focus for socially sustainable enterprise (Freeman 1984; Goodpaster 1991; Carroll and Nasi 1997). In 1984, R. Edward Freeman proposed a stakeholder theory of the modern corporation (1984, 1994, 1999, 2001) which takes as a starting point the premise that managerial capitalism pursues market transactions and customers in an unconstrained manner. Freeman acknowledges the property rights of shareholding classes, which he generalizes to be part of the wider stakeholder population with a special claim on the company; he then attributes shareholder-type rights to stakeholders, that is, to those groups or individuals who affect or are affected by, and/or whose rights are violated or respected by, corporate activity. The theory suggests that corporations have fiduciary obligations to "any individual (or group) that may claim to be affected by the achievement of an organization's objectives" (Freeman 2001, 57). Stakeholders may be defined, inter alia, "narrowly" or "broadly" (Freeman 2001, 59)—a narrow definition might consist of primary stakeholders, those who are "vital to the survival of a company" (Freeman 2001, 59) (such as shareholders, employees, customers, and suppliers) and wider definition would encompass "any group who can affect or is affected by the corporation" (Freeman 2001, 60–62).

Considering the wider definition in the context of global poverty, the management of an industrial corporation may be subjected to the claims of an almost unlimited number of interests (Jensen 2001; Campbell et al. 2002); some of which will be mutually incompatible (Child and Marcoux 1999; Beauchamp and Bowie 2001), and few of which will have any direct contractual or commercial basis (Hendry 2001; Marcoux 2003; Phillips 2003). While the interests of some stakeholder groups (shareholders, employees, and government) may be covered by regulation, many stakeholder claims will be implicitly moral rather than legal (Adams 2002). But it seems unlikely that it can be feasible for management to deal with and meet all these potentially incompatible claims (Unerman and Bennett 2004). Thus, most stakeholder theories limit their claims to a narrow definition of stakeholders.

For Milton Friedman, that which he calls the "socialist concept" of stakeholder theory is a dangerous one, which embraces a "fundamentally subversive doctrine" approaching "corporate fraud" (Friedman 1962, 133). Milton Friedman's *New York Times* article, "The Social Responsibility of Business is to Increase its Profits," is perhaps best known as an argument for a purely profit-based social responsibility of business. In this article, he notably argues that "there is only one social responsibility of business—to use its resources and engage in activities designed to increase its profits so long as it stays within the rules of the game, which is to say, engages in open and free competition without deception or fraud" (Friedman 1971).

From a utilitarian point of view Friedman and Freeman are not diametrically opposed. Friedman does not ignore ethical responsibility in his analysis; he is merely suggesting that decision makers are acting ethically if they follow their firm's self-interests. By pursuing these interests, which Friedman identifies with profits, a business manager functions to allocate resources to their most efficient uses. Consumers who most value a resource will be willing to pay the most for it, thereby profit is the measure of optimal allocation of resources. Over time, the pursuit of profit will entail continuous work toward the optimal satisfaction of consumer demand, which on one interpretation of utilitarianism, is a good. It should be noted, however, that Freeman and many other stakeholder theorists are not merely utilitarians and claim that in addition to the utility of stakeholder claims, stakeholders, as individuals and groups of individuals, are subject to rights claims as well (Freeman 1984; Freeman and McVea 2005).

It is the definition of corporate social responsibility (CSR), not the stakeholder-stockholder debate that gives rise to the duality, rather than a one-dimensional analysis of the "do-gooders" versus the "profit-maximizers." The duality depends on whether CSR is defined as those socially or ecologically accountable activities designed to meet the needs of a firm's myriad stakeholders (Miles and Covin 2000) (and aligned with a utilitarian model described earlier) or refers to activities that go beyond meeting the needs of particular and measurable stakeholders to the interests of society as a whole, which might be perhaps less measurable in terms of bottom line impact, but instead entails obligations to have a positive impact on society (Perrault and McCarthy 2002).

Difficulties with this debate rest upon two simple but narrowly framed mental models: 1) that profitability is the sole or primary aim of commerce, and 2) that stakeholder theory, in its original formulation, is adequate for describing global corporate activities. Concerning the first preoccupation, one will recall the Collins and Porras 1994 landmark study of successful companies, defined by long-term returns on investment and stock price. From their study of numbers of the largest U.S. companies James Collins and Jerry Porras conclude,

> Contrary to business school doctrine, "maximizing shareholder wealth" or "profit maximization" has not been the dominant driving force or primary objective through the history of visionary companies. Visionary companies pursue a cluster of objectives, of which making money is only one—and not necessarily the primary one. Yes they seek profits, but they are equally guided by a core ideology-core values and a sense of purpose beyond just making money. Yet paradoxically, the visionary companies make more money that the more purely profit-driven comparison companies. (Collins and Porras 1994, 6)

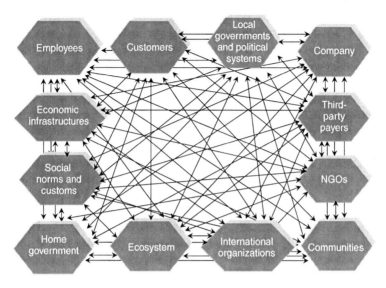

Figure 2.2 Stakeholder networks for global corporations to capture the complex network of relationships within which global companies operate.

Thus, even if many managers are preoccupied with shareholder wealth, according to Collins and Porras, they should not be, if their aim is to survive and do well in the long term.

Second, focusing now on stakeholder theory, the standard depiction of stakeholder relationships as wheel-and-spoke focuses our attention on the center—on the organization, despite claims that companies have equal reciprocal responsibilities between themselves and their stakeholders. Thus, our focus is skewed toward the corporation as the center of attention despite claims to the contrary. In a globalized flat economy, such a depiction fails to capture the complex network of relationships within which global companies operate. (See figure 2.2.) Indeed, what is often missing in global corporate thinking is such a morally imaginative networked systemic approach.

As Susan Wolf explained some time ago,

> [a] truly systemic view . . . considers how a set of individuals, institutions and processes operates in a system involving a complex network of interrelationships, an array of individual and institutional actors with conflicting interests and goals, and a number of feedback loops. (Wolf 1999, 1675)

A systems approach recognizes that, in a flat world, almost everything we can experience or think about is in a network of interrelationships such that each element of a particular set of interrelationships affects some other components of that set and the system itself; and almost no phenomena can be studied in isolation from other relationships with at least some other phenomenon. Global corporations are mezzo-systems embedded in many larger political, economic, legal, and cultural systems. These are all examples of "complex adaptive systems," a term used to describe open interactive systems that are able to change themselves and affect change through their interactions with other systems and, as a result, are sometimes unpredictable (Plsek 2001). In studying global corporate governance, if one focuses simply on a corporation's organizational structure, or merely on its mission statement, or its employees or customers, one obscures if not distorts the interconnections and interrelationships that characterize and affect that organization and its internal and external relationships. (Emanuel 2000; Werhane 2002).

Today, we commonly use a systems approach in talking about global corporate responsibility to the ecosystem, and we are expanding that responsibility to the human elements in the ecosystem in relation to employment through a concerted effort to critique companies that use sweatshop labor. But we have thought less about the responsibilities of companies to improve the conditions of those who are not recognized as their primary stakeholders. This is shortsighted for at least four reasons. First, in a global flat world, the manner in which one operates within a community affects that community, positively or negatively. Second, there are enormous untapped markets at the bottom of the pyramid, as C.K. Prahalad and Stuart Hart have argued. Third, if there is a positive value to economic well-being (and, surely, living in abject poverty, however culturally defined, is a social evil) and value in economic growth to achieve well-being, the potential market at the BoP is huge. If companies are able to provide affordable goods and entrepreneurial opportunities to this sector, both companies and these stakeholders can thereby prosper. There is an important caveat to this claim however. Unless companies also provide living-wage work in these sectors, there will be no new market development, since there will be no increase in customer purchasing power. Creating new markets *and* new consumers, however, should be sufficient motivation for global companies trying to survive, grow, and expand their core interests in what they do best. Fourth, if companies recognize the value in the third reason articulated above, they will be encouraged to remain vested in these stakeholders from a long-term perspective and are, therefore, both appropriate and effective constituents with which to partner in order to create sustainable solutions to the challenges presented by global poverty. Thus, corporate and community interests can come together. This is not a mandate for more corporate philanthropy, but rather an imaginative coming together of corporate interests: their core ideologies linked to their core competencies while serving unanswered community needs.

Global Corporate Initiatives: Addressing Poverty through Commerce

There are at least three forms of market-tested commercial initiatives that can successfully address poverty without converting to philanthropy. The first model is through operations of global corporations aimed at economic growth and poverty reduction, with particular foci on the developing BoP world. The second model is through bottom-up initiatives such as KickStart and microlending projects. The third initiative involves technology in the creation of partnerships between global companies and those at the bottom of the population pyramid.

There are a number of corporate initiatives focusing on profitable ventures with economically poor populations. For example, lack of access to clean water in many regions of sub-Saharan Africa is one of the greatest challenges to socioeconomic development. Safe drinking water is in great demand for more than 1 billion people at the bottom of the pyramid. The World Health Organization estimates that 2.2 million children die each year because of diarrheal diseases, which could easily be prevented by access to safe drinking water (P&G Health Sciences Institute 2007a). While large-scale infrastructure projects may be important in the long term, the demand for immediate relief persists. Since it is the small, home-based water purification systems that have drastically cut deaths caused by diarrhea, Procter & Gamble (P&G) designed PuR, a cost-effective water purification system that removes dirt and disease-causing pathogens from drinking water. Although P&G provides PuR at cost through its Children's Safe Drinking Water philanthropic outreach and uses the nonprofit Population Services International for marketing, the local distributors must make a profit for sustainability and access. As local distributors have learned, consumers did not value free give-aways (P&G Health Sciences Institute 2007b). P&G's involvement is not merely altruistic; with a positive brand image, new products for a billion potential consumers, and the proven high-volume, low-margin business model, P&G stands to increase its margins considerably.

Profitable ventures into the BoP do not just benefit corporations through new market opportunities but may have significant social benefits as well. In India there are an estimated 660,000 diarrhea-related deaths per year, a problem with known preventative measures as simple as hygienic education and access to antibacterial soap; however, the problem persists despite the work of NGOs, development agencies, and governments because of some daunting challenges. The problem has been seen historically as a public health issue falling under the domain of large-scale, expensive infrastructure projects (Prahalad 2005, 207–209). Even if one were to view the problem strictly from a public health perspective, that is, with the sole desire of maximizing hygienic education and access to soap, what is the best way to reach those goals?

Hindustan Lever's experience in the BoP suggests that distribution and hygienic education are challenges that at least some companies are equipped to address. First, however, it is important to give a brief history of why Hindustan Lever (HLL) ventured into the BoP to begin with. Karsanbhai Patel's Nirma detergent, a rising competitor of HLL's in the detergent market, had considerable success in selling to rural Indians. Once HLL had established the fact that rural Indians had the ability to buy goods, the company decided to go the extra distance to bring their goods to this new, unusual but sizeable, client group. With a clearer understanding of the market potential and a growing concern over a competitor's success, HLL still had significant issues to address to successfully venture into the BoP market. To win customers from Nirma, HLL had to develop a high quality product with good value and create brand loyalty. With the new market in mind, HLL developed a nontoxic, durable, highly functional, easily disposable product at a low unit cost. The new product for the new market still faced the daunting challenge of distribution (Ahmad, Werhane, and German 2004).

While HLL had an advanced distribution system in urban areas, it could not replicate them in rural areas. The sheer vastness of the task had discouraged many other MNCs from entering these areas, a challenge facing NGOs, developments, and government as well. In response to the particular challenges of reaching rural India, HLL set up a new distribution system based on population size and accessibility. Beginning with those villages near all-weather roads with a population of more than 2,000, HLL eventually developed Project Streamline to reach remote villages. Project Streamline used a network of local distributors (thus providing new job opportunities) to supply sub-stockists who, in turn, were responsible for transporting goods into the countryside for resale. By tractor or bullock cart, sub-stockists helped extend HLL's reach from 25 percent in 1995 to 37 percent in 1998 and currently directly impacts approximately 50,000 villages which allows the project to reach 250 million stakeholding consumers. (Hindustan Lever Limited, "Creating Markets" [2007], Retrieved from http://www.hll.com/brands/creating_markets.asp on October 2, 2007). Another innovative practice, Project Shakti, sold company products to rural women who in turn resold them at a profit. While companies like Amway and Avon had pioneered similar strategies, HLL was the first to apply it in remote regions (Ahmad et al. 2004b).

In addition to logistical problems, HLL also had to get its message to regions with poor media infrastructure and low levels of literacy. HLL used Ogilvy Outreach, the nonprofit arm of Ogilvy & Mather (Ahmad et al. 2004a). With the purpose of reaching those living in "media-dark" regions, Ogilvy Outreach offered some dynamic and creative solutions such as using street performers with entertaining jingles, traveling cinema vans, and various other performances at cattle and trade fairs. HLL and Ogilvy Outreach hired magicians, dancers, and actors to connect the brand and the residents, altering their scripts to accommodate differing dialects, religions, and education levels. Spanning six months and reaching over 2,000 bazaars, Ogilvy successfully ventured into media-dark regions, areas previously seen as inaccessible (Ahmad et al. 2004b).

HLL's case also reveals the close linkage between the public health interest in increased hygienic education, job opportunities, and the business interests of distribution, branding, and product education. One aim of Ogilvy Outreach was to ensure that when consumers purchased and used HLL's product, they were reminded of its popular value. In order to create brand loyalty and a sense of "missing out on something good," HLL marketing representatives used ultraviolet light sensors to scan villagers' hands, revealing the invisible germs present on unwashed hands that appeared to be clean. (Ahmad et al. 2004b).

From a public health perspective alone, that is, with the sole desire of maximizing hygienic education and access to soap, HLL's experience shows that for-profits make unique contributions to logistical challenges that others are not equipped to address. HLL's experience shows that the poor are brand conscious consumers and need to be seen as such in order to best address community needs. HLL also created new jobs in these markets, thus giving economic empowerment to people not always considered as employable.

Subsidiarity: From below Upward

The second model involves rethinking top-down directives or grand schemes for poverty reduction. One of the most troublesome biases concerning poverty alleviation is top-down thinking where sweeping ideas and elaborate projects dismiss the less obvious lessons or messages that often drive economic development. Contrary to top-down thinking is the notion of subsidiarity that comes from the Latin word meaning "to assist." It is an important principle for human communities, including business organizations (Melé 2004). The relative success of various initiatives in the last decade attests to the importance of bottom-up thinking, such as the KickStart irrigation pump, discussed earlier in the chapter.

An illustration of the positive impact of subsidiarity is that the growth of small business and vibrant commercial infrastructure can have a cascading effect. The success of Siongiroi Dairy in Kenya suggests that small business development is a great place for development experts to focus attention. Started in 1998 with the help of TechnoServe, Heifer Project International, and American Breeders Service, the Siongiroi Dairy buys 11,000 liters of milk per day from 2,000 local dairy farmers. Because of the Dairy Plant, farmers have an assured market for their milk and receive a fair price in a timely fashion. As a result, over 100 new businesses have emerged, including transportation services, veterinary supply stores, clothing shops, new restaurants, food stalls, butcher shops, hardware stores, and mechanic shops. Siongiroi villagers used to travel many miles to get to the market, now the market comes to them. William Yegor's new milk transportation business is but one example of the cascading effect. Since many farmers do not have their own means of transportation, Yegor developed Temik Milk Transportation. With a net profit of $1,000 a month, he now employs six people. As he explains, "I am opening up a new office to better coordinate my business. The future looks good for my family, thanks to the Dairy Plant." Even more impressive are the secondary social benefits on housing, healthcare, and education: the town now has three health clinics, two pharmacies, two new schools, and three new bookstores. Edward Manani, a dairy employee, attributes a great portion of the new development in Siongiroi to the Dairy Plant itself. In the words of Joseph Ubwei, "There are so many ways I have benefited from this dairy plant. I have children in secondary and primary school and it has helped me pay their school fees and their activity fees" (Technoserve 2007).

Technology Interactions between the Top and the Bottom of the Pyramid

A persistent and stubborn bias concerning the poor is that they do not need, will not appreciate, and cannot afford technology. C.K. Prahalad argues the opposite: not only do consumers readily accept advanced technology, they use it in transformative ways. Take, for example, the impact of ITC's e-Choupal on rural farmers in India. By placing a computer with an Internet connection in a *choupal*, a traditional village gathering place, ITC gives farmers access to many different *mandis* (government mandated marketplaces). Previously, farmers went to a single *mandi* where commission agents took full advantage of their leverage at the expense of farmers. With greater parity in access to information, social standing, and choice, rural farmers have begun to level the playing field (Prahalad 2005, 319–357).

From the Internet to cell phones, access to technology can be socially transformative. Vodacom has discovered that its community cell phones are an integral part of its core business strategy. Previous fixed-line efforts to establish service were not very effective given the expense of infrastructure development and maintenance. Vodacom's efforts to establish service and be South Africa's largest provider, however, have been very successful. Owned and operated by entrepreneurs, the Community Services Phone shops use refurbished shipping containers as phone shops, which provide service to areas of South Africa for the first time. Increased access to a cell phone is no frivolous luxury: from job hunting in distant cities to seeking medical advice, increased communication yields important social benefits. (Reck and Wood 2003). Not only do local entrepreneurs improve their income, but consumers save time and money by not having to travel to use a phone. Nobel Prize winner Muhammad Yunus may have started his Grameen project with a village bank lending money, but it has evolved into Grameen Telecom, Grameen Shakti (technical solutions for alternative energy), and Grameen Cybernet (Yunus 2003, 226–227). These examples also illustrate that poor, even illiterate people are NOT technologically challenged. They just need opportunities.

Critiques from the Top of the Pyramid

Challenging ideas always attract critics and the Bottom of the Pyramid propositions are no different. The evolution of strong linkage with the business community reaches back to the publication of two articles,

"The Fortune at the Bottom of the Pyramid" (Prahalad and Hart 2002) and "Serve the World's Poor, Profitably" (Prahalad and Hammond 2002). Aneel Karnani is perhaps the most significant critic of BoP propositions, which he calls a mirage (2006). His critique merits careful attention, among others, because it demonstrates the kind of problematic thinking that confronts the BoP proposition most directly. Karnani argues the BoP proposition is "a harmless illusion" at best and a "dangerous delusion" at worst. His critiques concern 1) the size of the BoP market, 2) the view of the poor as consumer, 3) the type of business that is most likely to benefit, and 4) the exploitative nature of BoP engagement. More recently, others have offered a fifth critique concerning the relative lack of global corporate involvement to date.

The Size of the Market

Karnani's first set of critiques concern the size of the BoP market and its relative opportunity. He believes the BoP proposition is guilty of false advertising: it is neither as big nor as profitable as Prahalad contends. Karnani believes the BoP market is around $1.2 trillion (2.7 billion poor people multiplied times $1.25 per day), closer to the World Bank's estimate in 2005 (2006, 5). Prahalad contends the market is $13 trillion (2005, 21). Karnani also argues that the "fortune and glory at the bottom of the pyramid are a mirage" because exaggerations of *size* are also exaggerations of *opportunity* for business (2006, 29).

The different estimates of the relative size of the BoP market are understandable given the debates in the field of economics about how best to measure poverty and the nature of the economic pyramid. (See, e.g., the *Economist* 2004 or Friedman 2005.) What Karnani's critique fails to recognize is that the Purchasing Power Parity metric is a relatively adequate tool, not the razor-sharp one he expects it to be. It is highly unlikely that there is soon to be a consensus among economists about the best metric for measuring poverty or the exact shape of the economic pyramid. The difference in scientific opinion only proves that consensus based on empirical data is slow, evolving, and tentative. This is not to say that consensus among economists does not make vital contributions to poverty alleviation efforts, but only to suggest that consensus around poverty metrics will always lag behind the relative gravity of the situation. After all, extreme poverty is a life-and-death matter. Efforts to alleviate it, therefore, do not have the luxury of waiting for a conclusive consensus and will always grope their way forward. Whether the BoP is $1.2 trillion or $13 trillion is less important than if there is any market at this segment of the economic pyramid. The answer to this question may take decades' worth of empirical data to arrive at a conclusive consensus.

Producers, Consumers, and Exploitation

Karnani's second critique is that viewing the poor as consumers is "an intellectually and morally problematic position." Instead, he argues, the poor should be viewed as producers. It is important to distinguish the intellectual claim from the moral one: the former concerns the accurate description of what the poor *actually* do and the latter concerns what the poor *ought to* do. The intellectual distinction between producer and consumer is dubious and potentially misleading. Take Felix Mururi's experience with KickStart's MoneyMaker Irrigation Pump, discussed above, as an example. Felix was first a consumer buying the MoneyMaker pump for $33. Because Felix had access to this new technology he was able to become a producer, selling his crop. Focusing on Felix solely as a producer is not only a conceptual limitation, it also dismisses the importance of KickStart's efforts to market and to sell its product in a sustainable fashion. Another example is the Siongoroi Dairy in Kenya that buys milk from local dairy farmers and thereby increases access to markets. From a broader perspective, the intricate link between consumers and producers and the multiple roles that people play concurrently all point to a complex web of interaction and activity.

On a moral front, viewing the poor through any rigidly defined lens, including "consumer" or "producer," is a form of distortive objectification (Buber 1996). There is no evidence that viewing the poor as consumers is inherently exploitative, as Karnani suggests. To the contrary, Prahalad argues that viewing the poor as consumers can actually have a humanizing effect through the dignity of attention and choice. From a pragmatic viewpoint, it was because P&G and Hindustan Lever attended to the poor as brand-conscious consumers that they were able to broaden their distribution of insecticide-treated bed nets and water purification systems. Secondly, the most pressing moral issues concerning poverty are not the abstract harms of consumerism, but the more concrete harms like starvation, malaria, and diarrhea, which are often the result of patterns of exclusion and the poverty penalty. An even greater moral affront than viewing the poor as a consumer is to avoid the BoP all together because it may not be immediately profitable. Ignoring the BoP market allows patterns of exclusion to persist. If Grameen Bank's success has any moral lesson, it is that the poor pay a poverty penalty because they do not enjoy the same access to goods and services that contribute to human flourishing.

The Role of Global Companies

Karnani's third critique is that most of Prahalad's case studies involve local microenterprises and nonprofits more than large global companies. He claims that Prahalad has exaggerated the role of these organizations in "taking the lead" (Karnani 2006, 16). Karnani's language of "roles" and "taking the lead" is quite revealing: both notions imply fixed roles and a hierarchical relationship. What Karnani seems to miss is the collaborative efforts that Prahalad describes in the ecosystem for wealth creation (Prahalad 2005, ch. 4).

It is true that to date there are few global corporate ventures into the bottom of the pyramid. The primary lesson delineated here is that various sectors *can* work together in ways that are beneficial to all, including global companies. The World Cocoa Foundation (an alliance of MNCs) illustrates the evolution in thinking quite well. Members of the WCF realized they all shared an interest in the region of the globe located 20 degrees north and south of the equator since it is the most suitable climate for harvesting cocoa. Through partnership with various sectors who shared similar interests, the WCF has benefited tremendously and has secured the conditions for the possibility of sustainable development. It did not, however, always have a clearly defined role and came relatively late to the alliance. Finally, focusing on a single actor in the BoP often dismisses the various institutions that contribute. Whatever the nature of the role, it is clear that collaboration is essential. Nonprofits, for example, often help to create the conditions favorable for corporate involvement.

The Most Dangerous Delusion

Karnani's most harmful critique is that the BoP proposition is a "dangerous delusion" to the poor themselves. He fears that corporate involvement in the BoP might reduce the welfare of the poor, since the poor "are vulnerable by virtue of lack of education . . . lack of information, and economic, cultural and social deprivations"

(Karnani 2006, 18). These deficiencies make the poor susceptible to exploitation and create a need for greater legal and social mechanisms. The poor do not often demonstrate the ability to make wise consumer choices, buying alcohol and whitening creams instead of useful products. The danger of the BoP proposition, he continues, is that it "de-emphasizes the role of the state in providing basic *services* and *infrastructure*" (Karnani 2006, 27, emphasis added).

The biggest concern of Karnani's dangerous delusion critique is that it reinforces the kind of objectification and paternalism that dominated the post–World War II development era. Karnani reveals an inherent skepticism that the poor are able to decide for themselves what is best. Viewing the poor as helpless victims leads to top-down thinking, where grand social-engineering projects are the primary vehicle of social progress. To the moral pragmatist, this path is both well-worn and unsuccessful. What are the needs of the poor and who determines them? Muhammad Yunus discovered the best way to approach this question is to ask the poor themselves. Albina Ruiz realized that the municipal authorities were incapable of collecting all of Lima's garbage, and that the solution *had to* emerge from the actions of private citizens. The most dangerous delusion is not that the poor will be exploited by corporate involvement at the bottom of the pyramid, but that sustainable economic growth can continue to come from shrinking markets at the top, if Stuart Hart's forecast is correct.

Karnani does raise an important concern, albeit indirectly. While his argument that the BoP proposition "de-emphasizes the role of the state" regarding basic services and infrastructure may be misguided, it is well founded when it comes to providing legal protection and recognition. Hernando de Soto's insight that participation in the informal, extralegal sector is more risky than participation in its formal counterpart is a serious concern worthy of greater attention. The BoP proposition does not deemphasize the role of the state, but sees it as crucial in creating favorable conditions for economic development, or transaction governance capacity in Prahalad's framework. Because corruption causes or exacerbates patterns of exclusion, fair, transparent governance is a vital agent in forming an ecosystem of wealth creation. The difference between Karnani's view and Prahalad's is not that governance is not important or does not play an important role, but that its role in providing services and infrastructure is varied and contextual, not fixed and predetermined. Patterns of exclusion are prevalent in the free market and in the public sphere of governance. The primary issue is not to clearly define the proper role of the state in economic development, but in removing the barriers that exacerbate the conditions of poverty. Karnani's concern about the role of the state is certainly worthy of critical attention, but it should not be an excuse for global companies to avoid the BoP market all together.

So Where are the Global Companies?

The most current critique of the BoP proposition is not about potential, but about the extent of actual involvement. If it is such a great opportunity, why are global companies not more consistently and fully involved? First, companies *are* getting more involved. Citigroup, P&G, Cisco Systems, ExxonMobil, Chevron, Nokia, Google, and even Wal-Mart are either directly involved already or have formal plans to get involved. Second, it is important to remember that the BoP proposition is a relatively new idea. In this time span, Citigroup has seen the potential of microfinance (Maitland 2005; Citigroup 2004); Wal-Mart has seen the potential of the Mexican and Indian markets; and ExxonMobil has worked on job opportunities and microfinancing in areas such as Chad and Cameroon where they are drilling for oil. Third, it is also important to note that some global companies and their managers will not take the plunge into the BoP at all since the bias of conceptualism and "common sense" fear of emerging markets tend to be more prevalent in managerial thinking than insight and innovation. Ventures into emerging markets tend to grope their way forward, which takes time.

Conclusion

The wisdom of the BoP proposition is twofold: 1) The United Nation's Millennium Development Goal to reduce poverty can be achieved only with substantive contributions of businesses as well as government and international organizations in ways that are sustainable and 2) poverty alleviation is a profitable endeavor both for companies and for the poor, when focused on corporate core competencies linking new market development with job creation and new product branding, not on the fringe of corporate social responsibility in the form of charitable contributions. Whether there is a fortune at the bottom of the pyramid or only sustainable profits is inconsequential. That there are profits in markets previously overlooked and ignored is of great consequence to both poverty alleviation efforts and to the sustainable development of global companies in the new flat world of the twenty-first century.

References

Adams, C. 2002. Internal Organizational Factors Influencing Corporate Social and Ethical Reporting. *Accounting, Auditing Accountability Journal* 15: 223–250.

Ahmad, P., J. Mead, P.H. Werhane, and M.E. Gorman. 2004a. Hindustan Lever Limited and Project Sting. *Darden Case Study UVA-E-0268.* Charlottesville, VA: Darden Business School Publishing.

———. 2004b. Hindustan Lever Limited and Project Sting. *Darden Case Study UVA-E-0269.* Charlottesville, VA: Darden Business School Publishing.

Ahmad, P., P.H. Werhane, and M.E. Gorman. 2004. Hindustan Lever and Marketing to the Fourth Tier. *International Journal of Entrepreneurship and Innovation Management* 4: 495–511.

Ashoka. 2007. Albina Ruiz. http://www.ashoka.org/node/3718 (accessed December 5, 2007).

Beauchamp, T.L. and N.E. Bowie. 2001. The Purpose of the Corporation. In *Ethical Theory and Business Practice*, ed. T.L. Beauchamp and N.E. Bowie, 45–50. Upper Saddle River, NJ: Prentice Hall.

Buber, Martin. 1996. *I and Thou.* Trans. Walter Kaurmann. New York: Simon & Schuster.

Campbell, D., B. Craven, and K. Lawler. 2002. Social Welfare, Positivism and Business Ethics. *Business Ethics: A European Review* 11: 268–281.

Carroll, A.B. and J. Nasi. 1997. Understanding Stakeholder Thinking: Themes from a Finnish Conference. *Business Ethics: A European Review* 6: 46–51.

Child, J.W. and A.M. Marcoux. 1999. Freeman and Evan: Stakeholder Theory in the Original Position. *Business Ethics Quarterly* 9: 207–223.

Citigroup. 2004. Microfinance. http://www.citigroup.com/citigroup/citizen/microfinance/index.htm (accessed December 5, 2007).

Collins, J. and J. Porras. 1994. *Built to Last.* New York: HarperBusiness.

Davies, James B., Susanna Sandstrom, Anthony Shorrocks, and Edward N. Wolff. 2006. The World Distribution of Household Wealth. http://www.wider.unu.edu/research/2006-2007/2006-2007-1/wider-wdhw-launch-5-12-2006/wider-wdhw-report-5-12-2006.pdf (accessed December 5, 2007).

De Soto, Hernando. 2000. *The Mystery of Capital: Why Capitalism Triumphs in the West and Fails Everywhere Else.* New York: Basic Books.

Easterly, William. 2006. *The White Man's Burden: Why the West's Efforts to Aid the Rest Have Done So Much Ill and So Little Good.* New York: Penguin Press.

Economist. 2004. Special Report: More or Less Equal?—Global Economic Inequality March 13. Vol. 370, Iss. 8366, p. 84. http://www.economist.com/displayStory.cfm?story_id=2498851 (accessed December 5, 2007).

Emanuel, Linda. 2000. Ethics and the Structures of Health Care. *Cambridge Quarterly* 9: 151–168.

Fisher, Martin. 2007. How a $33 Investment Helped One Family out Of Poverty. http://kickstart.org/documents/HipPump.pdf (accessed December 5, 2007).

Freeman, R.E. 1984. *Strategic Management: A Stakeholder Approach*. Pitman Publishing: Boston.

———. 1994. The Politics of Stakeholder Theory. *Business Ethics Quarterly* 4: 409–421.

———. 1999. Divergent Stakeholder Theory. *Academy of Management Review* 24: 233–236.

———. 2001. A Stakeholder Theory of the Modern Corporation. In *Ethical Theory and Business Practice*, ed. T.L. Beauchamp and N.E. Bowie, 56–65. Upper Saddle River, NJ: Prentice Hall.

Freeman, R.E. and J. McVea. 2005. Stakeholder Theory: A Names and Faces Approach, How Focusing on Stakeholders as Individuals Can Bring Ethics and Entrepreneurial Strategy Together. *Journal of Management Inquiry* 14: 57–69.

Friedman, Milton. 1962. *Capitalism and Freedom*. Chicago: University of Chicago Press.

———. 1970. The Social Responsibility of Business Is to Increase Its Profits. *New York Times Magazine*, September 13: 32–33, 122, 124, 126.

Friedman, Thomas L. 2005. *The World is Flat: A Brief History of The Twentieth Century*. New York: Farrar, Straus and Giroux.

Gentner, D. and E.W. Whitley. 1997. Mental Models of Population Growth: A Preliminary Investigation. In *Environment, Ethics, and Behavior: The Psychology of Environmental Valuation and Degradation*, ed. M. Bazerman, D.M. Messick, A.E. Tenbrunsel, and K. Wade-Benzoni, 209–233. San Francisco, CA: New Lexington Press.

Goodpaster, K.E. 1991. Business Ethics and Stakeholder Analysis. *Business Ethics Quarterly* 1: 53–73.

Gore, Al. 2006. *An Inconvenient Truth: The Planetary Emergency of Global Warming and What We Can Do About It*. New York: Melcher Media.

Gorman, Michael. 1992. Simulating Science: Heuristics, Mental Models and Technoscientific Thinking. Bloomington: Indiana University Press.

Hart, Stuart. 2005. *Capitalism at the CrossRoads: The Unlimited Business Opportunities in Solving the World's Most Difficult Problems*. New Jersey: Wharton School Publishing.

Hendry, J. 2001. Economic Contracts versus Social Relationships as a Foundation for Normative Stakeholder Theory. *Business Ethics: A European Review* 10: 223–232.

Hindustan Lever Limited. 2005. Creating Markets. http://www.hll.com/brands/creating_markets.asp (accessed December 5, 2007).

Jensen, M. 2001. Value Maximisation, Stakeholder Theory, and the Corporate Objective Function. *European Financial Management* 7: 297–317.

Johnson, Mark. 1993. *Moral Imagination: Implications of Cognitive Science for Ethics*. Chicago: University of Chicago Press.

Karnani, Aneel G. 2006. Fortune at the Bottom of the Pyramid: A Mirage. Ross School of Business Paper No. 1035. http://ssrn.com/abstract=914518 (accessed December 5, 2007).

Kickstart. 2007. Micro-Irrigation Technologies. http://www.approtec.org/tech/pumps (accessed December 5, 2007).

Langewiesche, William. 2000. The Shipbreakers. *Atlantic Monthly* 286(2): 31–49.

Lonergan, Bernard. 1971. *Method in Theology*. Toronto: University of Toronto Press.

Maitland, A. 2005. From a Handout to a Hand Up. *Financial Times*, February 3. http://www.ft.com/cms/s/c13c209e-7589-11d9-9608-00000e2511c8.html (accessed December 5, 2007).

Marcoux, A.M. 2003. A Fiduciary Argument against Stakeholder Theory. *Business Ethics Quarterly* 13: 1–24.

Melé, Domenec. 2004. *The Principle of Subsidiarity in Business Organizations*. Barcelona, Spain: IESE Business School—Universidad de Navarra. http://www.iese.edu/research/pdfs/DI-0566-E.pdf (accessed December 5, 2007).

Miles, Morgan P. and J.G. Covin. 2000. Environmental Marketing: A Source of Reputational, Competitive and Financial Advantage. *Journal of Business Ethics* 23: 299–311.

Morelli, Mark D. and Elizabeth A. Morelli, eds. 1997. *The Lonergan Reader*. Toronto: University of Toronto Press.

Oregon Public Broadcasting. 2007. The New Heroes. http://www.pbs.org/opb/thenewheroes/meet/ruiz.html (accessed December 5, 2007).

P&G Health Sciences Institute. 2007a. Safe Drinking Water. http://pghsi.com/safewater/ (accessed December 5, 2007).

———. 2007b. Social Marketing of PUR Purifier of Water by PSI. http://www.pghsi.com/pghsi/safewater/video_library.html (accessed December 5, 2007).

Perrault, W.D. Jr. and E.J. McCarthy. 2002. *Basic Marketing: A Global-Managerial Approach*. Burr Ridge, IL: McGraw-Hill.

Phillips, R. 2003. Stakeholder Legitimacy. *Business Ethics Quarterly* 13: 25–41.

Plsek, P. 2001. Redesigning Health Care with Insights from the Science of Complex Adaptive Systems. In *Crossing the Quality Chasm: A New Health System for the 21st Century*. Committee on Quality of Health Care in America, Institute of Medicine (Ed.) 309–323. Washington DC: National Academy Press.

Prahalad, C.K. 2005. *The Fortune at the Bottom of the Pyramid: Eradicating Poverty through Profits*. Upper Saddle River, NJ: Wharton School Publishing.

Prahalad, C.K. and Allen Hammond. 2002. What Works: Serving the Worlds Poor, Profitably. *Harvard Business Review*. (Original publication, 2002: Washington, DC: Markle Foundation and World Resources Institute.)

Prahalad, C.K. and Stuart Hart. 2002. The Fortune at the Bottom of the Pyramid. *Strategy + Business* 26: 54–67.

Reck, Jennifer and Brad Wood. 2003. *What Works: Vodacom's Community Services Phone Shops*. Washington, DC: World Resources Institute Digital

Dividend. http://www.digitaldividend.org/pdf/vodacom.pdf (accessed December 5, 2007).

Sachs, Jeffrey D. 2005. *The End of Poverty: Economic Possibilities for Our Time*. New York: Penguin Press.

Senge, Peter. 1990. *The Fifth Discipline*. New York: Doubleday.

Smith, Adam. 1759; 1976. *The Theory of Moral Sentiments*. Ed. by A.L. Macfie and D.D. Raphael. Oxford: Oxford University Press.

Technoserve. 2007. "Who Benefits?" http://www.technoserve.org/work_impact/locations/kenya.aspx (accessed December 5, 2007).

Unerman, J. and M. Bennett. 2004. Increased Stakeholder Dialogue and the Internet: Towards Greater Corporate Accountability or Reinforcing Capitalist Hegemony. *Accounting Organization and Society* 29(7): 685–707.

United Nations. 2007. United Nations Millennium Development Goals. http://www.un.org/millenniumgoals/ (accessed December 5, 2007).

United Nations Development Programme. 2006. Malawi Data Sheet. http://hdrstats.undp.org/countries/data_sheets/cty_ds_MWI.html (accessed December 5, 2007).

Werhane, Patricia H. 1999. *Moral Imagination and Management Decision-Making*. New York: Oxford University Press.

———. 2002. Moral Imagination and Systems Thinking. *Journal of Business Ethics* 38: 33–42.

———. 2007. Mental Models, Moral Imagination and Systems Thinking in the Age of Globalization. *Journal of Business Ethics*. Published online (only): SpringerLink Date March 20, 2007 DOI 10.1007/s10551-006-9338-4.

Wolf, Susan. 1999. Toward a Systemic Theory of Informed Consent in Managed Care. *Houston Law Review* 35: 1631–1681.

Wright, Robert. 2005. Reading Between the Lines: The Incredible Shrinking Planet. What Liberals can Learn from Thomas Friedman's New Book. www.slate.com/id/2116899 (accessed December 5, 2007).

Yunus, Muhammad. 2003. *Banker to the Poor: Micro-Lending and the Battle against World Poverty*. New York: Public Affairs.

Chapter Three

Innovative Business Approaches and Poverty: Toward a First Evaluation

Emmanuel Raufflet, Alain Berranger, and Alam Aguilar-Platas

Introduction

Business managers and leaders, and management researchers alike over the last decade have displayed an unprecedented interest in poverty related issues from several perspectives (Zadek 2004; Hopkins 1999), including marketing and market creation (Hammond and Prahalad 2002; Prahalad 2004), social entrepreneurship (Bornstein 1998; Ashoka Foundation), as well as the connections between nature conservation and poverty alleviation (PriceWaterHouseCoopers 2007). Research in this growing field has often tended to emphasize the identification of the potential contributions of business for poverty alleviation. However, it has not built on solid conceptual foundations of the key notions of poverty and development. This chapter aims to evaluate the potential contributions and shortcomings of three of these emerging business approaches to alleviating poverty using Amartya Sen's definition and framework of development. The three business approaches evaluated here in light of this framework are: 1) the Bottom of Pyramid, 2) Social Entrepreneurship, and 3) Business and Nature Conservation.

This chapter examines the potential contributions of business to poverty reduction and alleviation using the definition and framework of poverty proposed by Amartya Sen in *Development as Freedom* (1999). This chapter is organized in to three sections. We first introduce Sen's definition and framework of development as well as the analytical framework we built from this framework to evaluate the three approaches. The second section presents the analysis of the three approaches in light of this framework. The third section concludes this chapter and identifies implications of this research for researchers and practitioners interested in business strategy and poverty alleviation.

Sen's Definition and Framework of Poverty

Sen's definition goes beyond the more classical "low income" definition of poverty. This definition tends to misrepresent the level of well-being of an individual or of a community. Sen (1999) argues that most important to human beings is not income or consumption, but rather the capacity to realize their potential as individuals and groups and to achieve what they value. Sen views the removal of un-freedoms, or obstacles that impede human beings from achieving what they value, as a central element of poverty alleviation strategies and to achieve development.

In this approach, Sen does not deny the importance of income; although income is most often a means to achieve other dimensions of well-being, it is not the only condition nor the end of the process of development. His definition of poverty emphasizes other aspects of freedom as important as the material dimension of well-being— including the freedom to decide to be free of unreasonable constraint from government, from oppressive communities, and the freedom to work and trade with others as they choose. Sen thus conceptualizes freedom as a framework of interdependent dimensions of the well-being of individuals or groups that is sustained by institutions. These institutions are to be sustained by the government that has a proper role for regulation, rule of law, and the provision of public services such as education and health, that will contribute to the people's well-being (Wilson and Wilson 2006, 61).

The centrality of Sen's conceptual contribution on poverty and development has been recognized with the Nobel Prize in Economics in 1998, as well as in international development academic and practitioners' circles; this new conception of poverty and development has influenced the creation of Human Development Index by the United Nations Development Programme, which combines measures of per capita income with statistics for life expectancy, schooling, and literacy.

As such, this definition of development includes an institutional, more comprehensive view of freedom. It emphasizes five interconnected

Table 3.1   Analytical framework based on Sen's definition of poverty

Dimension	Short definition	Evaluative question
Political freedoms	Right and opportunity to participate in community life	To what extent does the approach contribute to increasing political freedoms, both individual and collective?
Economic facilities	Access to markets	To what extent does this approach foster improved access to markets and economic value creation?
Social opportunities	Education and openness	To what extent does this approach contribute to enhancing improved education and openness?
Transparency guarantees	Protection against arbitrariness	To what extent does this approach contribute to strengthening protection from arbitrariness?
Protective security	Health and security	To what extent does this approach enhance access to health and security of individuals and communities?

Source: Author created.

and interrelated components of development: 1) political freedoms—the right and opportunity to participate in community life, 2) economic facilities—access to markets, 3) social opportunities—education and openness, 4) transparency guarantees—protection against arbitrariness, and 5) protective security—health. In order to evaluate approaches generated in business, we derived an analytical framework from this definition, which is presented in table 3.1.

We focus here on the three approaches: Bottom of Pyramid, Social Entrepreneurship, and Business and Nature Conservation. We chose these three approaches as each of them emphasizes one of the three dimensions of sustainable development (economic development, social development, and ecology). Bottom of Pyramid emphasizes economic value creation and improved access to products and services; Social Entrepreneurship emphasizes social value creation; and Business and

Nature Conservation emphasizes the ecological maintenance through economic value creation. We proceeded as follows. For the sake of simplicity, we decided to focus mainly on the potential roles of international firms in developing countries. We did not include actions or policies that firms could formulate to address poverty-related issues in developed areas. We selected the literature as follows: books and articles from main practitioner's journals published since 2000 on Business and Poverty (these are key words in their titles and abstracts) as a nonexhaustive but representative sample of these approaches. For each of these articles and books we mapped the logical model that could connect business and poverty. Doing so, we aimed at surfacing the connections between actions conducted by businesses and their effects on the forms of poverty. The overall questions we attempted to answer were: how actions generated by business in this approach may generate what form of change in poverty alleviation? What kind of change generated by business may lead to which outcomes on poverty? We considered, as an independent variable, business behaviour/ actions/ policies, and the like, as a dependent variable, one/ several forms of change related to poverty situations in developing countries. Mapping the logical model allowed us to map links—or absence of links—between business actions and poverty, as well as to map what dimensions of poverty were addressed (or not) by these three approaches.

An Evaluation of the Three Approaches of Business Strategy and Poverty Alleviation

This section presents our analysis of the three approaches generated in business as approaches to alleviate poverty: 1) the Bottom of Pyramid, 2) Social Entrepreneurship, and 3) Business and Nature Conservation in light of Sen's framework.

The Bottom of Pyramid Approach (BoP)

The BoP approach was coined and promoted by C.K. Prahalad and the proposition contains the following key elements. The starting point is the existence of a gap between different sections of society: while businesses—mainly MNCs—tend to ignore the poor, poverty-alleviation organizations such as NGOs and governments, while they do not have the sufficient capacity to alleviate poverty without businesses, often ignore or mistrust businesses. The common challenge shared across society regarding poverty alleviation thus deals with the creation of a sense of interdependency between the sectors of society. Prahalad (2004, chs 1, 2) identifies several reasons why MNCs often ignore the poor as potential customers, such as 1) more affluent segments of developing societies are easier, more profitable target consumers, 2) the poor do not have uses for products from developed countries, 3) only developed countries appreciate and pay for innovation, 4) the cost structure of MNCs prevents them from serving the poor, 5) the market of targeting the poor is no source of innovation for MNCs, and 6) the markets of serving the poor lack attractiveness, which makes it hard to recruit for MNCs.

He argues that poverty alleviation and business development can be reconciled through a win-win situation that requires a shift in thinking. The challenge is to create an "inclusive capitalism" and to transform the poor into customers or into distributors of products created by business. His proposition is to "stop thinking of the poor as victims or as a burden and start recognizing them as resilient entrepreneurs and value-conscious consumers" (2004, 1). He argues that the poor represent a latent market for MNCs of 4–5 billion customers or $15 trillion. Business can reach the fortune at the Bottom of Pyramid by creating the capacity among the poor to consume through increased affordability, improved access, and availability. In concrete terms, MNCs will increase access through smaller packages, access to credit, more extended distribution channels in areas such as consumer products health, food, and housing. In sum, this marketing-driven approach proposes two interrelated models of social change: 1) business will alleviate poverty by creating products that the poor will be able to afford; doing so, the poor will become consumers of products previously financially unaffordable and physically nonaccessible to them and 2) business will alleviate poverty through enterprise channel, the employment of poor for distribution of products to other poor, such as in slums or rural areas. In the 2004 book, Prahalad provides several examples of successes of the BoP approach including HLL (Hindustan Lever Ltd) in India (27 instances), Casas Bahia in Brazil (22 instances), Cemex in Mexico (5 instances), and Aravind Eye Care System and Hospital (20 instances) among others.

Several authors have recently critiqued several dimensions of the BoP approach (Wilson and Wilson 2006; Karnani 2006). Karnani contested 1) the actual size of the BoP market: while Prahalad (2004, 4) claims that the market size is 4 billion poor with less than $2 a day and $13 trillion (Prahalad 2004, 21), Karnani (2006, 5), based on 2001 World Bank estimates, evaluates this market as $2.7 billion poor and $1.2 trillion, 2) the actual profitability for MNCs to really reach out to the poor would be limited, as an increased distribution of more products to the poor would increase distribution costs thus reducing profitability, 3) the lack of systematic research on the actual potential and the reliance on several superficially researched examples, and 4) actually denounced a dangerous illusion, as this approach could lead to increased exploitation of the poor, as these newly designed and distributed products could divert expenditure of the poor from necessary to non-necessary products (Karnani, 2006: 14). Wilson and Wilson, following Jenkins (2004) display scepticism on the effects of the BoP on actual poverty alleviation effects and mention that several of the examples cited by Prahalad are not firms but NGOs (2006, 34).

We more particularly focus here on evaluating the BoP approach in relation to Amartya Sen's framework of development. This framework comprises five dimensions. The first dimension concerns political freedoms, defined as the right and opportunity to participate in community life. The BoP approach, as a mainly marketing-driven approach does not address this dimension. It does not propose any direct relation between the approach and improved political freedoms. Examples of affordable, available products have perfectly coexisted in the past with repressive regimes and political exclusion, such as Apartheid South Africa (Raufflet 2005) in which "racial fordism" was implemented for more than four decades (1948–90). The second dimension deals with improved economic facilities/access to markets. The BoP proposes to include the poor as consumers of products made affordable. Prahalad emphasizes particularly the role of MNCs in developing countries, as they are the ones with more innovation and distribution capacity to reach the poor. However, MNCs altogether employ a limited number of people: as of 1998, MNCs employed around 18 million in developing nations, as compared to an overall poor population estimated at 2 billion (Karnani 2006), from which the poor tend to be excluded as they lack the skills and competencies to be hired (Raufflet 2004). Furthermore, most of the employment in several developing countries is created by small and medium companies and/or in the informal sector of the economy (Raufflet and Garcia 2005). Karnani has highlighted that the poor are unlikely to be relieved from poverty as consumers and that the only condition for them to improve their situation is to become producers and improve their livelihoods; affordable products remain out of reach if one lives with $1 a day. The BoP proposes limited opportunities to the poor to become more productive and to increase their livelihoods. As such, BoP, as a mainly consumer-oriented approach differs from microproduction-driven poverty alleviation approaches such as microcredit, which has proven relatively effective across several contexts to provide access to economic facilities (Daley-Harris 2006). The third dimension concerns social opportunities—education and openness. Prahalad (2004, 13) mentions the empowerment that women achieve when they distribute cosmetic products in their villages, as they are able to increase their livelihoods, and the empowerment that dark-skinned Indian women feel when they use a whitening cream (Prahalad 2004). These transaction-driven forms of empowerment, despite being important, are probably different from deeper, more substantial forms of social and political empowerment that aim at achieving social transformation. The examples mentioned by Prahalad on empowerment concern consumption and sales whereas access to education and openness involve deeper forms of empowerment. The fourth dimension is transparency guarantees—protection against arbitrariness. The BoP approach does not indicate how it aims at increasing transparency guarantees either directly or indirectly. The last dimension concerns protective security, and access to health. As such BoP may lead to improved hygiene and to healthcare as firms can collaborate with public health organizations. At the same time, as suggested by the case of access to medication in transmissible diseases such as malaria, TB, and HIV/AIDS, the obstacle to access is not distribution channel but cost, as the remedies in numerous developing countries were so expensive as to be out of reach for the poor.

In all, the BoP, as a marketing-driven approach, displays an extremely limited potential to increase political freedoms, social opportunities, transparency, and it has a limited potential to increase protective security—in particular, with healthcare. As an overall consumer-driven approach, its effects on increased economic facilities remain limited.

Social Entrepreneurship and Poverty Alleviation

The second innovative approach we evaluated is Social Entrepreneurship. In this section, we review the definitions of social entrepreneurs (SE), highlight the processes by which social entrepreneurs may alleviate poverty, and highlight the contributions to the different dimensions of our analytical framework.

The concept of social entrepreneur builds the works of two founding fathers of entrepreneurship and management: Schumpeter and Drucker. Joseph Schumpeter (1883–1950) saw entrepreneurs as the ones who drive the "creative-destructive" process of capitalism with a technological or business innovation that may create or destroy an industry, reorganize a supply chain, or open up new markets; therefore, for Schumpeter, entrepreneurs are the economy's agents of change. Drucker (1985) viewed the entrepreneur as an opportunity-exploiter, as he is always looking for opportunities that come with changes, such as consumer preferences, technology, or social norms; the entrepreneur is looking for new opportunities to satisfy the needs of changing times by venturing into a new project or idea may this be in a for-profit or in a not-for-profit (NFP) context.

Established in 1980, Ashoka Foundation finances and supports social projects with professional consultants. For Ashoka, SEs do not depend on the government or business sector to start a social change, and further more, they are willing to spread their innovative model abroad. The definition given by the Ashoka organization:

> Ashoka is the global association of the world's leading social entrepreneurs—men and women with system changing solutions for the world's most urgent social problems. Since 1981, Ashoka has elected over 1,800 leading social entrepreneurs as Ashoka Fellows, providing them with living stipends, professional support, and access to a global network of peers in more than 60 countries. (www.ashoka.org accessed on October 18, 2007)

A first area of academic research has emphasized the individual attributes of social entrepreneurs. Waddock and Post (1991) study social entrepreneurs in the public sector and highlight their role as catalytitic agents: they are private citizens who provoke public awareness of an issue of general public concern and with their actions, the public attention will cause an eventual change in a public problem (Waddock and Post 1991, 393). Dees (1998) defines the characteristics of a SE as not just a "catalytic agent," but a "change agent in the social sector" or a profile that has "a mission with social value" and which fosters "continuous innovation and learning" (Dees 1998, 4). The social entrepreneur is an active person whose mission is to create social value with the help of innovation and learning.

In 2004, Seelos et al. analyzed the role of a SE in sustainable development; in doing so the authors added two important contributions for the SE's literature: 1) corporate social responsibility and 2) government policies, funds, NGOs, and international organizations. This perspective establishes distinct levels of individual and cooperative action toward sustaining 1) alliances between SE's and international organizations such as the Ashoka and Schwab Foundation (Schwab Foundation for Social Entrepreneurship 2007), and the "World Bank which in 2003 awarded more than $6 million in seed money to be shared by 47 small-scale, innovative development projects from 27 countries" (Seelos et al. 2004, 9), 2) SE collaboration with firms to promote social projects such as the Ethos Institute promotes CRS in Brazil. In addition, they highlight differences in their initial motivation, either opportunity-driven entrepreneurs or necessity-driven entrepreneurs. An opportunity-driven entrepreneur is an individual who detects and ventures a project to alleviate social problem; however, he or she is not directly affected by the problem, the individual is an outsider of the main problematic (e.g., Yunnus and the Grameen Bank). The necessity-driven entrepreneur is an individual who is (or was) directly affected by social problem (e.g., Wangari Maathai and Greenbelt movement). Social value, defined as actions toward sustainable development considering individuals, communities, or societies and for future generations, can thus be a result of entrepreneurial activities, or the primary motivation per se. SEs are change agents looking for social development through new business models or organizational structures and they have different motivations. SEs can have strategic alliances to accomplish their goals with corporations, NGOs, and governments. Weerawardenaa et al. (2006) elaborate a list of the attributes that a SE must have. The authors define social entrepreneurship as a behavioral phenomenon expressed in a not-for-profit organization context aimed at delivering social value through the exploitation of perceived opportunities involving three dimensions: innovativeness, proactiveness, and risk management. Refer to table 3.2 for a systematic list of definitions of social entrepreneurship.

Paul Light (2006) cites four main problems related to the overall individualistic approach of social entrepreneurship that has prevailed so far in the literature: 1) a cult of personality that focuses on individual traits, 2) the tendency to ignore the role of network behind the SE that provides resources for pattern-breaking and social change, 3) the main point to success is not necessarily a new idea per se, but it is to have

Table 3.2 Definitions of social entrepreneurship

Author, Reference	Social Entrepreneur Definition
1 Waddock, Sandra A., Post, James E. (1991). *Social Entrepreneurs and Catalytic Change.* Public Administration Review	Social entrepreneurs are private sector citizens who play critical roles in bringing about "catalytic changes" in the public sector agenda and the perception of certain social issues. Although not involved in direct actions to solve public problems, their work sets the stage and context for policy making and policy implementation activities.
2 Dees, J. Gregory (1998). *The Meaning of Social Entrepreneur.* Graduate School of Business Stanford University	Social entrepreneurs play the role of change agents in the social sector, by: • Adopting a mission to create and sustain social value (not just private value), • Recognizing and relentlessly pursuing new opportunities to serve that mission, • Engaging in a process of continuous innovation, adaptation, and learning, • Acting boldly without being limited by resources currently in hand, and • Exhibiting a heightened sense of accountability to the constituencies served and for the outcomes created.
3 Seelos, Christian Seelos, Mair, Johanna (2004). *Social Entrepreneurship: The Contribution of Individual Entrepreneurs to Sustainable Development.* Anselmo Rubiralta Center for globalization and strategy center for business in society	Social entrepreneurs endeavor to create social value through innovative entrepreneurial business models. Social entrepreneurs must create novel business models and organizational structures, and unique strategies for brokering between very limited, disparate and often dynamic resources to create social value. SE find new and efficient ways to create products, services or structures that either directly cater to social needs or that enable others to cater to social needs that must be satisfied in order to achieve sustainable development.
4 Tan, Wee-Liang, Williams, John, Tan, Teck-Meng (2005). *Defining the "Social" in "Social Entrepreneurship": Altruism and Entrepreneurship.* Singapore Management University	A legal person is a social entrepreneur from t1 to t2 just in case that person attempts from t1 to t2, to make profits for society or a segment of it by innovation in the face of risk, in a way that involves that society or segment of it.
5 Light C. Paul (2006). *Reshaping Social Entrepreneurship*	A social entrepreneur is an individual, group, network, organization, or alliance of

Continued

Table 3.2   Continued

Author, Reference	Social Entrepreneur Definition
Stanford Social Innovation Review	organizations that seeks sustainable, large-scale change through pattern-breaking ideas in what or how governments, nonprofits, and businesses do to address significant social problems.
6 Weerawardenaa, Jay, Sullivan Mort, Gillian (2006). *Investigating Social Entrepreneurship: A Multidimensional Model.* Journal of World Business	Social entrepreneurship: • is responsive to and constrained by environmental dynamics. • strives to achieve social value creation through the display of innovativeness. • strives to achieve social value creation through the display of proactiveness. • strives to achieve social value creation through the display of risk management. • is responsive to and constrained by the need for organizational sustainability. • is responsive to and constrained by the social mission. • opportunity identification is responsive to and constrained by the organizational sustainability, social mission, and environmental dynamics.
7 Spear, Roger (2006). *Social Entrepreneurship: A Different Model?* International Journal of Social Economics	It differentiates between the conventional popular model of the individual entrepreneur creating their own enterprise from initiatives involving more than one person, and in particular looking at initiatives that involve a more formal, institutional focus of entrepreneurial activity. The social dimension of entrepreneurship is examined within the research: by exploring the extent to which social or community goals played a part in its formation and subsequent operation.
8 Dorado, Silvia (2006). *Social Entrepreneurial Ventures: Different Values So Different Process of Creation, no?* Journal of Developmental Entrepreneurship	They are nonprofit organizations entering into business to finance their social service operations. They can also be for-profit ventures that define their mission as having a double bottom line. Finally, they can be cross-sector SEVs, collaborative initiatives engaging nonprofit, profit, for-profit, and/or public organizations to solve particularly challenging social problems.
9 Ashoka, Social Entrepreneurship	Social entrepreneurs are individuals with innovative solutions to society's most pressing

Continued

Table 3.2   Continued

Author, Reference	Social Entrepreneur Definition
Organization. http://www.ashoka.org	social problems. They are ambitious and persistent, tackling major social issues and offering new ideas for wide-scale change.
	Rather than leaving societal needs to the government or business sectors, social entrepreneurs find what is not working and solve the problem by changing the system, spreading the solution, and persuading entire societies to take new leaps.

and provide the resources to pass from an ordinary good practice into a social context, and 4) a tendency to eclipse entrepreneurial activities within well-established organizations.

A second and more recent area of academic research has emphasized the connections between the individual entrepreneur and his/her network. It now emerges in the literature that SEs are not solo players active in front of social problems; they are also individuals who worry to make things different and can deliver profit to both society and themselves, risking their own capital; this is achieved thanks to a social network and different stakeholders (Tan et al. 2005, Spear 2006). Dorado (2006) highlights that the academic literature on social entrepreneurship is still limited and that there is disagreement among scholars on what they even mean by social entrepreneurship. Her article will join the previous efforts of defining SE and thus present three different categories (see table 3.2): 1) they are nonprofit organizations entering into business to finance their social service operations, 2) they can also be for-profit ventures that define their mission as having a double bottomline, and they can be 3) alliances of social entrepreneurial ventures (SEV) engaging nonprofit, for-profit and/or public organizations to solve particularly social problems. They are nonprofit organizations entering into business to finance their social service operations.

Three Processes of Social Entrepreneurship

Social entrepreneurs solve social problems in different dimensions—with profit, nonprofit strategies, alliances, knowledge transfer, and soon—as we have previously analyzed. However, we propose that the SE strategies and scopes of action to solve a predetermined social problem differ. In particular, according to their own abilities, knowledge, background studies, social concerns, we propose that each SE will use one of the following approaches to address a social problem: 1) commercial business skills, 2) knowledge and technology, and 3) catalyst innovation and creativity approach.

(1) Commercial Business Process Social entrepreneurs in this category (Bornstein 2004, Seelos et al. 2004, Tan et al. 2005, Dorado 2006, Light 2006, Weerawardenaa et al. 2006, Ashoka 2007) mobilize their knowledge and business skills to alleviate a social problem creating profits with innovative business models. SEs are either insiders or outsiders with respect to a social problem that is brought to conscious awareness by their internal motivations. The Grameen Bank illustrates this process as a profit-oriented and poverty-alleviation organization.

(2) Knowledge and Technology Process This strategy aims to solve social problems through the generation of employment and revenue by non-for-profit organizations (Dees 1998, Borstein 2004, Dorado 2006, Ashoka 2007) using knowledge and technology skills either directly from the SE or his or her network resource. The Kenyan Greenbelt movement founded by the 2004 Nobel Peace Prize winner, Wangari Maathai is a cited example on the literature. This nonprofitable organization mobilized rural women to combat deforestation in Kenya. The biologist Wangari Maathai transferred successfully her knowledge to a network of African women.

(3) Innovation and Creativity Process This process focuses on creating innovative ideas, though nonprofitable organizations or actions. The SEs strategy in this approach is to mobilize resources and serve as a catalyst in order to alleviate distinct poverty dimensions (Waddock 1991, Bornstein 2004, Spear 2006, Ashoka Foundation). The catalytic agent could be an organization or an individual that either encourages, finances, transfers and shares knowledge or technology, with close assistance and training programs (e.g., Ashoka Foundation, Ethos Institute, The Schwab Foundation). This approach described in the literature has a multiplier effect on social entrepreneurship, as aid programs may serve as incubators of social entrepreneurs, or just as a changing agent for social transformations (e.g., James Grant, cited in Bornstein 2004).

Social entrepreneurship aims at creating social and economic value. We define social value creation as generating development opportunities for a group of individuals who will later benefit a larger community and eventually to society in the five dimensions described by Sen. Economic value is defined as the capability of acquiring goods and services to satisfy needs, in economical terms the economic value can be measured with GDP, employment indicators, inflation, consumer price indicators, and macro economical indicators.

The first dimension described by Sen concerns political freedoms defined as the right and opportunity to participate in community life. Social entrepreneurship as catalyst individuals for new ideas (Bornstein 2004) or organizations (e.g., Ashoka Foundation, Ethos Institute, The Schwab Foundation, Greenbelt movement) encourage individuals to venture their own projects or to participate for their own community and with it encouraging the opportunity and the right to participate directly in the community life.

The second dimension deals with improved economic facilities/access to markets. Social Entrepreneurs as aforementioned, not only address to create social value but also improve economic facilities allowing individuals access to markets, creating opportunities not only to acquire products and services tailored for them but also the opportunity to create innovative ideas to satisfy communitarian needs (e.g., Microcredits).

The third dimension concerns social opportunities—education and openness can be created from Social Entrepreneurs by a project ventured especially for this. For instance, the Abrinquiq foundation was created by the SE Odej Grajew as an effort "to promote defence of the rights and the exercise of citizenship for children and adolescents" (Fundação Abrinq 2007). One of the foundation's focus is children's education "involving different educational dimensions such as: culture, sports, leisure, vocational preparation, and personal development" (Fundação Abrinq 2007).

The fourth dimension is transparency guarantees—protection against arbitrariness. Social Entrepreneurs are not solo players; behind them there is a social network that can produce pressure against social injustices and arbitrariness. For instance, the Ethos Institute founded by Odej Grajew mobilizes and helps "companies to manage their businesses in a socially responsible manner, making them partners in the construction of a fair sustainable society" (Ethos Institute 2007). The Ethos Institute promotes transparency guarantees for the Brazilian society with its network's aid.

The last dimension concerns protective security and access to health. Social Entrepreneurs' interests are vast and developing initiatives to promote health access in society are not an exception. James P. Grant, a social entrepreneur is a great example for this last dimension.

He headed UNICEF and promoted health programs all around the world and massively increased the number of children around the globe receiving vaccinations and essential micronutrients.

In all, social entrepreneurship is a vast multidisciplinary phenomenon that will attack almost any social problem and will promote development in all dimensions mentioned by Sen (1999), and it is limited only by the creativity ingrained by the SE motivations and resources. However, since social entrepreneurship is a recent phenomena studied by researchers, authors describe different streams and ideas for social entrepreneurs. Thus the frontiers of SE are not well established, creating ambiguous concepts, with it raising questions of validity and reliability among the existing literature.

Business and Nature Conservation

The third innovative approach we looked at is Business and Nature Conservation. Most of the world's rural poor live in biodiversity-rich regions of the tropics. The world's biodiversity is distributed largely in inverse proportion to the scientific and technological capacity (Macilwain 1998; Ten Kate and Laird 2000). Issues of deforestation and land degradation, habitat loss, low agricultural productivity, water scarcity, civil conflicts, and wars, all contribute to threats to biological diversity and its major losses. The poverty-environment nexus is a major development challenge based "on the time inconsistency problem between short-term survival strategies and longer-term environmental concerns" (Leyeka Lufumpa 2005) and the conservation of community natural resources.

> Too often, local people are forced to destroy the most precious capital they have—the biodiversity and ecosystems in their own backyard. Breaking this vicious cycle of poverty and biodiversity loss requires local ingenuity and the entrepreneurship to create new forms of income from the preservation rather than the over-harvesting of nature. (United Nations Development Programme 2007)

In international development circles it has been generally hypothesized that if local people can benefit from activities that depend on local natural resources, they would ensure their conservation and sustainable use. With the increased popularity of private sector development solutions for poverty reduction in international development since 2004, with the release of the Martin-Zedillo UN Report of the

Commission on the Private Sector and Development—"Unleashing Entrepreneurship: Making Business Work for the Poor," enterprise solutions to poverty reduction have been the darling of international aid agencies (Donor Committee for Enterprise Development 2007). However, it is also now established knowledge that conservation enterprise solutions are not always the only and best way of conserving biodiversity (Morris 2005, 2007). In Jennifer Morris' words (Personal Communication, February 24, 2005 and January 16, 2007), the key question posed "is the enterprise route the most cost-effective and time-efficient way to achieve the conservation objectives?"

The enterprise model for biodiversity conservation is no doubt applicable if it is not seen as a "magic" solution. In learning from experiences of silkworm rearing in the Garhwal Himalayas of India, for instance, community enterprises are not effective when they simply link producers to a market and are effective at conserving biodiversity when they are directly linked to the use of in-situ biodiversity, involve a community of stakeholders, and monitoring is participatory (Croucher 2007). In fact a number of other investigations in local Asia and Pacific communities have shown that a community-based enterprise strategy can lead to conservation, but only under limited conditions (Salafsky et al. 2001), as well as engender improved livelihoods and increased community empowerment and well-being (Senyk 2005). If one extends to definitions of poverty reduction that go beyond pure income growth to include improvements in political, environmental, and social freedoms (as Amartya Sen's [1999] argues so well!), then these findings are quite encouraging. See figure 3.1 for a logical flow-chart of a local enterprise model proposed by authors.

The biodiversity-business nexus has always been part of rural survival and development, including traditional livelihoods depending, inter alia, on medicinal plants, wild foods, livestock herding, bushmeat, fish, water, biomass fuel like wood and charcoal. The key issue today is the legal and sustainable use of natural and biodiversity resources. This nexus has taken on new meanings and forms, a slow evolution since the Convention on Biological Diversity (CBD) was signed in 1992. Governments are to facilitate access to genetic resources in return for fair and equitable sharing of benefits (CBD Article 1). One of the earliest and better known cases of ecosystem services and conservation payments is the Merck/INBio agreement in Costa Rica of September 1991 (Blum 1993). Markets and new market solutions to conserve biodiversity services are nascent and growing (Jenkins et al. 2004), and include land acquisition, ecotourism, conservation concessions and management contracts, tradable rights,

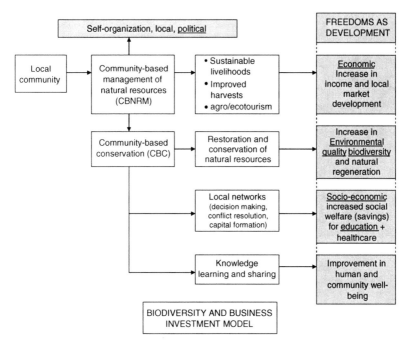

Figure 3.1 Biodiversity and Business—logical flowchart of local enterprise model.

eco-labeling and biodiversity-friendly emissions trading. The concept of "protecting through sustainable use" is taking form through five main sustainable businesses: ecotourism, natural forest and plantation management, afforestation projects that generate carbon dioxide reduction certificates under the Clean Development Mechanism of the Kyoto Protocol, use of wild animals, organic farming, and wild harvesting (PricewaterhouseCoopers 2007).

The financial markets are not standing still in the face of climate change and other global environmental challenges. As profits and value-appreciation are generated by environmentally friendly investments (carbon-emissions trading, biofuels, windfarms, etc.) and consumers and advocacy groups put pressure on investors and operators, the financial and capital markets are spinning off innovative ecological/sustainable investment products in the form of hundreds of environmental, ethical, and social investment funds of all kinds. The greening of the financial markets is still in its infancy with sustainable investments only

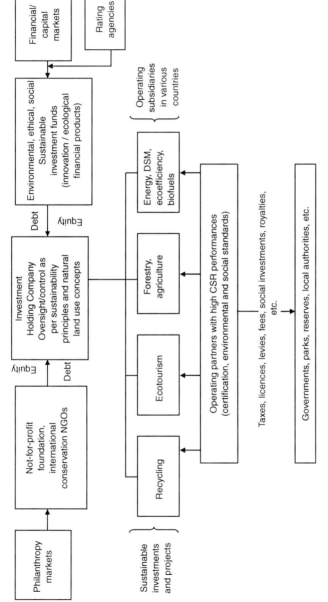

Figure 3.2 Sustainable investments for biodiversity conservation—financial/corporate structure.

Source: Adapted from PricewaterhouseCoopers (2007).

a very small fraction of all investments available. An investment model is flowcharted in figure 3.2 adapted from the PriceWaterHouseCoopers study for WWF. The originality of this model resides in the business case it makes for biodiversity conservation while ensuring that sustainability principles and natural land use practices are central to the oversight and control of the operating companies by an investment holding company controlled by not-for-profit international conservation NGOs and philanthropists. This instrument provides an opportunity for green philanthropy to blend with green capital markets, offering sustainability guarantees to both types of investors. When compared with local enterprise options, what differential impact might such large-scale investment models have at the community level? What differentiates the global and local enterprise models for biodiversity conservation in terms of business skills, access to markets, access to credit and, the role of the local communities?

Besides entrepreneurship and knowledge, the successful establishment of an enterprise also requires a set of multidisciplinary skills not easily found in rural communities where biodiversity is concentrated. When the sons and daughters of the community end up acquiring basic business skills, they most often do not return to their original villages. When faced with external threats to their local natural resources and related livelihoods, communities will respond in many different manners ranging from extremes of exile to violent resistance. If an enterprise strategy is part of the solution, it must slowly evolve through local leadership and requires a favorable enabling environment and key external inputs such as marketing and savings/credit. The business development value-chain analysis reveals that external resources are critical to local enterprises in at least two areas: marketing strategy and credit facilities.

Challenges

Access to Markets

Luxury barefoot ecotourism lodges (pristine sites with cultural heritage for instance, like Ibo Island, Mozambique or Siwa Oasis, Egypt) and wild-harvested gourmet chocolates, for instance, are two niche markets that encompass the challenges to market access for local enterprises. These end-use markets are very complex to reach, let alone do it profitably, and require sophisticated Web-based marketing tools, as well as other market intermediaries (Ecotourism at

Conservation International 2007, and The International Ecotourism Society 2007).

The marketing of wild-harvested cacao from Bolivian rainforests, through REPSA, transformed into "cru sauvage" truffles available on the Internet is truly a journey of wonder (Confiserie Sprüngli AG 2007). REPSA is a small Bolivian shareholder enterprise that provides an outlet for local rainforest cacao harvesters and most important the marketing expertise to move upstream into chocolate markets as well as the expertise, patience, and know-how to get organic certification. Local community livelihoods and traditional lifestyles are sustained while the upstream business is handled by intermediary entrepreneurs who make it a business to care about environmentally sound practices. Compare this approach with Kuapa Kokoo, Ghana's largest cooperative with a membership of 45,000 cocoa growers, which owns 45 percent of Divine Chocolate, a British chocolate company with an American affiliate, and has two seats on is board (*Economist* 2007). Divine bought 1,200 tonnes of cocoa from Kuapa Kokoo in 2006, all of it on Fairtrade terms (Fairtrade Labelling Organizations International 2007 and TransFair Canada 2007).

The degree of local empowerment and of other freedoms as development of the communities is a function of the enterprise model chosen or available and also of the route taken to access markets. However, the support and advice from international and local NGOs and from enterprise development and export support agencies are critical determinants to the ability and of the opportunity of the producers to move up the value-chain (Laven 2005).

The rapid growth of biodiversity-linked markets for certified organic foods and beverages, certified wood products, fair trade products and channels, and ecotourism is encouraging. However, the value added by local communities and intermediaries that care for them is most often not reflected in the profit-sharing and wealth creation. Typically, value-added increases upstream reflect factor costs increases along the value-chain. The social net benefits, the redistribution of net wealth creation, and the distributional impact of the value added rarely reverse the income inequities that build along the chain (Laven 2005).

Access to Credit

Biodiversity conservation finance is a challenge. Biodiversity-friendly livelihoods and business activities need to multiply if biodiversity conservation is to stabilize current losses and possibly reverse the trend. Innovative funding models and mechanisms need to emerge to tap the philanthropy and capital markets. The French development tax on flying and the recent practice in the United States of purchasing air travel offsets are two examples of such innovations. The 2007 CI partnership with Bank of America (Bank of America 2007) shows there is no lack of creativity or good ideas when it comes time to invest in corporate social responsibility. Minimizing socioenvironmental impacts of business on natural and biological resources has become a main-streamed corporate consideration, only limited for now by high investment barriers and sunk profits from past unsustainable practices (like red-mud lakes in bauxite mining).

The challenges of grassroots SME funding for biodiversity-linked products and markets (Rubino 2000) are of a different nature. These entrepreneurs are close to the habitat and the community (they act locally) but are globally informed (they think globally). The banking business services in the Global South are generally available in local currency for established businesses but unavailable for new entrants. Foreign exchange credits are very hard to obtain legally throughout the developing world and black markets often prevail. The funding gap between microcredit loan amounts and large domestic or investment banking loans for established businesses is quite an obstacle to entrepreneurial activities in biodiversity-linked businesses. The situation is similar with venture capital, especially in Africa. The sector is so nascent in Africa and so sophisticated in the Northern financial places that investments portfolio (deal flow) is totally inadequate, even for social venture capitalists. Too much capital chasing too few projects!

Trade-offs in Poverty Reduction between Income Growth and Freedoms as Development

In the large investment model, the community benefits in a different way if it organizes its own local enterprise. In the latter, its local political empowerment and economic freedom will be maximized while in the former its income and social benefits as a result of formal-type employment will probably be higher. In the large investment model, the smart outside company will call for community involvement that is still less empowering than if there is community ownership through shareholding and control over operating policies through the board of directors elected among shareholders.

Conclusions and Implications for Researchers and Managers

This chapter used Sen's framework to assess the recent approaches proposed by business and management scholars to alleviate poverty. It particularly aimed to map where the most and least promising contributions of business could be in the light of this comprehensive and multidimensional definition.

Our analysis highlights that these approaches have strengths and limitations. On a conceptual level, they are still "in their infancy": they lack solid conceptual definitions and rigorous models of social change; these approaches would probably gain from systematic research that would evaluate their effects on poverty alleviation.

On the connections between business strategy and development, our analysis suggests that these approaches seem to have more potential to address economic dimensions of poverty—increasing incomes; creating economic value—than on "softer," less tangible dimensions of development, such as participation in community, or political dimensions.

Implications for Management Researchers

Debates on the links between business and poverty have long been absent both among management academics and business practitioners circles. Connecting business strategy (the independent variable) with poverty (dependent variable) is new to management research. For a long time, debates on poverty—the dependent variable—have mainly been located in public policy, development economics (Stiglitz 2003), and more generally, international development studies. This was mainly the domain of government and international cooperation/aid (Easterly 2002, 2006); social anthropologists (Crewe and Harrison 1999), development economics (Sachs 2005), and critical thinkers (Banerjee 2003, Castro 2004). International businesses were long criticized as exploiters of the poor in developing countries (Ziegler 2002). Recent studies from management scholars on international firms and their local milieus in developing countries have documented these interactions and provided more nuanced account of these interactions (Pedersen and Huniche 2006, Bird, Raufflet, and Smucker 2004, Bird and Herman 2004).

Our core competency, as a group of management scholars, is to understand what is going on in business organizations and to propose recommendations for action to managers and business leaders. As such, venturing out into a new field such as the connections between business strategy and poverty alleviation is simultaneously promising and dangerous. The promise is to identify new avenues—both conceptual and action-oriented—that previous researchers from other disciplines had not explored or identified. Business deals with wealth-creation—it is obvious that wealth-creation is part of the solution to poverty. Our position as management researchers, as "specialists" of management and business organizations gives us an edge in doing so: in providing a deeper understanding of the functioning of business organizations. However, there are two dangers for us in these explorations. The first one is conceptual: the danger of "venturing out" of the behavior of the business organization, our independent variable, which has been our main unit of analysis and field of interest for many years might lead us to oversimplify the complexities of poverty and development and the dependent variable: after all, as seen from this analysis of three approaches that connect business and poverty, poverty is still a poorly conceptualized concept in management and business in general.

The second danger concerns our collective responsibility vis-à-vis managers and business leaders who do have a sheer interest in addressing poverty-related issues. Our potential role is to help them make sense of these connexions to really increase the positive impact they intend to have. The danger is to propagate naïve statements and fallacies that may lead to the demise of this new interest among management debates into demise. Unfortunately, poverty-related challenges are daunting and real. Providing systematic and reliable knowledge and understanding is an important endeavor ahead. Here lies a responsibility for our field and for the problem at hand.

Implications for Business Leaders and Managers

Over the last few years there has been an increasing interest in order to make business part of the solution to poverty. Several approaches have been developed, proposed, and diffused from both practice and research. In this chapter we have used a simple framework grounded on a solid definition of poverty and development to evaluate three of these new approaches. We propose three implications of this chapter for business leaders and managers interested in the connections between business strategy and poverty alleviation. The first one is conceptual: we have confronted here business approaches with a definition and framework generated in political sciences/economics. This confrontation has allowed us to go beyond the "halo effect" of these approaches and to identify their strengths and limitations. The second one is methodological. We used this framework for these three approaches, which revealed the strengths and limitations of these on poverty and development. We could suggest the use of this simple framework for evaluating business actions on poverty alleviation. After all, managers and business leaders use management and business concepts to describe and understand business and management dimensions of their work. It might be advisable to use adequate poverty and development concepts to describe, define, and understand poverty and development realities. The third one is more practical. Business does not operate in a vacuum, nor can it ignore local milieus it may contribute to positively—in addressing poverty-related issues for instance. Managers and business leaders could become more acquainted to the local milieus in which they operate by integrated national and local poverty strategy plans into their business strategy objectives.

References

Ashoka. 2007. http://www.ashoka.org (accessed on December 5, 2007).

Banerjee, Subhrata Bobby. 2003. Who Sustains Whose Development? Sustainable Development and Reinvention of Nature. *Organization Studies* 24(1): 143–180.

Bank of America. 2007. https://www.bankofamerica.com/index.jsp (accessed December 5, 2007).

Bird, F. Raufflet, E. and J. Smucker. 2004. *International Businesses and the Dilemmas of Development: Case Studies on Global Responsibilities and the Practices of Businesses in Developing Areas.* London: MacMillan.

Bird, Frederick and Manuel Velasquez. 2006. *Just Business Practices in a Diverse Developing World. Essays on International Business and Global Responsibilities.* New York: Palgrave Macmillan, p. 301.

Bird, Frederick and Stewart W. Herman. 2004. *International Business and the Challenges of Poverty in the Developing World. Case Studies on Global Responsibilities and Practices.* New York: Palgrave Macmillan, p. 247.

Bornstein, David. 2004. *How to Change the World. Social Entrepreneurs and the Power of New Ideas.* New York: Oxford University Press, p. 320.

Blum, E. 1993. Making Biodiversity Conservation Profitable: A Case Study of the Merck/INBio Agreement. *Environment* 35(4): 16–20, 38–45.

Castro, Carlos J. 2004. Sustainable Development. *Organization and Environment* 17(2): 195–224.

Confiserie Sprüngli AG. 2007. http://www.spruengli.ch/Shop/geschenkideen-katalog.php?lang=en&catalog=1008 (accessed December 5, 2007).

Crewe, Emma and Elizabeth Harrison. 1999. *Whose Development? An Ethnography of Aid.* New York: Zed Books, p. 214.

Croucher, J. 2007. The Enterprise Model for Biodiversity Conservation: A Critique. http://www.ansab.org/research_papers/ntfp_paper_JC.pdf (accessed December 5, 2007).

Daley-Harris, Sam. 2006. State of the Microcredit Summit Campaign Reort 2006. http://www.microcreditsummit.org/pubs/reports/socr/2006/SOCR06.pdf (accessed December 5, 2007). Washington, DC: Microcredit Summit Campaign.

Dees, J. Gregory. 1998. *The Meaning of "Social Entrepreneurship."* http://www.fntc.info/files/documents/The%20meaning%20of%20Social%20Entreneurship.pdf (accessed December 5, 2007).

Donor Committee for Enterprise Development. 2007. http://www.enterprise-development.org/ (accessed December 5, 2007).

Dorado, Silvia. 2006. Social Entrepreneurial Ventures: Different Values So Different Process of Creation, No? *Journal of Developmental Entrepreneurship* 11(4), 319–343.

Drucker, P.F. 1985. *Innovation and entrepreneurship: practice and principles,* New York: Harper and Row.

Easterly, William. 2002. *The Elusive Quest for Growth. Economists' Adventures and Misadventures in the Tropics.* London: The MIT Press, p. 342.

———. 2006. *The White Man's Burden. Why the West's Efforts to Aid the Rest Have Done So Much Ill and So Little Good.* New York: The Penguin Press, p. 436.

Economist. 2007. Chocolate—Thinking out of the Box. *Economist,* April 7, 2007, p. 65.

Ecotourism at Conservation International. 2007. http://www.ecotour.org (accessed December 5, 2007).

Ethos Institute. 2007. http://www.ethos.org.br (accessed December 5, 2007).

Fairtrade Labelling Organizations International. 2007. http://www.fairtrade.net (accessed December 5, 2007).

Fundação Abrinq. 2007. http://www.fundabrinq.org.br (accessed December 5, 2007).

Hammond, J. and C.K. Prahalad. 2002 Serving the Poor, Profitability. *Harvard Business Review,* October, 12–21.

Hopkins, Michael. 1999. *The Planetary Bargain. Corporate Social Responsibility Comes of Age.* New York: St. Martin's Press, p. 229.

Jain, Trilok Kumar. 1999. *Entrepreneurship for Social Cause: A Study of Western India.* Ph.D. Dissertation report. Department of Business Management Faculty of Management Bhavnagar University, p. 219.

Jenkins, Michael, Sara J. Scherr, and Mira Inbar. 2004. Markets for Biodiversity Services: Potential Roles and Challenges. *Environment* (July/ August 2004): 32.

Karnani, Aneel G. 2006. *Fortune at the Bottom of the Pyramid: A Mirage, How the Private Sector can Help Alleviate Poverty.* Working paper no. 1035, Version November 2006, University of Michigan, Ross School of Business, p. 40.

Laven, A. 2005. *Relating Cluster and Value Chain Theory to Upgrading of Primary Commoditie: The Cocoa Chain in Ghana.* December, AMIDSt, University of Amsterdam, unpublished, p. 67.

Leyeka Lufumpa, Charles. 2005. The Poverty-environment Nexus in Africa. *African Development Review* 17(3): 335–591.

Light C. Paul. 2006. Reshaping Social Entrepreneurship. *Stanford Social Innovation Review* 4(3) Fall 2006: 47–51.

Macilwain, C. 1998. When Rhetoric Hits Reality in Debate on Bioprospecting. *Nature* 392(9) April 1998: 535–541.

Mair, Johanna, Jeffrey Robinson, and Kai Hockerts. 2006. *Social Entrepreneurship.* New York: Palgrave Macmillan, p. 280.

Pedersen Rahbek, Esben and Mahad Huniche. 2006. *Corporate Citizenship in Developing Countries. New Partnership Perspectives.* Denmark: Copenhagen Business School Press, p. 277.

Prahalad, C.K. 2004. The Market at the Bottom of the Pyramid, The fortune at the Bottom of the Pyramid, *Wharton School Publishing.* Upper Sadle River, NJ: Pearson Education.

PricewaterhouseCoopers. 2007. Sustainable Investments for Conservation: The Business Case for Biodiversity. A study on behalf of the World Wide Fund for Nature (WWF), p. 56.

Raufflet, E. 2005. International Businesses in the Political Economy of South Africa. In *International Businesses and the Dilemmas of Development,* ed. Bird, Raufflet, and Smucker, 36–56. London: Macmillan.

Raufflet, E. and C. Garcia de la Torre. 2005. A la recherche du Pérou: Un regard sur les études organisationnelles péruviennes 1960–2000. *Management International* 9(2) Spring 2005: 61–75.

Rubino, M. 2000. Biodiversity Finance. *International Affairs* 76(2) 2000: 223–240.

Sachs, Jeffrey D. 2005. *The End of Poverty. Economic Possibilities for Our Time.* New York: The Penguin Group, p. 397.

Salafsky, N., H. Cauley, G. Balachander, B. Cordes, J. Parks, C. Margoluis, S. Bhatt, C. Encarnacion, D. Russell, and R. Margoluis. 2001. A Systematic Test of an Enterprise Strategy for Community-based Biodiversity Conservation. *Conservation Biology* 15(6): 1585–1595. Schwab Foundation for Social Entrepreneurship. 2007. http://www.schwabfound.org/ (accessed December 5, 2007).

Seelos, Christian and Johanna Mair. 2004. Social Entrepreneurship: The Contribution of Individual Entrepreneurs to Sustainable Development. Working paper no. 553. University of Navarra. IESE Business School. Center for Business in Society, p. 17.

Sen, Amartya. 1999. *Development as Freedom.* New York: Anchor Books, p. 366.

Senyk, J. 2005. *Lessons from the Equator Initiative: Community-based Management by Pred Nai Community Forest Group in the Mangroves of Southeastern Thailand.* Unpublished, Centre for Community-Based Resource Management, University of Manitoba, p. 55. http://www.umanitoba.ca/institutes/natural_resources/pdf/Tech%20Report%20Thailand%20-%20Jason%20Senyk.pdf (accessed December 5, 2007).

Spear, Roger. 2006. Social Entrepreneurship: A Different Model? *International Journal of Social Economics* 33(5–6): 399–410.

Stiglitz, Joseph E. 2003. *Globalization and its Discontents.* New York: W.W. Norton, p. 288.

Tan, Wee-Liang, John Williams, and Teck-Meng Tan. 2005. Defining the "Social" in "Social Entrepreneurship": Altruism and Entrepreneurship. *International Entrepreneurship and Management Journal* 1(3) September: 353–365.

Ten Kate, K. and S.A. Laird. 2000. Biodiversity and Business: Coming to Terms with the "Grand Bargain." *International Affairs* 76(I): 241–264.

The International Ecotourism Society TIES. 2007. http://www.ecotourism.org (accessed December 5, 2007).

TransFair Canada. 2007. http://www.transfair.ca (accessed December 5, 2007).

United Nations Development Programme. 2007. Euator Ventures. http://www.undp.org/equatorinitiative/equatorventures/EquatorVentures.htm (accessed December 5, 2007).

Waddock, Sandra A. and James E. Post. 1991. Social Entrepreneurs and Catalytic Change. *Public Administration Review* 51(5) September: 393–401.

Weerawardenaa, Jay and Gillian Sullivan Mort. 2006. Investigating Social Entrepreneurship: A Multidimensional Model. *Journal of World Business* 41(1): 21–35.

Wilson, Craig and Peter Wilson. 2006. *Make Poverty Business. Increase Profits and Reduce Risks by Engaging with the Poor.* UK: Greenleaf Publishing Limited, p. 192.

Zadek, S. 2004. *The Path to Social Corporate Responsibility, Harvard Business Review*, December 23–32.

Ziegler, Jean. 2002. *Les nouveaux maîtres du monde et ceux qui leur résistent.* Paris: Fayard, p. 264.

Chapter Four

Information and Communication Technology for Poverty Alleviation through Education and Healthcare— The India Experience

Nilay M. Yajnik

Introduction

The Indian economy is growing at a spectacular growth rate and is one of the fastest growing economies of the world. However, if one analyzes the statistics one will see that the growth is not inclusive.

As per the Economics Intelligence Report of the Reserve Bank of India, the population of people in India earning less than $500 per year is nearly 40 percent (Economics Intelligence Unit 2003). At 8 percent growth that India is achieving, only 1 percent have come out of the BPL (Below the Poverty Line). Nearly 250 million people in India are still below the poverty line. Statistics also reveal that the services sector in India will account for nearly 53 percent of the GDP of India but will employ only about 14–18 percent of the Indian population.

Teledensity (number of telephones per 100 people) is another measure of the growing division in society. While the urban teledensity in India is around 33, the rural teledensity is only around 2 (Yajnik 2005b). Research has shown that there is a direct correlation between teledensity and the GNP of a nation (Yajnik 2003, 35). Therefore, it is very important that to help alleviate poverty in India, the rural people have to be brought into the telecom revolution that is happening in India today.

In 2005 the literacy rate for the urban male in India stood at 69 percent but for the rural male it stood only at 47 percent. The situation in healthcare is even worse. The population per hospital bed in urban India stood at 1,110 while in rural India the population covered per hospital bed was 5,300. A lot more work has to be done on the education and healthcare front in rural India. It is very important that people in the rural areas of India as well as the underprivileged must be literate and also healthy to be able to work productively.

Education for Poverty Alleviation

To help alleviate poverty in India nearly 30 million jobs have to be created per year. India today has nearly 550 million people who are below 25 years of age. Providing education to them is of great importance. Information and Communication Technology (ICT) can help enable this.

The Indian Census of 2001 has stated that only about 65.38 percent of the Indian population is literate. One of the biggest challenges facing Indian education is the number of dropouts at the undergraduate level (first degree at college level). For example, approximately 23 million children per year take up primary education (kindergarten to fourth standard) but only about 15 million children per year take up secondary education (fifth standard to twelfth standard). This figure gets drastically reduced at the undergraduate level to only about 2.3 million students per year. This implies that only 10 percent of children who join school at the primary level go to college. Furthermore, the Census 2001 also brings out another alarming statistic that out of the total literacy rate of 65.38 percent, only about 59.40 percent of rural Indian population is literate as compared to about 80.30 percent of the urban Indian population (Yajnik 2005b). Nearly 70 percent of the Indian population lives in villages in the rural parts of the country. Many of these villages do not have schools or have schools without basic infrastructure and teachers. It is very critical therefore for India to quickly educate these vast number of people living in the rural parts of India who do not have access to good education. Information and Communication Technology can help make education available and affordable to the rural and remote parts of India. Good quality education to these people will give them the confidence to earn their own livelihood and thus help alleviate poverty in India.

Technology Issues and Applications in Education

This section will discuss the following technology and applications to enable quality education in rural India:

1. ICT for distance learning
2. Open Access
3. Digital libraries

ICT for Distance Learning

There are a large number of universities and colleges in India offering fairly good to excellent quality of education. Many of the faculty of these institutions of higher education are excellent and of a world-class stature. However the main problem in developing and emerging nations such as India is that these institutions are in the urban parts of India in tier I cities (large cities) and tier II cities (smaller cities). A student in a semi-urban or rural part of India is cut off from these institutions. This problem is even more acute at the primary education level.

Information and Communication Technology can help enable distance learning very effectively in developing nations. In India there are many success stories of ICT for distance learning. One of the earliest experiments in making education reach out to remote villages was in the 1970s when the Satellite Instruction Television Experiment was launched (Yajnik 2005a). In this experiment, the Indian Space Research Organization (ISRO) used a satellite to beam programs of educational content on television to villagers. The villagers would gather at a location in their village where a TV set would have been installed and would watch the program developed in their own language on topics such as irrigation, crop management, and other such issues that would be of interest to them. This experiment demonstrated the power of ICT to reach out to villagers in remote locations. The success of this project, which covered nearly 2,400 villages way back in the 1970s when ICT was not as developed as it is in 2007, encouraged ISRO to launch more projects in this area of delivery of education through satellite technology. The Jhabhua Developmental Communications Project and the launch of an exclusive training and developmental communications channel were all steps in this direction. However the most notable of such projects has been the EDUSAT project, which is the world's first satellite to have been launched exclusively for education purposes. Launched in 2004, the EDUSAT project covers the entire Indian nation through the following governmental institutions:

1. The All India Council of Technical Education
2. The University Grants Commission
3. The National Center for Education, Research and Training
4. The Indira Gandhi National Open University
5. The Indian Council for Agricultural Research

The state of Karnataka in South India is where this project was initially implemented and now many other states in India such as Jammu and Kashmir, Haryana, Rajasthan, Uttranchal, Madhya Pradesh, Kerala, Punjab, West Bengal, and Tamil Nadu will be covered through EDUSAT (EDUSAT India 2007). Schools and colleges in remote locations will get the benefit of learning from faculty of leading institutions in India without leaving their village or town (Information for Development 2007).

There are also several ICT for distance learning projects in India run by educational institutions in the private sector. Listed below are some examples of such institutions:

1. NMIMS (The Narsee Monjee Institute of Management and Higher Studies) in Mumbai is one of the pioneers in the usage of ICT for distance learning of management education. About a decade back, NMIMS tied up with a local TV channel, Zee, to offer various diploma level courses to students outside the city of Mumbai. However this was not an interactive medium. Nearly four years ago, NMIMS tied up with a U.S.-based VSAT service provider, Hughes, to offer various management programs through this mode. This was a highly interactive medium in which the NMIMS faculty would deliver their lectures live from a studio in Mumbai and the lecture would be beamed via satellite to around 33 cities in India. Students from these cities could ask questions to the faculty that could be heard by all and the faculty's response would be immediate, which could also be heard by all students. It was a simulation of a classroom except that the students were spread all over India and were not confined to a classroom in Mumbai. This author has participated in this project almost since its inception and has observed that one of the major issues, apart from technology, was that a change in mindset for both the teacher and the student were required for learning through this medium. This medium can be used to make the entire lecture highly interactive, but both the teacher and the

student have to adapt to this alternate mode of learning and teaching (NMIMS Department of Advanced Modes of Learning 2007).

2. BITS Pilani (The Birla Institute of Technology and Science at Pilani) is also one of the pioneers in the usage of ICT for distance learning. BITS Pilani has set up a BITS Virtual University. In this case, the alumni of the institute (this author is also an alumnus of this institute and has participated in this project) raised nearly a million dollars though the BITS Pilani Alumni Association and planned, designed, and implemented one of the largest campus-wide broadband networks in Asia. The project called BITS Connect connects all faculty and students over a 300-acre campus. This has now been extended throughout India by which any student based anywhere in the world can interact with BITS Pilani faculty at a mutually convenient time, or can participate in a regular scheduled class. The student can participate online through video conferencing over IP. BITS Pilani alumni spread all over the world also give guest lectures through this medium (Birla Institute of Technology and Science 2007).

3. The Indian Institute of Technology (IIT) Bombay has also implemented ICT for its distance learning program. In the case of the IIT, a regular lecture at the IIT Bombay campus at Powai in Mumbai is beamed live via satellite to several locations across India and the class in Mumbai becomes an extended classroom spread across India (Indian Institute of Technology, Bombay 2007).

4. The National AIDS Research Institute and the BJ Medical College in Pune get extensive training and research discussions from the Center for Clinical Global Health Education of the Johns Hopkins University through video conferencing using a U.S.-based service provider, Polycom. Continuous training of doctors, nurses, and paramedical staff is very important to ensure that they provide quality medical attention to their patients. It is not possible for people living several thousand miles away in a developing nation to afford traveling to the United States frequently to attend training programs. However, through powerful ICT, experts at the Johns Hopkins University are able to provide the required training to medical people in India without the necessity of their traveling the distance (Johns Hopkins Center for Clinical Global Health Education 2007).

5. Several private network service providers have come up in India recently. Many institutions have tied up with these service providers to offer distance education. As an example, the Indian Institutes of Management at Ahmedabad, Indore, and Kolkota have tied up with a private Indian company, NIIT, to offer courses over NIIT's network called Imperia (NIIT Imperia, Centre for Advanced Learning 2007).

Digital Libraries

ICT for the delivery of education programs to remote sites in India is gaining substantial momentum. However, for a student to learn effectively, access to libraries is also very important. A student in a remote village in India would not have access to a large university library physically. It is therefore very important that the student should be able to access the latest books, journals, magazines, and educational content remotely. Digital Libraries is one application of ICT that has tremendous potential in nations such as India (Yajnik 2001). Digitizing various learning resources and making them available to people in remote locations is the essence of a digital library. There are many examples of digital libraries in India, the most well known amongst them being the Digital Library of India (Digital Library of India: Indian Institute of Science 2007) in which thousands of books in regional Indian languages have been digitized and are available free to anyone who has access to the Internet. This is a very ambitious project and is a collaborative effort of the Indian Institute of Science, Ministry of Communications and Information Technology of the Government of India, and Carnegie Mellon University

Some of the other innovative digital library projects in India include the Honeybee project of the National Innovation Foundation in which grassroots innovation done by villagers to solve their specific problems are captured and shared with other villagers, thereby sharing innovation (National Innovation Foundation 2007), and the Traditional Knowledge Digital Library in which the traditional Indian knowledge for various medicinal plants has been captured and made available in a digital library (Yajnik 2004).

Open Access

It is imperative that access to these digital libraries be made freely available to all. The concept of open access is very relevant here. In the IT industry globally, the open source movement has changed the dynamics of the IT industry and has given users the power to be free from proprietary software. Similarly, the open access movement is gaining momentum around the world. Open access means access to information and scholarly works would be made available free and without any copyright issues, as long as the user gives the concerned author due credit for referring to his works. There are many movements globally which are driving the open access concept.

The Budapest Initiative, the Open Society Institute, FIGARO (a consortium of universities and publishers), the Public Library of Science started by researchers of the University of California at

Berkley and Stanford University, MIT, and Hewlett Foundation Open Courseware are some examples of open access movements (Yajnik 2005c, 2006). In India too, in addition to the Digital Library of India, there are many organizations that are provide open access to their journals. Open access initiatives in India include several publications (Kumari 2005) of the Indian Academy of Sciences (Indian Academy of Sciences 2007), e-print archives of the Indian Institute of Science (ePrints at the Indian Institute of Science Bangalore, India 2007), Indian Medlars Center (Indian Medlars Center 2007).

Sustainability of open access journals and books would be through sponsorships from private companies, very much similar to the business models adopted by companies such as Google.

The experience of all the above experiments in India on the usage of Information and Communication Technology for distance learning, digital libraries, and open access can be used to reach out to the under-privileged people as well as people who live in the rural parts of India. These technologies and their applications can be used to help enhance the literacy level of India. The more the literacy level, the greater is the capability of people to make a living, thereby alleviating poverty to a great extent

Healthcare for Poverty Alleviation

Healthcare is another area of concern in developing nations such as India. Healthy people can work harder and smarter thereby uplifting their own economic status and thus alleviating poverty. However, in developing nations access to quality healthcare is a major issue. In fact, even though a very large population of India live in the villages, nearly 75 percent of doctors in India live in cities (Bagchi 2006). Information and Communication Technology can be of great help to make quality healthcare accessible and affordable to the village folk in India.

One of the earliest applications of ICT for healthcare applications in India was in 1994 when the Indian Healthcare Project was initiated jointly between the industry and the Government of India. The Government Healthcare System in India is a very large program and is spread over nearly 650 million people across all the states of India. The healthcare worker physically visits various rural households assigned to him/her, collects demographic data, and advises the villagers on various health related issues. Huge amounts of paperwork was involved resulting in data inaccuracy. Hence, as a pilot project in

Ajmer in Rajasthan, the government tied up with Apple Inc to provide hand held computers to the healthcare workers who would enter the data into the computer and then report the same back to the district headquarters where it would be consolidated. This resulted in lesser data errors and also helped to build a database of health related issues, village and household wise (Yajnik 2003, 72).

ICT has advanced substantially since then and from an offline mere data collection application of IT in 1994 to an online interactive remote diagnosis through satellite. Telemedicine is gaining substantial momentum in India and there are several examples of telemedicine projects in India.

One of the earliest telemedicine projects in India was in 2002–03 when doctors attending to patients at a hospital in Siliguri (a remote hilly location in the northeastern part of India) could take expert advice from doctors based in Calcutta through the Internet. Internet was mainly used as a medium to send test reports of patients in an offline mode. Since then, there have been many more telemedicine projects in India using advanced technologies (Yajnik 2003, 74).

Apollo Hospitals

The Apollo Hospitals have been making significant progress in telemedicine in India. The Apollo Telemedicine Networking Foundation has been set up by the Apollo Group of hospitals and has provided telemedicine facilities to the state of Mizoram in the remote northeastern part of India. In fact, the Apollo Group has also prom- ised free teleconsultations to the people of Mizoram. The hospital group has also begun a pilot telemedicine project in Aragonda, a village in the state of Andhra Pradesh in South India (Neurosurgery on the Web 2007). The hospital in this village is equipped with web cameras and advanced video conferencing equipment. More than 200 telecon- sultations have already been done, with the patient being present at the village hospital and the expert being available at the Apollo Hospital at Chennai. The hospital now even transmits digital images of CT scans, X-rays, and ultrasound images to the experts based in Chennai, which is several hundred kilometers away from the village (Apollo Telemedicine Networking Foundation 2007).

The Apollo Hospitals have also been providing telemedicine facilities to a small village about 100 kilometers from Chennai called Sriharikota. This village is where the Indian Space Research Organization launchpad exists and a virtual outpatient department is run by Apollo Hospitals for the families of the ISRO employees based at Sriharikota through VSAT connectivity. The Indian Space Research Organization has already connected nearly 22 super-specialty hospitals in India with 78 hospitals in remote and rural parts of India across several remote, rural, and difficult terrains such as Jammu and Kashmir, Andaman and Nicobar islands, the Lakshadweep islands, and northeastern parts of India.

The goal of the ISRO is to connect the nearly 650 district hospitals, 3,000 taluka (sub-district) hospitals, and around 23,000 primary health centers across India with several super-speciality hospitals (Bagchi 2006). ISRO also plans to launch a satellite, HEALTHSAT, which would be dedicated to healthcare on the lines of EDUSAT.

Telemedicine projects to reach out to the rural parts of India appear to work well when a public–private partnership model is adopted. One of the projects where such a model is being experimented involves a government agency—the ISRO, a private company—Philips, a voluntary service organization—Dhan, and a super-specialty hospital group—Apollo (through the Apollo Telemedicine Networking Foundation). Philips had commissioned a market research firm AC Nielsen to survey the various aspects of rural healthcare and one of the findings of this study was that the villager based in the rural parts of India actually ends up paying more for his/her healthcare needs than his/her urban counterpart (Philips Electronics News Center 2007). A large part of the expenses go toward traveling to and from the village to the nearest specialty hospital, which would be based in an urban location. Hence this project was conceptualized in a village near Madurai called Theni in South India and Philips provides a mobile clinical van equipped with various advanced medical instrumentation with VSAT connectivity. ISRO provides the satellite and communication facilities, the Apollo Hospital at Madurai serves as the referral base station hospital for the mobile clinical van, and the Dhan VSO provides the local community interface.

Aravind Eye Hospital

The Aravind Eye Hospital (AEH) has been practicing telemedicine for several years. The hospital has set up an Aravind Tele-Opthomology Network (ATN) for this purpose. AEH has real time consultation with the rural eye hospital at a place called Theni and the specialty eye hospital at Madurai. This is also done in an offline mode so that the patient does not have to travel all the way to the town just for a diagnosis. The hospital also has a mobile van with advanced opthomological equipment and VSAT connectivity to the base station hospital. In this case, the patient goes to the mobile van where his/her eyes are tested and screened and sent via satellite to the base station hospital. The specialist at the base station hospital gives the prescription within an hour. At times, if the doctor wishes to talk to the patient, it is done via video conferencing from the van itself (Aravind Tele-Ophthalmology Network 2007).

Sankara Nethralaya

This is a leading eye hospital in India that has also been practicing telemedicine for several years. The hospital has set up the Sankara Nethralaya Tele Opthomological Foundation (SNTOP). The experiment in telemedicine by Sankara Nethralaya started in 2001 when teleconsultations were carried out on a trial basis between two campuses of the hospital separated by a few hundred meters. Subsequently, the hospital started a teleconsultation unit in Bangalore connected via ISDN lines to the main hospital at Chennai. The hospital further progressed with a collaborative model comprising the hospital—Sanakara Nethralaya, a government agency—the ISRO, and VSOs—the MSSRF (Monkombu Sambasivan Swaminathan Research Foundation) and the Jamsetji Tata National Virtual Academy for Rural Prosperity to set up a mobile van equipped with medical equipment and VSAT connectivity (Express Healthcare 2007a, Sankara Nethralaya Medical Research Foundation 2007).

Narayana Hrudalaya

This is a specialist cardiac care hospital located in the city of Bangalore and has been practicing telemedicine for several years. The hospital has set up the NH Telemedicine Network and has conducted nearly 12,000 teleconsultations. It has also set up an ECG network that connects several general practitioners in remote areas of India with an ECG system and connection via telephone lines to transmit ECG data connected to the Narayana Hrudalaya Hospital in Bangalore to get expert advice on cardiac issues (Express Healthcare 2007b, Narayana Hrudayalaya Hospitals 2007).

Conclusions

Both education and healthcare are two of the most important elements in the alleviation of poverty in India. The rural parts of India cannot be left out of the technology, economic, and services boom that India is witnessing now. Powerful information and communications technology can help make education and healthcare accessible to the rural parts of India. There are already several successful examples in both the government and in the private sector in the applications of ICT for education and healthcare for rural India. The experience of these case studies can be used to quickly scale up and have many more such cases through a public–private partnership model, thereby helping to alleviate poverty in India.

References

Apollo Telemedicine Networking Foundation. 2007. www.telemedicineindia. com (accessed December 5, 2007).

Aravind Tele-ophthalmology Network. 2007. www.aravind.org/telemedicine (accessed December 5, 2007).

Bagchi, Sanjit. 2006. Telemedicine in Rural India. *PLoS Medicine Journal* 3(3): e82. http://medicine.plosjournals.org/perlserv/?request=get-document&doi= 10.1371%2Fjournal.pmed.0030082 (accessed December 5, 2007).

Birla Institute of Technology and Science. 2007. http://discovery.bits-pilani.ac. in/index.htm (accessed December 5, 2007).

Digital Library of India: Indian Institute of Science. 2007. www.dli.ernet.in (accessed December 5, 2007).

EDUSAT India. 2007. http://www.edusatindia.org/ (accessed December 5, 2007).

ePrints at the Indian Institute of Science Bangalore. 2007. http://eprints.iisc. ernet.in/ (accessed December 5, 2007).

Express Healthcare. 2007a. April 2007 issue. www.expresshealthcaremgmt. com/200704 (accessed December 5, 2007).

———. 2007b. February 28, 2007 issue. www.expresshealthcaremgmt.com/ 20050228 (accessed December 5, 2007).

Indian Academy of Sciences. 2007. www.ias.ac.in (accessed December 5, 2007).

Indian Institute of Technology, Bombay. 2007. www.iitb.ac.in (accessed December 5, 2007).

Indian Medlars Center. 2007. http://medind.nic.in/ (accessed December 5, 2007).

Information for Development. 2007. www.i4donline.net (accessed December 5, 2007).

Johns Hopkins Center for Clinical Global Health Education. 2007. www.ccghe.jhmi.edu (accessed December 5, 2007).

Kumari, Lalitha. 2005. Global Access to Indian Research: Indian STM Journals Online. (Spring 2005) *Issues in Science and Technology Librarianship*. www.istl.org/05-spring (accessed December 5, 2007).

Narayana Hrudayalaya Hospitals. 2007. http://www.narayanahospitals.com/ tele_medicine_centers.html (accessed December 5, 2007).

National Innovation Foundation. 2007. www.nifindia.org (accessed December 5, 2007).

Neurosurgery on the Web. 2007. http://www.thamburaj.com/telemedicine. htm (accessed December 5, 2007).

NIIT Imperia, Centre for Advanced Learning. 2007. www.niitimperia.com (accessed December 5, 2007).

NMIMS Department of Advanced Modes of Learning. 2007. http://nmims. edu/daml (accessed December 5, 2007).

Philips Electronics News Center. 2007. http://www.newscenter.philips.com/ (accessed December 5, 2007).

Sankara Nethralaya Medical Research Foundation. 2007. http://www. sankaranethralaya.org/tele_activities.htm (accessed December 5, 2007).

Yajnik, Nilay M. 2001. Digital Libraries for Indian Rural Development. Proceedings of the International Conference on Asian Digital Libraries organized by UNESCO, Ministry of Science and Technology, Indian Institute of Information Technology Bangalore, December.

———. 2003. Information Technology and its impact on aspects of Human Development in Rural India. Ph.D Dissertation, unpublished, September 2003, University of Mumbai.

———. 2004. Digital Libraries to Bridge the Digital Divide. Paper published in the Proceedings of the International Conference on Digital Libraries by The Energy Research Institute(formerly known as Tata Energy Research Institute) and Commonwealth of Learning, Canada, February.

———. 2005a. Bridging the Knowledge Divide in Developing Nations— Issues and Perspectives. Paper published in the Proceedings of the International Conference on Information Management in a Knowledge Society, organized by Indian Association of Special Libraries and Information Centers and Ministry of Culture on February at Mumbai. This paper has been published by Allied Publishers Ltd.

———. 2005b. E-Learning and the Digital Divide. Paper published in the Proceedings of the National Conference on E-Learning and E-Learning Technologies organized by Centre for Development of Advanced Computing, Ministry of Communication and Information Technology, Government of India and Media Lab Asia, Hyderabad, August.

———. 2005c. Open Access: A Teachers' Perspectives. Paper published in the Proceedings of the National Conference of IIT Chennai organized by IIT Chennai & Indian Association of Special Libraries and Information Centres [IASLIC], Chennai, December.

———. 2006. Bridging the Digital Divide through Open Access to Digital Libraries. Paper published in the Proceedings of the International Conference on Digital Libraries organized by UNESCO, Department of Scientific and Industrial Research, Government of India, TERI and ACM, New Delhi, December.

Chapter Five

A Collaborative-Systemic Strategy Addressing the Dynamics of Poverty in Guatemala: Converting Seeming Impossibilities into Strategic Probabilities

James L. Ritchie-Dunham

Introduction

Business strategy practice and scholarship have developed frameworks and processes for understanding and acting within complex social systems that are proving valuable for multi-stakeholder, intersectoral, societal issues such as poverty. These frameworks and processes have evolved over the last 50 years to incorporate the assessment of: 1) economic efficiency within and across organizations, industries, sectors, and nations, 2) power structures within and across networks, and 3) compliance-driven rule structures that promote or restrict equitable and market-driven incentives within and across these boundaries.

We are stronger now at knowing who controls what and how to get them to compete more freely or equitably: until we reach the seemingly "intractable"—issue domains where the conflict is so high and the trust so low that: 1) divergent stakeholders will not come together, 2) will not share the same understanding of the issue domain, and 3) will not act together to address the issue. These three observations are arising as core assumptions facing strategists looking at many intractable issues, such as corruption, biodiversity loss, global warming, and terrorism. Poverty in Guatemala is another such issue, and this chapter describes an exploration through collaborative-systemic frameworks and processes that were able to bring together 26 conflicted stakeholder groups, reaching a shared understanding of the dynamics of poverty, and initiating a collective action plan toward addressing poverty. From the shoulders of the giants who incorporated economics and sociology into business strategy frameworks and processes, we can now begin to ask the next level of questions around intractable issues like poverty, learning from exploratory work in collaborative-systemic business strategy.

Situation 2004

The highlighted case study starts in Guatemala with CARE, the international aid agency, as it was assessing its capacity to end poverty. In 2004, CARE envisions a world of hope, tolerance, and social justice, where poverty has been overcome and people live in dignity and security (CARE 2004). On most key developmental indicators, CARE had excelled for 50 years. Through its projects in over 70 countries since 1945, CARE had reached millions of people every year, supporting thousands of communities. A mark of CARE's success was its growth to $515 million in annual donations and its continued, very high level of operational efficiency (CARE 2004, 2; Barrett 2004; Navigator 2005; Yaqub 2002). But, the percentage of the world population in extreme poverty, earning less than $1 per day, was increasing—20 percent worldwide and 23 percent in Guatemala, a country of 12 million inhabitants (UN Secretary-General 2002; Vandemoortele 2002; Gobierno de Guatemala 2003; Sachs 2005b; World Bank 2005).

To address this increase, as part of a large, collective effort that culminated in the United Nation Millennium Development Goals, CARE shifted its vision in 1999 from poverty alleviation to poverty eradication—halving the world's population in extreme poverty by 2015. While CARE and the global community took on this vision in 1999, it was clear in 2004, that Guatemala was no closer (CARE LAC Regional Council 2003; Sachs 2005).

In Guatemala, the CARE staff noticed that many other groups were asking similar questions, "how can we be doing well, from our organizational perspective, yet the overall situation of the very problem we are fighting is getting worse?" Assessing the growing percentage of people in extreme poverty in Guatemala, it seemed impossible to fix, yet it was clear to the CARE team that they had to try.

Structuring the Approach

Sitting with this situation, CARE's leadership began an exploration of people, frameworks, and processes that might shed light on the seeming intractability they faced. In this exploration, they found earlier work that CARE sponsored around urban planning in Tegucigalpa, which pulled together multiple stakeholders into a systemic strategy process for reimagining after Hurricane Mitch (Puente and Forrest 1999). This led to an invitation to the Institute for Strategic Clarity to assist in the design and implementation of process for understanding the underlying dynamics of poverty. This section explores core assumptions surfaced, criteria for shifting these assumptions, expected outcomes of the process, the multi-stakeholder, intersectoral, strategic framework that was used, criteria for selection of the participants, and the institute's research questions that guided the process.

Core Assumptions

Initial conversations about multi-stakeholder processes with CARE's leadership team in Latin America and stakeholders with extensive experience in the Guatemala context surfaced many core assumptions about what was possible and what was not. Essentially, it is not possible to get all of the major stakeholders together, they cannot understand each other, they cannot arrive at a shared understanding of the context, and they cannot act together.

They will not come together. Guatemala has a rich history of conflict, across many sectors and societal dimensions, peaking in the twentieth century in a decades-long civil war that ended officially with the 1996 Peace Accords. While the civil war was over, the complete lack of trust and accompanying social tensions continued. Many attempts to gather stakeholders either failed outright or were short lived. For a hopeful multi-stakeholder gathering in 1998 that initiated a set of commonly developed scenarios for the future of Guatemala, see (UNDP 2007; Kahane 2004).

They will not come to a shared understanding. Guatemala is uniquely multiethnic in Latin America, being composed of over 24 linguistic communities and cultures dating back thousands of years. Additionally it has one of the world's largest gaps between the wealthy and the poor. Adding to these differences in cosmovisions and economic perspectives, differences among perspectives on poverty from government, civil society, and business are extreme. Thus, the common experience was that these differences in worldview proved too strong to overcome for a group to achieve a shared understanding of the drivers and underlying dynamics of poverty. Even if they came together, they could not understand each other and could not arrive at a shared understanding.

They will not act together. While hundreds of organizations actively address dimensions of poverty in Guatemala, bringing billions of dollars in resources into the country, there is scarce cooperation among them, with each organization working on its piece, often in different areas. For example, while one organization constructs school buildings in the central part of the country, another organization works on getting families to send their daughters to school in the north, and yet another works on getting multicultural education developed in the western region. While each has its own logic, the lack of the efforts often leads to failure, and in the best cases, any possible synergies are completely missed. Further evidence of this independence in action is the newness of coordinating groups such as CORNASAM (Coordinadora Interinstitucional del sector de recursos naturales y ambiente de San Marcos), working to integrate efforts of 20 NGOs and government with 50 communities around micro-watersheds in San Marcos. Due to the often-extreme difficulties in getting conflicted stakeholders together and arriving at a shared understanding, almost no work is done to get them to work together.

Criteria for Shifting Assumptions

If valid, these core assumptions would lead to conflict-avoiding poverty studies based on third-person, observable data and behaviors, such as census data and expert investigation of the socio-political-economic forces that drive poverty in Guatemala. This focus represents most of the national-level studies done (LCSHD 2003; UNDP 2001; Gobierno de Guatemala 2003). While these descriptive and normative studies based on objective data and expert interpretation contribute to the understanding of the character, state, and distribution of poverty in Guatemala, they remain fragmented in their prescriptions of where to focus resources and unsupported by the vast majority of organizations working on poverty-related issues in Guatemala. This project sought to integrate these fragmented studies and to incorporate the voice of the stakeholders leading the efforts and of the affected communities, something rarely done. Robert Chambers and C.K. Prahalad document the general absence of these voices in recommendations about their future, as well as providing brilliant examples of the integration of these voices (Narayan et al. 2000; Prahalad 2005).

To understand the society-level dynamics of poverty required a multi-stakeholder, intersectoral approach. Freeman describes a stakeholder as any group or individual that influences or is influenced by the achievement of the social system's objectives (Freeman 1984). Waddell describes intersectoral as integrating the economic, social, and political systems through business, civil society, and government (Waddell 2005b). These three sectors unite to promote, respectively, growth, social cohesion, and societal health (Ritchie-Dunham forthcoming).

For a multi-stakeholder, intersectoral process to work, the three core assumptions were turned upside-down, to highlight new core assumptions. To incorporate the multiple voices, so they might come together, required a highly participatory process. In participatory processes stakeholders codesign and coimplement. In initial meetings, Guatemalan leaders emphasized the importance of transparency in the process, so they might understand each other and achieve a shared understanding, as trust among the stakeholders was very low, at best. Transparency International defines transparency as "a principle that allows those affected by administrative decisions, business transactions or charitable work to know not only the basic facts and figures but also the mechanisms and processes. It is the duty of civil servants, managers and trustees to act visibly, predictably and understandably" (TI 2007). Additionally, individual, organizational, and interorganizational accountability were critical for them to be able to act together. Thus, to incorporate the voices of highly conflicted and differentiated stakeholders, shifting the core assumptions, this project focused on a highly participatory, transparent, and accountable process.

Expected Outcomes

The expected outcomes of this project focused on: 1) learning about the core society-level dynamics of poverty in Guatemala, 2) learning about the utility of highly collaborative-systemic strategic processes in low-trust, high-conflict situations, 3) determining collective strategies for intervening in these poverty dynamics, and 4) shifting CARE's existing organization from its historical role of "project manager providing social services to local populations" to its new role as a catalytic facilitator of change (Waddell 2005).

Research Questions

This research asks whether a collaborative-systemic strategy process might provide insight into: 1) understanding the core dynamics of poverty in Guatemala, 2) characterizing complex social systems to inform mental models, and 3) developing an intersectoral systems understanding collaboratively.

Understanding the Core Dynamics of
Poverty in Guatemala

What are the core dynamics of poverty in Guatemala? While many groups have studied poverty dynamics in general, as well as specifically in Guatemala, the groups directly working with the poor in Guatemala report that these previous studies have had little impact on their work.

Does a systems thinking approach provide a more relevant understanding? The lack of shared framework and understanding among the many stakeholders studying and working in poverty led the CARE Latin America regional management unit to believe that a systemic approach to understanding poverty dynamics might shed new light.

Characterizing Complex Social Systems
to Inform Mental Models

Can a systems mapping of poverty dynamics improve the understanding of how different efforts combine to generate poverty? Much anecdotal data supports the claim that systems thinking improves individual and collective understanding of complex social systems (Brehmer 1992; Vennix 1996; Sterman 2000; Ritchie-Dunham 2002, forthcoming).

Developing an Intersectoral Systems
Understanding Collaboratively

Does exploring and integrating the perspectives of stakeholders from different sectors provide an understanding that promotes a collaborative understanding? While seemingly obvious, we found no evidence of this being done in Guatemala.

Does it provide a more complete understanding, simply by asking them? Can a group of conflicted stakeholders with very low trust, overcome this lack and arrive at mutual understanding? What processes achieve this collaboration most quickly, efficiently, and effectively?

Methods and Validation

This systems analysis was informed by primary and secondary data sources (Ritchie-Dunham 2007).

- Primary data: Focused on individual interviews, group reflection, and group exercises with representatives of multiple sectors working in and around poverty.
- Secondary data: Included literature reviews in different prominent perspectives on poverty, including economic, social, psychological, developmental, and spiritual, which are included in the bibliography.

The frameworks developed were validated with the interviewees, CARE employees, and a wider group of stakeholders addressing poverty.

Multi-stakeholder, Intersectoral Strategic Framework

To orient the integration of the strategic processes in this project, five criteria were used to gauge the degree to which the integration bridged the rigorous characterization of social systems and the rigorous characterization of the individual and collective intentional mental models of those social systems (for a survey of the research on individual and collective mental models, as they apply to strategic understanding of complex social systems, see Ritchie-Dunham 2002). The CRISP criteria ask whether the process is sufficiently comprehensive, rigorous, integrative, simple, and purposeful (see table 5.1) (Ritchie-Dunham 2004, forthcoming).

This section presents the criteria for building the framework that integrates the strategic processes of systems thinking, resource-based view, collaborative appreciative inquiry, across multiple sectors with multiple stakeholders, highlighting the related strategy literature.

Systems thinking, as popularized by Senge, Stacey, and Oshry, suggests how different parts of a system relate over time, providing a language for making these systems understandings explicit, so they can be shared and improved (Senge 1990; Oshry 1996; Stacey 1996). The systems thinking dimension of the process uses

Table 5.1 The five CRISP criteria used to gauge whether the process is sufficiently comprehensive, rigorous, integrative, simple, and purposeful

CRISP Elements	Brief Explanation	Process Assessment	Description
Comprehensiveness	What elements are included	High	While the process does not include all stakeholders in Guatemala society, the collective of 26 stakeholders felt it was sufficient for a rich conversation, about the system dynamics of self-determination.
Rigor	How the stakeholder understandings and analysis are tested	Medium	All maps of individual interviews were validated individually and the maps integrating them were validated collectively. Analysis added to the rigor of relationships. Nonetheless, the process is based on qualitative data.
Integrative	How the process relates the individual elements	High	The process shows how all the individual maps fit together, through the integrated map, according to many collective conversations.
Simple	How the elements in the process are understood	Medium	While very complex, in integrating many perspectives, everyone was able to engage it fully within two hours of conversations and then present it to others.
Purposeful	Why the process was created	High	Purpose focused the collective (self-determination). Each interviewed individual's purpose was made explicit and this drove the process.

system dynamics modeling to make explicit the intentional mental models of each individual stakeholder and integrate them into a single map (Sterman 2000). A wide variety of systems and decision analysis tools were used to discover the micro-, meso-, and macro-level dynamics in the integrated map (Ritchie-Dunham and Rabbino 2001).

The resource-based view of strategy provides an integrating, dynamic perspective on the accumulation dynamics of the resources that enable the developing and sustaining of these resources that drive value for the organization's stakeholders (Foss 1997; Ritchie-Dunham and Rabbino 2001; Ritchie-Dunham forthcoming). Essentially, a system's health can be determined by the strength of the tangible and intangible resources it brings to bare on satisfying its purpose. These resources accumulate over time, thus they erode over time and require investment to grow and be sustained. The level of these resources influences the accumulation of other resources. For example, a utility's infrastructure of pipelines has to be built up over time and it erodes over time, so to keep this resource's capacity at the same level over time, the utility has to continuously invest. This applies as well to intangibles like a firm's reputation, an individual's ability to self-determine, or a culture's support of education.

To the dynamic systems perspective, collaborative appreciative inquiry (Cooperrider and Whitney 2005) provides guidelines for creating a high trust environment within which conflictive stakeholders can reflect on their own intentional mental models and those of others (for more on collaborative systemic inquiry, see Spann 2007, Ritchie-Dunham 2007). The intersectoral perspective highlights the importance of including the perspectives of the economic, social, and political sectors from the beginning (Waddell 2005).

Taking a CRISP view of societal strategy processes, many stakeholders influence the flow of resources into and within the systems we lead, live in, and depend on. Not including their perspective in our understanding does not mean their influence is zero. Understanding the perspective they espouse leads to greater correspondence between our understanding and what is actually happening.

Participant Criteria

In a consultative process with a large, diverse group of stakeholders, we developed the criteria for the selection and invitation for the stakeholders in the process: 1) that they represent one of the many perspectives that exist within the Guatemala context from civil society, business, and government and 2) with a high level of credibility and trust among their peers and among other stakeholders. While this group represents many

sectors with vast experience and networks of relationships in these
sectors, they were individuals open to participating in this exploratory
process.

To shift the three core assumptions that we could not get the
stakeholders to come together, they would not arrive at a shared
understanding, nor act together, this project pulled on well established business strategy frameworks for designing a highly participatory, transparent, and accountable process that integrated multiple
stakeholders, collaborative appreciative inquiry, systems thinking,
and the resource-based view of the firm into a simple, four-stage
process.

The Process

Having highlighted above the criteria and elements used for the design
phase, this section focuses on the process and what resulted from it
over six visits. The process and its products are described in the
chronological order of the six visits. The products are presented
graphically, in chronological order, in figure 5.1.

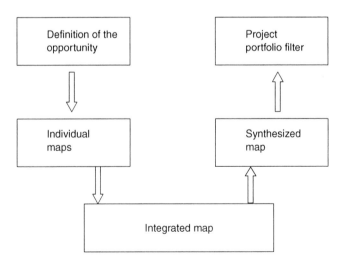

Figure 5.1 Products from the process of producing opportunity into individual
and then integrating mappings and projected portfolios.

Source: Ritchie-Dunham, James L. (2007).

Visit 1: Definition of the Opportunity
(February 2004)

The first visit started with individual interviews of 10 of the CARE Guatemala staff, including a cross-section of the organizational functions, processes, and hierarchical levels. The interviews explored the individuals' deeper intentions in their work, the organization's ability to achieve that, and what would need to change in the individuals and the collective to achieve success. This 45- to 60-minute interview served multiple purposes: 1) creating rapport between the process facilitators and the individuals, which would be critical during the group process and 2) providing a space for deeper reflection about their experience in addressing poverty and what needed to change, in others and in themselves.

These interviews served as input for a two-day exercise with 10 CARE Guatemala staff. This exercise culminated in a collective, synthesized definition of what they were working to create collectively. This was an important shift in CARE's conversation and that of other stakeholders, whose organizations' missions focused on what they were ridding the world of, rather than what they were collectively creating in the world.

In the synthesis process, the terms of freedom, mutual respect, solidarity, and self-determination emerged. The alignment of these terms became clear, with freedom focusing on my ability to be myself, mutual respect focusing on how we see each other, and solidarity focusing on our relationship to the whole, as we participate in the collective. With agreement on the ability to self-determine as the element that synthesized the group's responses, we then looked at how Guatemala had fared.

As seen in figure 5.1-a, the y-axis was set with a high "ability to self-determine" as being a state of real democracy and justice, and with a low "ability to self-determine" as being a state of slavery and authoritarianism. On the x-axis, the group chose a time horizon of one generation going back and going forward as the time over which one could see an impact on this overall indicator of the system's health. The group agreed that one generation ago the average Guatemalan's ability to self-determine was very low, and that up to the Peace Accords it improved. With the signing of the accords, it leveled off and then dropped precipitously with the entering of the FRG (Frente Republicano Guatemalteco) into political power, returning to levels of ability to self-determine just above civil war

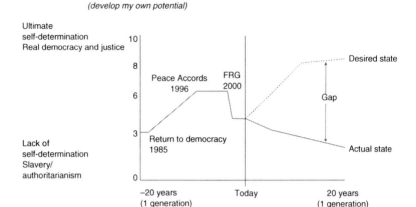

Figure 5.1-a   Definition of the opportunity.
Source: Ritchie-Dunham, 2007.

levels. Looking forward, they all agreed that if things remained as they were, given all of their hard work, things would most probably continue to deteriorate—given the current way decisions were made and resources allocated among all of the stakeholders in Guatemala, it was only going to continue to worsen, quickly at that, to below civil war levels. Nonetheless, everyone agreed this was unacceptable and that it had to improve drastically, within the next decade to levels higher than after the Peace Accords, and then it had to sustain at these levels.

Once this was drawn out, incorporating in a simple graphic, their reality and their deepest intentions, the gap between the two futures shocked them. Many reported months later that this image was the motivating force for their subsequent decision to change—themselves and their work—as continuing the same was not improving the situation.

We were all very involved emotionally—it was not just about work—and I remember one of my team members was crying. We do not usually share things. The way we were asked to think of something personal, we were asked to think about the first time that we decided to dedicate part of our life to address poverty. It was so clear that everyone came with these strong emotional moments in our life. I had not spoken before about that. It was very revealing, and I found out it was a long time ago when I was a kid and that was a discovery for me. After this exercise . . . it put everyone on the same page, really willing to talk deeply. (Luis Paiz, Assistant Country Director, CARE Guatemala [Waddell 2005])

This exercise helped us shift our focus, as a team. This framework reflects our understanding better than $/day. It is also clear now that we need to bring in more diverse points of view. (CARE Guatemala staff, two-day offsite, February 2004)

Visit 2: They Come Together (June 2004)

This synthetic redefinition of poverty, focusing on what was being collectively created in the world—the ability to self-determine—was validated with a large group of stakeholders during a two-day workshop in the second visit. The group of stakeholders and CARE Guatemala staff as this time defined the criteria for who would be included in the subsequent stakeholder interviews, with credibility, trust, and accountability being very important to be able to continue the process (for a list of the stakeholders who validated this, see Ritchie-Dunham 2007).

Visit 3: They Arrive at a Shared Understanding (October 2004)

The third visit started with individual interviews of 10 stakeholders responsible for a wide range of activities related to "the ability to self-determine"—from education of young girls to military officers, from land reform to localized capitalism, from the indigenous poor to the presidency, and the peace accords. In a 90-minute interview, these stakeholders were each asked: 1) what is your personal vision for Guatemala as a country and for your community? 2) speaking in your present role as a leader, what is the goal of your organization? 3) what are the top three to five things that you must be able to do to achieve this goal? and 4) what are the core resources required to achieve those? (for a list of who was interviewed and the details of each interview, see Ritchie-Dunham 2007). We mapped the response of each interview individually and into an integrated map (see figure 5.1-b).

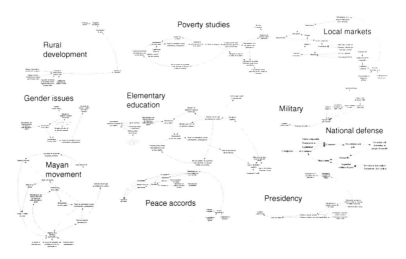

Figure 5.1-b Individual maps.
Source: Ritchie-Dunham, 2007.

In the first day of a two-day offsite with the CARE Guatemala team, the maps of the individual stakeholders were presented, demonstrating the intention that person brought, their story about their work, and contribution to self-determination in Guatemala, and how it was mapped. This process was important in helping the CARE team to be able to see and believe the story told by stakeholders they normally mistrusted. Each participant was then asked to tell the stakeholder's story, in a way that would convince the stakeholder they had been heard. Thus, the CARE participant shared the stakeholder's intention and story, using the map to guide their logic. Going through the individual maps, one by one, also accelerated everyone's ability to identify with each and all of the stakeholders.

The second day was dedicated to exercises to understand the map that integrated all of the stakeholder individual maps (see figure 5.1-c). The CARE team then led the same exercise in a one-day workshop with an invited group of stakeholders.

> In this process, we saw a huge shift in our CARE Guatemala staff from presenting our CARE point of view and asking others to comment, the traditional process, which is a defensive posture, to a process of inquiry into what they have heard in the integration of many stories of others. (Colen Beckwith, Country Director, CARE Guatemala, CARE LAC meeting in Ecuador, June 22, 2005)

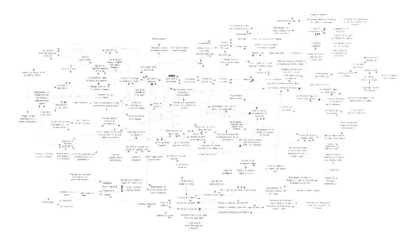

Figure 5.1-c Integrated map.
Source: Ritchie-Dunham, 2007.

Visit 4: They Arrive at an Understanding of How to Act Together (February 2005)

In the fourth visit, in a two-day workshop, the CARE Guatemala worked through a series of conversations to determine collectively which variables in the map

- indicated the overall health of the system, along with "the ability to self-determine" (outcome variables)
- if shifted would change the behavior of the whole system, as reflected in the outcome variables (instrumental variables)
- if addressed collectively would shift the instrumental variables (intervention variables)

The CARE team repeated the same exercise the next day with an invited group of stakeholders, arriving at very similar results. A combination of the two was synthesized in figure 5.1-d.

The synthesized map shows the key dynamics of the ability to self-determine. As Guatemala's intercultural identity increases, its social structures and processes strengthen, which in turn strengthen the social fabric and economic opportunities. As the economic opportunities

Figure 5.1-d   Synthesized map.
Source: Ritchie-Dunham, 2007.

increase, one's ability to self-sustain increases. With a higher ability to self-sustain and a stronger supporting social fabric, one's ability to self-determine increases. Coupled with the stronger social fabric, an increase in the ability to self-determine leads to a stronger intercultural Guatemalan identity, thus re-enforcing the original behavior. This is the positive spin through the dynamics of increasing the ability to self-determine in Guatemala.

These dynamics likewise provide a story for the dynamics that keep Guatemala poor. Given a weak Guatemalan intercultural identity, as it is deeply fractured and conflictive, the social structures and processes are unsupported by a clear identity, leading to a weak social fabric and few economic opportunities for much of the nation. With few economic opportunities, many struggle to self-sustain. Coupled with a weak social fabric that does not support them, high vulnerability from the inability to self-sustain, leads to a weak ability to self-determine, which further exacerbates the potential richness intercultural Guatemalan identity.

This approach to using systems mapping, reflection, and conversation to tap into the collective wisdom of the multiple voices present provided many insights that were rigorously validated through analysis and subsequent exercises with a wide group of stakeholders (for more on the validation through analyses and stakeholder engagement, see Ritchie-Dunham 2007, Waddell 2005).

Visit 5: They Define How to Act from This Understanding (October 2006)

The CARE Guatemala team had now lived with the map for 18 months, shared and validated it with their staff nation-wide and engaged many stakeholders around it. In a two-day workshop, they began to design strategic metrics and project portfolio filters from their systemic understanding of the dynamics of self-determination in Guatemala (see figure 5.1-e).

Pulling from the original definition of the ability to self-determine as the ability to relate to oneself, to another, and to the whole, the CARE team collectively designed strategic metrics for each of the six elements of the synthesized map, which reflected the level of: 1) the freedom of the individual to achieve high levels of that element, 2) the level of equality for everyone in achieving high levels of that element, and 3) the level to which the whole community benefited from high

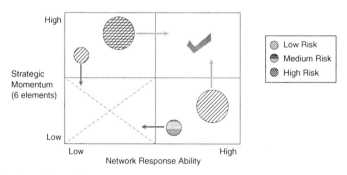

Size -- Impact (# people)
Color -- Risk (CARE's ability to respond)

Figure: 5.1-e   Project portfolio filter.
Source: Ritchie-Dunham, 2007.

levels of that element (for detailed strategic measures at each level for each element, see Ritchie-Dunham 2007).

Key Findings

This approach to incorporating and integrating voices from across sectors and levels that would never come together provided both unique insights into the dynamics of poverty and self-determination in Guatemala, as well as providing a common platform for deep dialog about how these voices and their organizations and communities might start working together toward these shared goals and understandings. This section summarizes these insights, the roles for the different sectors, and business opportunities and obstacles.

From this exercise, the involved stakeholders came to a shared understanding that the path they are on will not get them out of poverty—it reinforces poverty. Looking at poverty through the lens of the elements of self-determination highlights where they might be failing. The gap between the current path and the desired path is large and growing. There are a series of historic structures that limit the growth of the system away from poverty and self-determination. These structures indicate how they might be able to act to address these limits, together in harmony, strengthening the system's ability to pull itself out of poverty, focusing on the whole of each level in sequence.

Additionally, blaming each other and advocating solely for their own interests is not helping, after all it seems that they are each right, when you look at each situation. And, everyone sees that the desired direction is vastly different than today. By shifting how they work, together, they can harmonize efforts on some interventions in the system that significantly boost the system with other efforts that support the new levels of development further down the road.

These three perspectives point to two high-leverage points, focusing on a collective agreement of the integral nature of poverty (self-determination) dynamics and who is providing leadership in rural communities.

Role of Sectors

This intersectoral view of societal dynamics highlights two perspectives on the roles each sector can play: intrasectorally and intersectorally.

Intrasectorally, each sector focuses on those areas with which it is most accustomed. In the synthesized map, this means that:

- business focuses on growth in the economic sector, providing resources for the nation's social structures (i.e., infrastructure, energy, schools, hospitals); dignified economic opportunities for women and men across linguistic communities; and resources for people to be able to self-sustain.
- civil society focuses on social cohesion in the social sector, strengthening institutions that support processes for an intercultural Guatemalan identity, developing and supporting social processes, and strengthening the social fabric, all in support of increasing everyone's ability to self-determine.
- government focuses on societal health in the political sector, ensuring the social processes and structures that support equal individual and collective access to basic services and rights.

Intersectorally, each sector has the opportunity to integrate its key strengths with those of the other sectors, providing a uniquely strong and sustainable future for Guatemala. In the synthesized map, this means that:

- business contributes its deep understanding and experience in creating, managing, and leading for-growth engines to the efforts required to strengthen and scale-up organizational capacities for developing intercultural Guatemalan identity and ramping up the required social structures required for a higher level of coexistence (for recent examples of massive scaling up of investment in basic infrastructure in developing countries, see Giridharadas 2007).
- civil society contributes its wealth of experience in motivating and inspiring sustainable social cohesion to the creation of sustainable economic opportunities that best meet the talents and skills of each individual, as well as helping individuals to develop these gifts into marketable skills, and building communities that help each other self-sustain during difficult times.
- government contributes its capacity to promote societal health by providing equal access to markets, economic opportunities, and self-sustenance during particularly vulnerable times (i.e., hurricanes, mud slides).

Business Opportunities/Obstacles

In addition to the aforementioned for-growth roles of business, this project identified specific opportunities and obstacles for business in strengthening every Guatemalan's ability to self-determine.

Various civil society and government-led initiatives provide potential for-growth *opportunities for business.* There are many projects where an understanding of actual market forces and structuring incentive-based, for-growth contracts would significantly increase the amount of investment and opportunity available within Guatemala. One striking case of this is the work of Rodolfo Paiz, presidential commissioner for local development, where the commission works with local communities throughout Guatemala: to identify their "local treasures," which abound in this very fertile, scenic, and creative country; to create demand for their treasure; to create market access for the treasures; and to administer these resources according to world-class standards of sustainability. Another business opportunity that is having a major impact on the poorest communities is microfinancing, whereby microcredit, as little as $100, is provided to the very poorest. Payback rates are proving to be much higher than traditional banking. For more on the impact of the world-wide microcredit movement on poverty, see the Microcredit Summit Campaign Web site (http://www. microcreditsummit.org/). Another great resource for business is the entrepreneurial spirit of Guatemalans, especially the youth. Broad campaigns, such as the Youth Employment Summit and Junior Achievement are active in Guatemala—enterprising businesses might be able to support this entrepreneurship and develop unique offerings out of this bountiful land. To all of these projects, business contributes a solid basis for identifying and managing sustainable growth, typically a weakness for civil society and government.

There are equally many *obstacles to business* in making significant contributions to eradicating poverty and radically increasing the ability to self-determine. Principal among these obstacles are: business's inability to see the value of organizations that focus on social cohesion (civil society) and on societal health (government); their inability to see how to integrate with these organizations, both existing and from the beginning. Businesses working in conjunction with civil society and government toward increasing self-determination must be able to:

- integrate their for-growth and for-efficiency point of view with the for-social-cohesion and for-societal-health perspectives, instead of imposing it on them

- be highly transparent and accountable in highly participatory processes

While this integration from the beginning seems antithetical to most business practices, indeed there are many business organizations that are now understanding the value of this integration (Waddell 2005).

In summary, the integration of collaborative-systemic strategy processes in this project led to increasing levels of clarity in relationships and understanding capable of overcoming the three core assumptions, allowing for the first incorporation of stakeholder voices across sectors not integrated before. This produced a shared understanding and conversation for action quite different from previous poverty studies and fully owned and internalized by the participants.

Situation 2006

The achievement of the project's goals by no way means that Guatemala's problems are now resolved, two years later. In fact, from one perspective, the situation is worse—there is an increase in crime and hurricanes and general strikes have weakened the poorest. And, CARE Guatemala and the stakeholder groups involved are completely different (Waddell 2005)—not only in their understanding, but also in their relationships and ability to develop and communicate probably pathways out of poverty, toward self-determination for every Guatemalan, which previously most thought was impossible. This section highlights what we found worked best, what did not, and we revisit the core assumptions and take a look forward.

What Does/Does not Work

In the process of this project, we have learned much along the way about what works and what does not work in bringing together a wide group of conflictive stakeholders toward shared understanding and shared action. Many process and technical assumptions we brought with us were either severely challenged or outright turned upside-down.

While our processes lean heavily toward inquiry, we were immediately and continuously reminded of implicit imposition assumed by bringing any "expert" lens to issues with which we had no personal experience, such as poverty and discrimination in Guatemalan when we were three white men from the United States and Canada. This led to using our "expert analysis" as just another voice in the room—we used it to inform our own offerings into the group discussion, but gave it no more weight than other voices, which worked very well, as we developed solid rapport with the stakeholders. This also pushed the process much more to discovery through reflection and dialog than presentation of our findings, which ended up providing much greater ownership, individually and collectively, and wonderfully surprising to us, they came up with many of the same insights.

We also faced many challenges in convening the diverse group of stakeholders in a timely manner. The initial sponsoring organizations, including CARE, did not initially have formal relationships with many of the stakeholder groups, so we had to find them and develop them through other colleagues. As we advanced, the work we did with the stakeholders who participated engaged them enough so that they helped us engage additional stakeholders. Many of these relationships are now strong across all of the participants, as evidenced by the bilateral and multilateral conversations and projects that have emerged.

The most challenging processes were developmental, both individually and collectively. Due to their long history of deep conflict, there was a very strong us-them viewpoint in the participants, as well as a deep focus on one's own interests. Over the year, most of the stakeholders, especially the CARE team, were able to shift developmentally from seeing "me-and-you" to seeing "we," from just one's own interests to holding one's own contribution, another's contributions, and the needs of the whole. In interviews one year later, in March 2006, many reported significant developmental breakthroughs along these lines, and that they had been permanent, which we subsequently experienced in the fifth visit.

Finally, working in a challenging environment like Guatemala requires greater flexibility than we originally designed in our project. National strikes, massive hurricanes, and general unrest forced us to shift meetings, once when we were already in Guatemala, and delay meetings by months.

Revisiting Core Assumptions

Revisiting the three core assumptions that we had uncovered in the beginning of the project, in 2004, by 2006 we saw that:

They did get together. We were able to bring together stakeholders from across all three sectors and all levels of society, from often very conflictive groups.

They did arrive at a shared understanding. By shared understanding we mean that: 1) the stakeholders were able to agree on the overall goal they were all trying to create, the ability to self-determine, 2) they were able to see how they and all of the others contributed to that goal, 3) they were able to see how their actions influenced each other and the goal, often generating the very dynamics they were fighting, and 4) what they each needed to contribute to shift the whole system.

They are acting together. From the first meetings, bilateral and mutilateral conversations emerged within the group. By the end of the year, projects had emerged. With greater clarity, CARE Guatemala has now drastically shifted its focus.

The final assumption we added at the end of the first year. Most skeptics suggested that even if we were able to do all of the above, it would take many years. The stakeholders involved dedicated seven days over one year and the CARE Guatemala team dedicated an additional eight days over that first year.

Scenario

So, as of February 2007, is Guatemala out of its difficulties? No. Has the downward trend in the ability to self-determine trend turned up? No. Since 2005, Guatemala has faced Hurricane Stan and lost, has faced a strong increase in gang warfare from the Maras from El Salvador and is losing that battle as is the United States, and has faced continuing drug trafficking from Colombia to the United States and widespread corruption. Does this mean the project was not a success? That depends. When we interviewed participants in March 2006 and then again in the fall of 2006, we heard the following messages:

Power of imagination. In February 2005, all of the stakeholders, while wanting a better Guatemala, thought it was impossible, given their situation. Today, even though the situation is possibly worse, these same leaders know it is possible. While nobody suggests that this will fix all ills, it seems clear that when we leaders know the situation is impossible, it is. And when we know it is possible, something else happens. Margaret Mead reminds us of the power of imagination when she tells us that a small group of people who can see a new possibility where others see impossibility is the only force that has ever changed the world.

Multisectoral integration. It is entirely possible to see that what has been perceived for decades as deep conflict and competition for scarce resources, even when all of the organizations involved purport to working on the same goals (i.e., a better Guatemala), that indeed most of the stakeholders across these sectors are in fact working on different dimensions of the same system, and that if their intentions, understanding, and actions can be integrated, they might actually support each other versus fight with each other.

Going into 2007, the initial efforts of this project have expanded in various directions. For example, at the national level, many conversations and projects have been initiated across sectors and stakeholder groups. At the community level, CARE and GAN-Net have initiated a project to bring a dozen global action networks and local government together with the leadership of 50 communities around microwatersheds in San Marcos, devastated by Hurricane Stan, to apply the framework and process to community-level issues.

Thus, we have attempted in this project to building on the long history in business strategy scholarship on economic markets, power structures, compliance, with different core assumptions about who is involved and how they are involved.

References

Barrett, William P. 2004. Special Report: America's Most (And Least) Efficient Charities. *Forbes.com*, November 24. http://www.forbes.com/2004/11/23/04charityland.html (accessed December 5, 2007).

Brehmer, Berndt. 1992. Dynamic Decision Making: Human Control of Complex Systems. *Acta Psychologica* 81: 211–241.

CARE. 2004. *CARE USA 2004 Annual Report* http://www.care.org/newsroom/publications/annualreports/2004/2004annualreport.pdf. (accessed December 5, 2007).

CARE LAC Regional Council. 2003. *Advancing the LAC Region's Strategic Priority.* Internal Memorandum, January 28. Atlanta: CARE's Latin America and Caribbean (LAC) Regional Council.

Charity Navigator. 2005. Top 10 Best Charities. http://www.charitynavigator.org/index.cfm/bay/topten.detail/lstid/18.htm. (accessed December 5, 2007).

Cooperrider, David L., and Diana Whitney. 2005. *Appreciative Inquiry: A Positive Revolution in Change* San Francisco: Berrett-Koehler.

Foss, Nicolai J., ed. 1997. *Resources, Firms and Strategies: A Reader in the Resource-Based Perspective.* New York: Oxford University Press.

Freeman, R. Edward. 1984. *Strategic Management: A Stakeholder Approach.* Boston: Pitman.

Giridharadas, Anand. 2007. "Second Tier" City to Rise Fast Under India's Urban Plan. *New York Times*, May 13. http://www.nytimes.com/2007/05/13/world/asia/13nagpur.html?_r=1&oref=slogin (accessed December 5, 2007).

Gobierno de Guatemala. 2003. Estrategia de Reducción de la Pobreza: 2004–2015. Ed. M.T. Editores. Guatemala City: Gobierno de la República de Guatemala.

Kahane, Adam. 2004. *Solving Tough Problems: An Open Way of Talking, Listening, and Creating New Realities*. San Francisco: Berrett-Koehler.

LCSHD. 2003. Poverty in Guatemala. Washington, DC: Poverty Reduction and Economic Management Unit, Human Development Sector Management Unit, Latin America and the Caribbean Region, World Bank.

Narayan, Deepa, Robert Chambers, Meera Kaul Shah, and Patti Petesch. 2000. *Voices of the Poor: Crying Out for Change*. New York: Oxford University Press.

Oshry, Barry. 1996. *Seeing Systems: Unlocking the Mysteries of Organizational Life*. San Francisco: Berrett-Koehler Publishers.

Prahalad, C.K. 2005. *The Fortune at the Bottom of the Pyramid: Eradicating Poverty through Profits*. Upper Saddle River, NJ: Wharton School Publishing.

Puente, Luz Maria, and C. Jay Forrest. 1999. Aplicación de Pensamiento Sistémico al Desarrollo del Plan Urbano de Tegucigalpa. Tegucigalpa: CARE Honduras.

Ritchie-Dunham, James L. 2002. Balanced Scorecards, Mental Models, and Organizational Performance. PhD. Thesis, Department of Management Science and Information Systems, University of Texas, Austin, Texas.

———. 2004. A Framework for Achieving Clarity for You and Your Organization. *The Systems Thinker* 15(7):7–8.

———. 2007. *The End of Poverty—The Beginning of Self-determination*, Wilton, NH: Institute for Strategic Clarity.

———. forthcoming. *Thinking Clearly within Complex Social Systems*. New York: Elsevier.

Ritchie-Dunham, James L., and Hal T. Rabbino. 2001. *Managing from Clarity: Identifying, Aligning and Leveraging Strategic Resources*. Chichester: John Wiley & Sons.

Sachs, Jeffrey D. 2005. *The End of Poverty*. New York: Penguin Press.

———. 2005. *Investing in Development: A Practical Plan to Achieve the Millennium Development Goals*. Sterling, VA: UN Millennium Project.

Senge, Peter M. 1990. *The Fifth Discipline*. New York: Doubleday Currency.

Spann, R. Scott. 2007. *Collaborative Systemic Inquiry*. Wilton, NH: Institute for Strategic Clarity.

Stacey, Ralph D. 1996. *Strategic Management & Organizational Dynamics*. 2nd ed. London: Financial Times.

Sterman, John D. 2000. *Business Dynamics: Systems Thinking and Modeling for a Complex World*. Boston: Irwin McGraw-Hill.

TI. 2007. What is Transparency? http://www.transparency.org/news_room/faq/corruption_faq (accessed December 5, 2007).

UNDP. 2001. Choices for the Poor: Lessons from National Poverty Strategies. In *Pro-Poor Policies*, ed. UNDP Poverty Strategies Initiative. New York: United Nations Development Programme. http://www.undp.org/dpa/publications/choicesforpoor/ENGLISH/index.html (accessed December 5, 2007).

———. 2007. Democratic Dialogue: A Handbook for Practitioners Democratic Dialogue Network.

UN Secretary-General. 2002. Implementation of the Millennium Declaration. New York: United Nations General Assembly.

Vandemoortele, Jan. 2002. Are We Really Reducing Global Poverty? United Nations Development Programme, Bureau for Development Policy.

Vennix, Jac. 1996. *Group Model Building: Facilitating Team Learning Using System Dynamics*. New York: Wiley.

Waddell, Steve. 2005a. A Learning History: The CARE-LAC—Institute for Strategic Clarity Guatemala Poverty Project. Wilton, NH: Institute for Strategic Clarity.

———. 2005b. *Societal Learning and Change: How Governments, Business and Civil Society Are Creating Solutions to Complex Multi-Stakeholder Problems*. Sheffield, UK: Greenleaf Publishing.

World Bank. 2005. The Global Poverty Numbers Debate. http://web.worldbank.org/WBSITE/EXTERNAL/TOPICS/EXTPOVERTY/EXTPA/0,contentMDK:20242512~menuPK:435040~pagePK:148956~piPK:216618~theSitePK:430367,00.html (accessed December 5, 2007).

Yaqub, Reshma Memon. 2002. America's 100 Best Charities. http://www.worth.com (accessed September 28, 2007).

Chapter Six

In Search of Sustainable Social Mission Ventures to Alleviate Poverty

Shelby McIntyre, Albert Bruno,
and Patrick Guerra

Introduction

What can a university do to help alleviate poverty worldwide?

This chapter describes a program established at Santa Clara University in 2003 that answers this question. The program is named the Global Social Benefit Incubator (GSBI) that is housed within the Center for Science, Technology, and Society. Business incubators are organizations that support the entrepreneurial process, helping to increase survival rates for innovative startup companies. Incubators provide entrepreneurs a specialized menu of support resources and services that might include: provision of physical space, management coaching, help in making an effective business plan, administrative services, technical support, business networking, advice on intellectual property, and sources of financing.

This chapter is an introduction to this program and constitutes one university's attempt to help alleviate poverty by "helping the helpers" who are social entrepreneurs. This is an attempt to provide an infrastructure to improve the success rate of innovation and the use of technology in the quest to help those at the Bottom of the Pyramid.

The Social Entrepreneur

Often referred to as "society's change agent," Wikipedia describes a social entrepreneur as "someone who recognizes a social problem and uses entrepreneurial principles to organize, create, and manage a venture to achieve social change. Whereas business entrepreneurs typically measure performance in profit and return, social entrepreneurs measure their success in terms of the impact they have on society." Of course there are more extensive definitions available.

For instance, the Spring 2007 *Stanford Social Innovation Review* contains an article titled "Social Entrepreneurship: The Case for Definition," by Roger Martin and Sally Osberg. These authors provide the following more intricate definition:

> We define social entrepreneurship as having the following three components: (1) identifying a stable but inherently unjust equilibrium that causes the exclusion, marginalization, or suffering of a segment of humanity that lacks the financial means or political clout to achieve any transformative benefit on its own; (2) identifying an opportunity in this unjust equilibirium, developing a social value proposition, and bringing to bear inspiration, creativity, direct action, courage, and fortitude, thereby challenging the stable state's hegemony; and (3) forging a new stable equilibrium that releases trapped potential or alleviates the suffering of the targeted group, and through imitation and creation of a stable ecosystem around the new equilibrium ensuring a better future for the targeted group and even society at large.

Social entrepreneurs, in turn, create what may be called "Social Mission Ventures," whose primary purpose is the transformation of an economic or social injustice. These ventures provide products and services to disadvantaged groups at below currently established market rates, while generating sustainable earned income streams from related activities and deliverables. The profits or economic surplus generated by the social mission venture provides comparable financial returns to commercial investments while at the same time delivering socially transforming results. Note that economists define "surplus" as the revenue received over and above the direct cost of the goods or services provided.

The GSBI

The mission of the GSBI at Santa Clara University is to contribute to the sustainability and scaling of social mission enterprise innovations.

The vision is a more inclusive world through knowledge sharing, capacity building, and facilitation of the flow of capital to deserving social mission ventures that accelerate development and diffusion of technologies serving the urgent, unmet needs of humanity.

The GSBI is an intensive two-week residential program at Santa Clara University that teaches entrepreneurial principles and business skills. It combines classroom instruction in finance, marketing, organizational development, and business planning with case studies, best practices, and, most importantly, carefully matched mentoring support. The invited entrepreneurs have already demonstrated "proof of concept" in applying technology or other innovations to address urgent human needs in the most adverse of circumstances around the world. GSBI participants have achieved recognition through the rigorous selection processes of the prestigious Tech Museum Technology Benefiting Humanity Awards, the World Bank's Development Marketplace, the Global Junior Challenge, or the business plan competition at the Skoll Foundation Social Edge Web site (Social Edge 2007). Many of the attendees have also been recognized as Skoll, Schwab, or Ashoka Fellows.

Measures of Success

The GSBI is focused on serving social mission ventures that seek to complement grant revenue with earned income streams. Therefore, development or enhancement of self-sustaining sources of funding in the ensuing years is an important measure of GSBI near-term impact. The second key measure of success is demonstrating impact against criteria and targets relevant to the respective ventures. Stated differently, this means meeting the growth and reach objectives of the venture.

The Context for Incubating Global Ventures

In 2004, the UN Commission on the Private Sector and Development, released its findings to the Secretary General of the United Nations, in a report entitled "Unleashing Entrepreneurship: Making Business Work for the Poor" (Commission on the Private Sector and Development 2007).

The report identifies three pillars that are essential for entrepreneurship to thrive:

1. A level playing field
2. Access to financing
3. Access to skills and knowledge

The GSBI program is focused on skill building and knowledge transfer. Knowledge transfer is a culture-based process (considered as informal or "invisible") by which adaptive organizational knowledge that lies in people's heads is exchanged with others (Information Technology Toolbox 2007). The curriculum specifically addresses issues of financial planning, sustainability, and scaling relevant to small social benefit enterprises. Here, sustainability refers to both economic continuance in terms of revenues and grants being greater than costs as well as embracing the concept of an environmentally sustainable world.

Silicon Valley is renowned for incubating and scaling thousands of companies whose innovations and technology transform our daily lives. The GSBI draws on the lessons and mentors of Silicon Valley to adapt, transfer, and apply these lessons in entrepreneurship for the benefit of initiatives aimed at making the world a better place.

While the GSBI does not attempt to influence policy, its alliance partners certainly promote policy solutions that can provide a more fertile environment for social mission ventures and thus accelerate their ability to scale.

At the business plan presentations in the second week, called the GSBI Summit, a review panel critiques each presented plan. The review panelists are drawn from foundations, Silicon Valley high technology companies, and the venture capital community of Silicon Valley. The panelists give suggestions and insights to the social mission entrepreneurs regarding the "fundability" of their plans, and in some cases, have actually been interested in further discussions regarding specific funding. Several GSBI fellows have received financial support and have recruited board of director members as a result of these presentations. The curriculum also provides background and knowledge about foundation processes and grant and investment priorities, in addition to providing an overview of the latest developments in the world of social venture capital.

Finally through ongoing research and the postresidence Accelerator Program, the GSBI provides "on the ground" assistance to entrepreneurs with tactical implementation issues that they may encounter. This type of engagement provides essential feedback for the continuous improvement of the overall program and contributes to advances in both practice and the body of knowledge. Figure 6.1 summarizes the GSBI program in graphic form.

Living and learning together, GSBI participants develop common conceptual skills and a true sense of community. This process fosters peer-to-peer collaboration and receptivity to expert mentoring from seasoned Silicon Valley entrepreneurs. The business plan presentation summit culminates the two-week, in-residence experience. At this

The GSBI

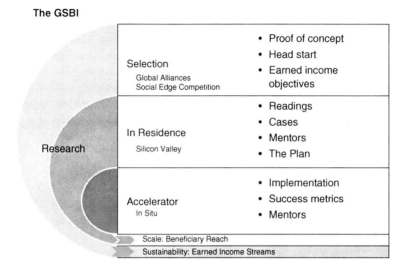

		• Proof of concept
Selection Global Alliances Social Edge Competition		• Head start • Earned income objectives
In Residence Silicon Valley		• Readings • Cases • Mentors • The Plan
Accelerator In Situ		• Implementation • Success metrics • Mentors

Scale: Beneficiary Reach
Sustainability: Earned Income Streams

Figure 6.1 The GSBI platform: a program for social entrepreneurs to assist those who endeavor to alleviate poverty world-wide.

Source: GSBI 2006, Santa Clara University, Santa Clara, CA.

summit, panelists, some of whom are venture capitalists, evaluate the extent to which the innovative adaptation of technology and models of social change can bring positive benefits to the forgotten and desperate part of the human family. Attendees discover how practical knowledge in marketing, finance, organizational development, and business models can be applied to enhance the prospects for a better life for populations marginalized by the uneven march of economic progress.

In a broader perspective, the GSBI and similar university-based centers can be viewed as an enabling technology, or process, perhaps an infrastructure that finds and leverages the endeavors of fledgling social entrepreneurs in order to make them more successful. It is analogous to the first derivative of the function of alleviating poverty by improving the processes (or slope) of those who endeavor to achieve social change. In some cases, there is an attempt to put the venture on an entirely new curve, to achieve more assured sustainability and greater beneficiary reach.

Much like a venture capitalist who creates a portfolio of projects, the GSBI measures its performance by the subset of attendees who achieve substantial success. This is because one way to view the process of alleviating poverty is through the placement of many "bets" where the survival of the best approaches will result in the *evolution* of a society without poverty. Poverty in this context means living below subsistence levels where life spans are forced far below potential. However, just placing bets is not enough, because each of these bets needs to be given the best chances of adapting successfully to its environment, so as to achieve (and improve) sustainable mission results. The goal of the GSBI is to ensure that each venture achieves such best possible adaptation.

The Role of Formal Business Planning

On first thought, it would seem that formal business planning would be essential for a new venture to achieve its vision of success. However, research about this association has shown only a very limited correlation between the degree of formal business planning and business success (Lange et al. 2007). Sometimes, business planning can become paralyzed by analysis if all the planning slows down the execution and implementation. Possibly, this is so because there is only so much management time and effort available. Our take-away from this lack of association is that formal business planning should be focused, intense, benefiting from many perspectives, and particularly the perspective of experienced experts. Furthermore, it should have a clear end point where after execution, implementation becomes the main focus. The GSBI boot camp experience is designed as just such an encapsulated business review and planning session. The GSBI summer program is short, focused, and supportive. It provides many perspectives and culminates in a "best plan." However, as Eisenhower observed: "Plans are nothing, but planning is everything," which suggests that the participants be instructed to use their plans only as a launch pad from which to adapt as new information and experience shows that changes are needed. With the background of planning, the adaptation needed in the heat of battle (implementation) will be more appropriate and more forceful in its certitude.

Ventures That Have Come Through the GSBI

As of December 2006, a total of 54 social mission ventures have passed through the GSBI program including entrants from 23 different countries. A complete list of the participating ventures is included in table 6.1.

Table 6.1 GSBI venture entrepreneurs by Cohort Year

Class of	Name	Source	Country	Description
2003	Omar Dengo	1	India	Promote the use of digital technology for education
	Vaancha ICT	1	India	Overcoming telecommunication access, illiteracy, and basic skills
	Katha	1	India	Information technology to enhance literacy and build community
	CLEAN	1	India	Environmental assessment, awareness, and action to develop cleaner environments
	SchoolNet	1	Nambia	Internet service and training
	OrphanIT	1	Philipines	Training and employment in IT service for online businesses
2004	CT-x Green	2	Canada	Carbon-neutral biodiesel-fueled energy for Orissa
	Digital Divide Data	2	Laos	Digital IT services providing training and employment
	EcoSystems	4	Nepal	Wire bridges and hand or pedal-powered generators for poor
	Equal Access	5	USA	Digital satellite broadcasting and solar energy with local content for global markets
	Eatset Blood Transfusion	5	Nigeria	Appropriate medical devices—recirculating blood transfusion pump—for poor
	Freeplay Foundation	5	South Africa	Wind-up and solar powered radios and life-saving information
	Gram Vikas	5	India	Vertical shaft brick kiln for home building materials
	GreenMap System	5	New York	Promoting awareness of natural and cultural environments using new media
	Greenstar	5	Seattle	Solar-powered Internet-enabled PC's for microenterprise development

Continued

Table 6.1 Continued

Class of	Name	Source	Country	Description
	INBio	5	Costa Rica	Bioinformatics and data storage for enhancing biodiversity resources
	The League of Women	5	USA	Smart Voter for informed voting and participation in the democratic process
	STARBRIGHT	5	USA	Provides support electronically to help ill children to cope
	THASA	5	Argentina	Reinforced concrete tomography for nondestructive building inspection
	Transclick	5	New York	Digital translation for email and mobile text messaging
	United Group	2	Jordan	E-commerce supply chain and Web tools for women's handicrafts
2005	Aguada Guzmán	6	Argentina	Develops markets and revenue opportunities for poor sheep-farmers
	Asociación Abj'atz Enlac.	5	Guatemala	Use of information and communication technologies for indigenous peoples
	Bee Conservation Project	7	Nigeria	Honeybees as a livelihood for the urban and rural poor
	Book Trust	6	Colorado	Utilizes existing schools for poor youth to purchase books
	Comitê para Democratization	1	Brazil	Provides free computers, software, training for the poor through IT schools
	Cognisense Labs	5	California	Land reclaimed for safe use by GPS software to remove land mines
	e-Mobilizer	8	California	Cellular mobile technology to connect microentrepreneurs to online marketplace
	eShopAfrica	1	Ghana	WWW to preserve cultural artifacts and enhance livelihood for traditional artisans

Continued

Table 6.1 Continued

Class of	Name	Source	Country	Description
	Frost Protection Corp	5	Uruguay	Provides solutions for frost damage of fruit producers in developing world
	Fundacion Paraguaya	7	Paraguay	Economic literacy and entrepreneurship training to micro-loans in rural areas
	iEARN-USA	5	New York	Enables students to interact with individuals from different cultures over the internet
	Ikamva Youth	1	South Africa	Transitions poor youth through a focus on technical skill development
	NetHope	5	California	Information platform for NGOs to coordinate global relief and services
	Phulki	7	Bangladesh	Day care facilities for poor women to achieve economic emancipation
	Unidos	2	Mexico	Offers the poor who are disabled new models of hope and empowerment
	XayanIT	1	Bangladesh	Helps poor university students enter local employment in IT outsourcing operations
2006	B2Bpricenow.com	2	Philippines	Provides price information to rural farmers by creating an electronic marketplace
	BushProof	2	Madagascar	Water and sanitation products that impact the health and well-being of the poor
	Cows to Kilowatts	3	Nigeria	Installs biogas plants at slaughter houses to create a source of domestic energy
	Dress for Development	2	Bolivia	Education and employment of disadvantaged and handicapped female seamstresses
	Drishtee	2	India	Bridging the digital divide for remote and economically poor rural communities

Continued

Table 6.1   Continued

Class of	Name	Source	Country	Description
	Enterprise Professional.	2	Kenya	Improving slum living by a used oil collection and recycling facility
	Helps International (HINT)	1	Cameroon	Provides computer literacy for the illiterate poor through ICT centers
	if People	3	Georgia	Delivers to the poor online collaboration and strategies for value-driven enterprises
	International Development	5	India	Improves conditions for amilies in need by harnessing market forces
	Kiva	3	California	Leverages microfinance via personal lending on the web to poor entrepreneurs
	Scojo Foundation	2	New York	Creating livelihoods through the sale of reading glasses to the poor
	MIT OpenCourseWare	5	USA	Free access to MIT educational materials worldwide for non-commercial purposes
	Sprinkles	3	Canada	Packets containing a blend of nutrients in powder form to be sprinkled on food
	Sustainable Healthcare	2	Kenya	Franchising clinics for nursing services and drugs to the poor
	Thamel Dot Com	3	Nepal	Services for migrant workers in developed nations sourced locally
	Enterprise Works/VITA	2	Ghana	Solutions to problems of small-scale producers around the developing world
	Whirlwind Wheelchair	5	California	Wheelchairs used in developing countries and training in building wheelchairs

Source: GSBI 2006, Santa Clara University, Santa Clara, CA.

Several observations are important about this portfolio of entrepreneurial efforts. Most of them involve applying information technology either as a direct approach (e.g., computer training centers for poor youth) or an indirect approach (e.g., a Web site for people in the developed world to make direct loans to poor entrepreneurs in the underdeveloped world via microfinance partners). Those ventures that do not involve computer or Internet technologies, apply other technology often by translating to a more locally appropriate technology (e.g., methods for land mine removal that work in a particular country, or wheelchairs applicable to third-world settings, low cost water purification systems, etc.). What all of the ventures share is a need that natural market forces have been slow to address or are not viable through purely profit seeking (e.g., normal) market-based activity. In essence, the GSBI assists social entrepreneurs who use "a leapfrog approach"; leap-frogging market forces in adapting technology (Hart and Milstein 1999) to social mission ends and then applying the notions of value creation to support the endeavor (at least partially) with earned income streams.

One of the concepts fostered by the GSBI is to encourage thinking about the concept of a double-bottom line (Christen et al. 2004), wherein social mission entrepreneurs have first a social mission bottom line (numbers of beneficiaries served or similar related metrics of social impact), and second, a business bottom line (not profit but breakeven or surplus).

Recent GSBI Success Stories

Several examples from the GSBI roster can serve to clarify its mission:

Kiva.org

In the class of 2006, the GSBI enrolled Matt Flannery who was in the process of founding and scaling up a Web-based endeavor known as Kiva.org (Kiva 2007). This venture was inspired by the microfinance movement first started in 1972 by Mohammad Yunus with his now well-known Grameen Bank. The Grameen Bank provides small loans for utterly poor people in Bangladesh. As most readers will know, the methods of the Grameen Bank have spread widely so that today thousands of microfinance institutions exist in over 50 countries. This spreading success is why Mohammad and the Grameen Bank were awarded the Nobel Peace Prize for 2006.

Kiva.org is the first person-to-person microlending Web site where individuals from the developed world can make direct loans to relatively poor entrepreneurs in the less-developed world. At the GSBI summer in-residence program, Matt scrutinized and fine-tuned the business model and advanced the venture's traction with Silicon Valley companies and venture funds. Kiva.org became know as a high potential leveraging of the original microfinance idea onto the Web. Traditional microfinance institutions work in partnership with Kiva.org to actually implement the program, since it is they who post the loan opportunities from among their best loan applicants. They then monitor the progress, collect the repayments as they come due, and post those back to the Web site. This provides a three-way win-win-win solution as the poor person gets the loan, the microfinance company can expand its program, and the person providing the loan gets his or her funds returned along with progress reports about the business. The person making the loan can then take the money out of the program, or more likely reloan it to another applicant. This creates a way for individuals to connect with and make personal loans to small businesses in developing countries.

Kiva spent much of its first year finding and vetting local microfinance partners worldwide. These partners screen each microentrepreneur and after finding them credit-worthy, post a profile of them on Kiva's site. Kiva then aggregates funds from the Internet community and transfers them to the local microfinance partner for funds distribution and collection. Anyone with a PayPal account or credit card can choose a specific low income entrepreneur and make a 0 percent interest loan in $25 increments. The impact of each loan is recorded on Kiva's Web site and Internet lenders are usually repaid within 12 months.

The company is incorporated as a nonprofit so that it can be funded by foundations and 501c3 charitable donations, as it builds its way toward the day when it receives legal status as a bank and can then provide interest to those individuals who provide the loans.

The good work of Kiva.org has gained growing support from Silicon Valley and now receives free payment processing from PayPal so that 100 percent of loaned funds can reach the microentrepreneur and 100 percent can be repaid to the Internet lender.

It is also felt that the microfinancing mechanism provides a way around government involvement and the unfortunate corruption that often exists through other existing financing channels. Even when there is no corruption, the microfinance institutions, leveraged by the Kiva.org Web approach constitute much needed competition and alternatives for the entrepreneurs working from the Bottom of the Pyramid. Since going through the GSBI program, Kiva.org has become the most trafficked site in microfinance and has been featured in major blogs, news publications, and global conferences such as the Clinton Global Initiative. Kiva.org is headquartered in San Francisco, CA. and can be found on the web at www.kiva.org.

Since its launch and mentoring at the GSBI, Kiva.org has scaled up nicely and is positioned to make a substantial impact on a global basis.

Digital Divide Data (Digital Divide Data 2007)

A key employee from Cambodia, Mai Siriphongphanh, attended the GSBI in the summer of 2005 and subsequently led the expansion of Digital Divide Data (DDD) services into Vientiane, Laos. A recent development update confirms that she has a staff of 200 and "lots of success stories in terms of business growth."

DDD provides high-quality, low-cost data entry and digital services in Cambodia and other nearby countries. It was established through a partnership of international advisors and local Cambodian leaders. The Cambodian participants had a wide range of proven experience in the business sector as well as in nonprofit and social ventures. Talented workers were hired from Cambodia's most disadvantaged groups—such as the disabled, land mine victims, and women. DDD provided them with opportunities that are not normally accessible to such individuals.

The business model for DDD states that it operates as a self-sustaining cooperative of data entry and digital services, with all profits being reinvested in the business to provide fair salaries, ongoing training, and healthcare for its employees.

Thus, DDD has a balanced dual mission—one to its customers and another to its employees: to customers, DDD provides highly accurate, well priced digitization services (e.g., Web page design, etc.) that meet customer needs at competitive prices. To employees, DDD facilitates human development by providing fair wages, healthcare, education, and career advancement opportunities. DDD has served more than 50 satisfied customers and employs hundreds of people, nearly all of whom are continuing their education. The plan is to expand upon this base across many cities and countries.

Clearly DDD is gaining traction with its GSBI honed business plan to localize its approach from one city to another while at the same time keeping focused on its original mission of quality digital services at low prices.

Equal Access International
(Equal Access 2007)

Ronni Goldfarb, president and executive director of Equal Access International attended the GSBI in the summer of 2005. Since her time at the GSBI, Ronni has led Equal Access in scaling their services to millions of beneficiaries and several new countries across Asia. At the GSBI, she refined a business plan that clearly articulates Equal Access' mission, business model, value proposition, and desired outcomes.

Equal Access, an international not-for-profit was founded with the mission to create positive social change for millions of underserved people in the developing world by providing critically needed information and education. As a development communications organization, that combines the power of media with grassroots community mobilization, Equal Access (www.equalaccess.org) is headquartered in San Francisco with country offices in Nepal, Afghanistan, Cambodia, and a partner office in India. The organization creates customized communications strategies and outreach solutions that address the most critical problems affecting people in the developing world such as basic education, health, human rights, women's empowerment, and livelihood training.

Equal Access supports the majority of its services through earned revenue and grants from international development agencies and governments, with some additional support from private foundations and individual philanthropy. Equal Access derives revenue from designing and producing communications and outreach programs for these international development agencies and governments that meet their goals and objectives of improving health, education, and social development compatible with Equal Access' own mission.

Equal Access was founded with the goal of closing the information gap for communities in the developing world. The vision of the organization is firmly rooted in the belief that people everywhere should have equal access to information and education and should have the opportunity to join the dialogue as both recipients and contributors of content. Indeed, Equal Access views access to information and education as a basic human need and believes it is an indispensable tool in bridging the gap between poverty and opportunity. Yet, in many parts of the world, information is a scarce and inaccessible resource. Many individuals, especially in rural communities, do not perceive a lack of education, information, and social services as a violation of basic rights. Without this perception of injustice, the few development efforts that reach rural areas struggle to empower these underprivileged, semi-literate communities. While most commercial media reinforces the status quo, community-oriented media has the power to portray positive role models and local solutions that inspire emulation and positive change in audiences.

Equal Access' integrated solution consists of three core services:

1. Locally designed and produced content: Equal Access develops innovative needs-driven radio and multimedia programming that is culturally appropriate and incorporates feedback directly from audiences. By designing and producing compelling local language programs in-country, the organization catalyzes behavior change in target audiences. Working with local partners to create customized communications strategies and outreach solutions, Equal Access determines the most effective program formats, such as chat shows, dramas, magazine shows, and many more.

2. Information dissemination through cost effective and appropriate technology: Equal Access' technology solutions take advantage of the rich oral histories of the developing world and overcome low literacy rates. These solutions are designed to effectively reach the vast majority of people living in the developing world—people who lack regular or reliable access to telephone service, the Internet, and even FM radio. According to local needs and infrastructure, Equal Access employs a combination of satellite FM/AM radio, multimedia, and solar technologies to provide access to information and education. Digital satellite receivers deliver programs directly to remote communities where organized listening groups discuss program content following broadcasts. When community and national radio stations are connected to the satellite network, FM/AM listeners anywhere also have access to the programs. Receivers can also be connected to computers to access a Web browser-like display of social development information direct from the satellite with no telephony required.

3. Community engagement: Social and economic development is not possible without the meaningful and sustained ownership by local communities. To foster this capacity and empowerment, Equal Access trains local leaders to organize listening and discussion groups in their communities, record voices and opinions from the field, and mobilize positive change based on the powerful role model, stories, and information provided by the programming.

Performance: It is interesting to examine Equal Access's performance in a double-bottom line context. First, from a fiscal performance perspective, in the past three years, the organization has tripled its earned revenue, diversified its revenue streams, and is covering the majority of its operational costs through earned revenue. During the same time period, they have increased the number of beneficiaries served by tenfold.

Feedback: Ronni Goldfarb, the founder of Equal Access, concludes that GSBI was very useful in refining and implementing their innovative business model, developing insights on how to market the organization's services, measuring performance, and enhancing long-term sustainability.

Drishtee (Drishtee Development and Communication 2007)

Satyan Mishra enrolled in the GSBI class of 2006. He represented the organization named Drishtee, which was established to deliver information services to rural villages all over India. During his stay at the GSBI, he honed the business plan and delivered a compelling case at the GSBI Summit that year. The investment crowd was most impressed with her plans.

Drishtee developed a very broad vision indeed: to reform the sociopolitical scenario of the Indian village. The organization is making a paradigmatic shift in the delivery of information services to rural villages by serving villagers directly through information kiosks rather than through intermediaries. Drishtee has signed contractual arrangements with the different state governments within India who provide the platform upon which Drishtee has been able to build a network of sustainable franchise relationships. Local franchise entrepreneurs contract with Drishtee to provide customized Information and Communication Technology (ICT) services to a group of proximate villages. The services are localized and typically include job postings, educational programs, and commercial services such as insurance, among many others.

More than anything else, Drishtee is an IT infrastructure for rural India. More than 600,000 villages of India house two-thirds of its people, and they earn one-third of the national income. A report by the National Council of Applied Economic Research (NCAER) in India shows that rural consumers represent more than 50 percent of consumption and are the prime target market for consumer goods and essential services such as education, healthcare, and employment. Despite such an open market, around 68 percent of the rural economy still lies untapped. Villagers are desperate for appropriate services at affordable costs—from education to market access, from telecom to healthcare, from financial intermediation to entertainment. But the nonavailability of such services linked to the lack of perceived opportunities in rural areas by investors creates a dead end for progress—a dead end that Drishtee is overcoming.

In rural India, villagers live without easy access to trade, government, business, and health services. This makes them easy prey for intermediaries who control the supply chain of products and services and can demand high payments to allow villagers access to these commodities. Drishtee is a for-profit organization that has implemented a sustainable, scalable platform of entrepreneurship enabling the development of rural economies and societies through the use of ICT.

Through a tiered franchise and partnership model, Drishtee facilitates the establishment of ICT nodes, enabling access to information as well as local services to the rural community at nominal cost. The business model is driven by the village entrepreneur, who owns the village node and operates a self-sustaining, profitable kiosk. The kiosk provides access to information like government records, agricultural data, and health insurance; help in filing of applications for licenses, certificates, compensations, and benefits; commodity product rates in different markets; education like computer courses and English classes.

Performance: As of March 2007, Drishtee is serving over 1.5 million villagers and has partnership associations with Intel, Microsoft, ICICI, Airtel, and many other corporations that help enhance the Drishtee services.

Bee Conservation (Bee Conservation Project 2007)

Tunde Fabunmi, president and CEO of Bee Conservation, attended the GSBI in the summer of 2006 to further develop his food-producing enterprise in Nigeria.

Bee Conservation preserves honeybees as an ecological resource in Nigeria and as a source of livelihood for the urban and rural poor. While Kiva, Drishtee, DDD, and Equal Access might be viewed as "meta" initiatives, the Bee Conservation venture represents somewhat more of a "traditional business." This example is one of the few that the GSBI accepts, which is where "the rubber meets the road," so to speak. Kiva, for instance, funds hundreds and hundreds of such enterprises all over the world. Businesses like the Bee Conservation are an important venture in the portfolio of GSBI projects in order to keep close to the businesses that are more traditional but still with a component that has a social mission.

The Bee Conservation is a sustainable agriculture initiative that combines beekeeping and honey processing knowledge, and value chain practices and innovations for the mission of alleviating poverty in rural Nigeria. It also contributes indirectly to the alleviation of poverty by cultivating and expanding the bee hive populations that are critically important to local agricultural ecosystems.

Bee Conservation exists against a backdrop of a nation that is compromising its environmental sustainability by massive bee hunting and deforestation in rural regions. Here 70 percent of Nigerians (mostly those in rural settings) live on less than $1 a day; few jobs are available; 60 percent of college graduates are unemployed; food security is a matter of life and death; 11 percent of women have chronic malnutrition, and 42 percent of children have stunted development.

Bee Conservation seeks to empower a segment of Nigeria's rural poor with "bee wealth" as Tunde likes to call it. He is an Ashoka Fellow who systematically builds a "honey products and services" network and value chain by providing beekeeping training, equipment, and supplies to rural apiarists. The apiarists harvest and process the honey from the hives to Bee Conservation standards while the company markets the final product to urban food centers. Bee Conservation is also a source of nutritional information about honey and bee and honey therapies. This single, integrated commercial venture has fostered an economic development cluster that includes beekeepers, honey processors, honey marketing, sales and distribution, as well as the production of beekeeping hives, kits, and equipment.

Bee Conservation has some aggressive scaling and benefit-reach objectives:

- 900 rural beekeepers achieve a minimum income of $400 per year through honey production in the next five years
- 50 college graduates employed in marketing annually
- Expand honey-based care to 2,000 people annually
- Educate an additional 5 rural communities on the environmental, health, and nutritional benefits of bees and honey each year

Statistics show that 70 percent of Nigeria's 130 million people do not have a sustainable livelihood, but a large portion of the 52 million urban residents are potential domestic honey consumers. Through Honey Fairs, Bee Forums, and public service advertising, Tunde brands his organic, domestically grown honey, providing a significant value proposition over other domestic sources of questionable quality and the higher priced, imported honey products. Since demand for high-grade honey is beyond the capacity of Bee Conservation and other beekeepers in Nigeria, this bodes well for continued growth. Bee Conservation has seen a revenue increase of 33 percent over the past three years, while it is estimated that the beneficiaries in the value chain have grown 75 percent over the same period.

Performance: Tunde Fabunmi's bee-keeping cooperative increased its earned income by 33 percent and doubled its net income in a two-year period. During the same time period, the Bee Conservation increased the number of beneficiaries served by 75 percent.

Feedback: Tunde assessed the GSBI's contribution to the success of his cooperative as being very positive.

What Lessons Have Been Learned?

It is important to recall that the GSBI is a dynamic organization and process. Experience from each class is beneficial in adjusting the process to expand what works best and to reduce, modify, or eliminate the rest. Among some of the subtle lessons learned over time are the following:

   1. Language is important. The GSBI has discovered that social mission entrepreneurs are often quite sensitive about terminology that they consider to reflect the "crass side of business," such as target market, profit, cash flow, and the like. In a number of instances, attendees have been outspoken in expressing irritation at what is the natural language of business. Thus, there is somewhat of a culture clash at first and then a growing acculturation as these types of social entrepreneurs come to better appreciate the potential business side of their endeavors and how to integrate that business perspective into their otherwise altruistic mission to make it more viable, more powerful, and more sustainable. One job of the GSBI is to win over these individuals and help them build a more robust and sustainable vision and mission, one

that can be more enduring and thus actually more fulfilling than their original vision. This is easily accomplished when notions of value creation and monetization of value are linked to sustainability and less dependency on the vagaries of the nonprofit funding processes.

2. Left versus right brain dichotomy. Many GSBI attendees are charismatic, inspirational founders of a social mission venture that they are passionate about. This being said, they are also typically very "right brain" in their orientation and as a result do not naturally embrace the concepts, tools, and analytical methods of business. However, in some ways this is the strength of the program because analytical methods and business plan development concepts are teachable skills that can very much benefit from mentoring and coaching. If it were the other way around, the situation might not be as viable because instilling charisma and inspiration is not viable.

3. Educational model versus venture capital model. During the in-residence program, the GSBI has consistently treated each attendee equally. For example, providing equal resources, advice, and consultation has been the norm from inception of the program. This policy has been in place in spite of the fact that some social mission ventures may have more potential for impacting society than others.

Once the social mission entrepreneurs complete the in-residence portion of the program, the GSBI must use its limited resources to support those endeavors that have the highest probability for sustaining themselves and scaling to greater beneficiary reach. Thus, the accelerator needs to place larger emphasis on a subset of all in-residence attendees. This includes, particularly, the intensive on-the-ground support from GSBI partners such as Accenture.

4. The human side of participants. There can be no more heterogeneous set of classmates than those that typically arrive in any GSBI cohort. Attendees from Central and South America, Asia, India, Africa, Europe, and occasionally North America bring an amazing combination of different needs, expectations, and daily challenges. One individual from Africa had never experienced air travel, a menu without red meat at *every* meal, and air conditioning. Another candidate had his visa application rejected by the U.S. State Department because his ex-wife was on the red alert list. One person was an avowed communist, another was a university professor, and a third had been the former mayor of a city who had dealt with rebel insurgents. The diversity is simply astonishing.

The Future of the GSBI

The GSBI itself is adapting, learning, and gaining from the experience of each cohort of social entrepreneurs that pass through its process. There are episodes of reflection and learning from across all of the ventures in one group and then from one year's group to the next. What is beneficial about the process is identified and expanded and what is less beneficial is reduced, modified, or eliminated. Also, as the GSBI develops a track record and a clearer vision, it can and will attract more resources enhancing its ability to provide benefit and be self-sustaining as it learns to extract a small tax from that benefit. The GSBI faces several challenges as it attempts to scale:

1. Admissions. Each year, as the GSBI continues to gain visibility, it has adapted its application process. The number of applications for the 20 or so slots has increased in 2006 to approximately 100 per year. Typically, 50 percent of the applications are rejected because the GSBI aspires to admit only those that the process can most help. Around 30–40 applicants are typically subjected to intense interviews and 20 are accepted. This is also driven by an operating constraint related to the amount of attention each attendee needs in order to fulfill potential. For example, each attendee is assigned two mentors, experienced entrepreneurs from the local Silicon Valley community, who volunteer their time. While the growing awareness of the GSBI in the Silicon Valley business community is attracting more mentors, there is clearly a constraint on this "supply side" of the program. Clearly, the number of attendees per cohort class is a limiting factor in GSBI's growth. Possibilities that are being explored include multiple GSBI sessions per year, and satellite GSBI sessions offered in parallel at other locations.

2. Content/case material. The best learning environment includes the use of cases, lecture examples, and the material that "relates" in a practical way to the participant's own experiences. While more resources are emerging, it is clear that better material needs to be developed since a significant amount of current course material is not totally appropriate for the audience. This is improving with each year's program as the institution bootstraps itself from experience and continual adaptation for each year's "crop" as well as the continual search for outside material that is better.

3. Learning challenge. Most of the attendees find it difficult to be away from their work for more than two weeks. Given this constraint, it is very challenging to design a two-week curriculum that is

sufficiently comprehensive and yet not overwhelming. On the other hand, this "break away from the current situation" to take a holistic, 360 degree review and assessment of the situation is the heart of the program and arguably it's most important aspect. These social entrepreneurs are transported away from their environment and forced to focus objectively and analytically on what they are doing, how they are doing it, and what kind of a plan can lead to better success at it, particularly in terms of making it more viable and particularly sustainable. So, while being able to break away from execution and implementation for two weeks is the key challenge, it is also what really defines the opportunity.

4. Funding. Historically the GSBI has received funding support from several foundations. Last year for the first time, partial tuition was paid by one GSBI attendee. The hope is to increase the number of participants who pay tuition (for those who can) and continue to provide full support (tuition plus room and board) to those who cannot otherwise afford to participate. Clearly, to scale the GSBI, funding sources must be consistent with any scaling plans.

Conclusion

The Global Social Benefit Incubator is an example of what universities are good at; providing knowledge and *know-how* to build skills and capabilities amongst social mission entrepreneurs. The goal of the GSBI is to expand its reach and impact by exposing social mission entrepreneurs to the GSBI curricula, and to selectively impact those social mission initiatives that can scale. We believe that the GSBI can support the growing interest in the U.N.'s millennium development goals (MGDs). We believe that universities can provide support to this growing movement and that university students will be energized by the example and opportunities to participate in programs like the GSBI.

References

Bee Conservation Project. 2007. http://www.beeconservation-nigeria.org/about. html (accessed December 5, 2007).

Christen, R.P., R. Rosenberg, and V. Jayadeva. 2004. "Double Bottom Line": Implications for the Future of Microfinance. Consultative Group to Assist the Poorest (CGAP). Occasional Paper.

Commission on the Private Sector and Development, a division of United Nations Development Programme. 2007. http://www.undp.org/cpsd/report/index.html (accessed December 5, 2007).

Digital Divide Data. 2007. http://www.digitaldividedata.com/ (accessed December 5, 2007).

Drishtee Development and Communication. 2007. http://www.drishtee.com/ (accessed December 5, 2007).

Equal Access. 2007. http://www.equalaccess.org/ (accessed December 5, 2007).

Hart, S.L. and M.B. Milstein. 1999. Global Sustainability and the Creative Destruction of Industries. Sloan Management Review. http://www.latec.uff.br/mestrado/DS/Sustainability and the Creative Destruction.doc (accessed December 5, 2007).

Information Technology Toolbox, Knowledge Management Section. 2007. http://knowledgemanagement.ittoolbox.com/topics/t.asp?t=324&p=324&h1=324#(accessed December 5, 2007).

Kiva. 2007. www.kiva.org (accessed December 5, 2007).

Lange, Julian E., Aleksandar Mollov, Michael Pearlmutter, Sunil Singh, and William D. Bygrave. 2007. Pre-startup Formal Business Plans and Post-startup Performance: A Study of 116 New Ventures. http://blog.guykawasaki.com//Bygrave.doc (accessed December 5, 2007).

Martin, Roger and Sally Osberg. 2007. Social Entrepreneurship: The Case for Definition. *Stanford Social Innovation Review* 5(2) Spring: 28–39.

Social Edge, a Program of the Skoll Foundation. 2007. http://www.socialedge.org/ (accessed December 5, 2007).

Chapter Seven

Scrutinizing the Link between Poverty and Business Strategy: What Can We Learn from the Case of Shuttle Traders in Laleli, Istanbul?

Mine Eder and Özlem Öz

Introduction and Background

The literature on strategy has long been silent as regards the possible link between poverty and business strategy, and the subject matter has only recently begun to attract attention in this particular line of thinking. The main debate shaping this newly emerging literature (e.g., Rankin 2001; Prahalad 2005) seems to revolve around one basic idea, which advocates that a long-term solution to the problem could be attained if the poor become active participants in business life. Accordingly, the discipline of strategic management should help in this endeavor by working on ways to transform the poor into consumers and/or into producers/entrepreneurs. This argument is, in fact, not new in the broader literature on poverty, and the responses to this stream of thought range from those emphasizing the possibility that there might be instances in which such an approach might or might not work (thus there is a need to conduct ethnographically informed studies), to those severely criticizing the idea on both ideological and substantive grounds (Blowfield 2005; Darrell 2005; Walsh, Kress, and Beyerchen 2005).

The idea of transforming the poor into "consumers" that rests on the view that low-priced goods should be made available for the poor by business organizations, and the poor should then decide for themselves how they would like to allocate their limited resources among the alternatives provided (commonly used examples include TV versus education or cell phones versus health), has been severely criticized as it invites an exploitation of the poor (Karnani 2006). The idea is equally problematic in ethical terms when approached from another angle. It is questionable, for instance, that whether or not achieving what seems to be the ultimate purpose of the Bottom of the Pyramid (BoP) paradigm proposed by Prahalad (2005) (i.e., the poor equipped with low quality/low priced goods, probably at the expense of some basic needs) could be considered a successful outcome. The idea of transforming the poor into entrepreneurs, on the other hand, has been criticized on the grounds that the number of entrepreneurs that eventually become successful in their business ventures is in fact not that high in any given society (Karnani 2006). The empirical evidence regarding the Nobel Prize-winning microcredit system, for instance, is rather mixed, as it has been found out that microcredit does not always result in the alleviation of income poverty (Morduch 1998; Hoque 2004; Islam 2007).

More generally, these two perspectives, involving transforming the poor into consumers or entrepreneurs, can be considered among the varieties of the so-called indirect approach to poverty alleviation. This approach mainly relies on a stimulated economic growth's potential to create wealth and employment, which are in turn expected to help alleviate poverty, albeit indirectly. Those who favor a more direct approach (with an emphasis on social welfare issues including health, education, and housing) argue that an increased economic growth will not automatically alleviate poverty (World Bank 2003) and that "we need to target programs specifically at poverty reduction rather than just wait for the general multiplier effect to kick in" (Karnani 2006, 25). Although it seems that there is a consensus in the literature on the need to employ direct and indirect approaches simultaneously to alleviate and perhaps eventually eradicate poverty, the debate about whether the direct or indirect approach should be given priority in a specific context continues, given that the likelihood of success of different approaches might change from location to location and according to the period of implementation (Senses 2001).

It is necessary, at this juncture, to clarify the stance taken in this chapter regarding the above mentioned differences in opinion. We first argue that the issue at hand is too serious to be left solely to voluntary attempts in the society, and that the state apparatus, within the framework of a social policy, should lead and get involved in the design and implementation of schemes targeting a reduction in poverty. While underlining the necessity of seeing poverty essentially as a public policy issue, however, given the extent of poverty in the world (according to the World Bank [2006], one-fifth of world's population is poor), the value of engaging multiple actors and processes with simultaneous benefits in all fronts (public policy, NGOs, businesses) is also very apparent, which in turn leads us to favor an integrated approach.

Seeing poverty alleviation essentially as a public policy issue, in other words, does not preclude the possibility that businesses might assume some important and complementary roles in addressing this crucial task. It is a fact, however, that alleviation of poverty is not currently viewed as a strategic priority by many business organizations. This suggests that there is a need, before anything else, for a change in mindset on the part of business organizations, starting with the very basics; first, by developing an awareness of the problem and second, by acknowledging their responsibility for poverty alleviation. Businesses must realize that their operations are likely to generate positive or negative effects on different forms of poverty, albeit unintendedly. It has been pointed out, for instance, that a coexistence of hunger and food exports are observed in many famines (Sen 1999) since, ironically, successfully exported crops may become unavailable/unaffordable for the local population (Singer 2006). It can be argued that such entrepreneurial activity may nevertheless contribute toward alleviating some instances of poverty (e.g., by creating additional wealth and new jobs), but it is well-known by now that creation of additional wealth does not guarantee poverty alleviation, as mentioned above. All this, in turn, implies the need for a deliberate integration of the subject matter into the strategies of business organizations.

This being said, we can shift our focus to another dimension of the link between poverty and business strategy, which is a rather understudied aspect, and constitutes the central concern of the present chapter. The limited literature on the link between poverty and business strategy focuses mainly on how strategies of companies might have an impact on alleviating poverty. We argue, in this chapter, that the issue at hand is much more complicated in nature, given the possibility that individual entrepreneurs' reaction to the condition of poverty might itself trigger the emergence of new areas of maneuver in terms of business strategy. It has been, well documented, for instance, that in Turkey there is a link between poverty and informality (Carkoglu and Eder 2006), but there is little work that connects this stream of research to the area of strategic management. Digging into the details of this link is one of the main purposes of this chapter, which will investigate the workings of the complex relation between poverty and business strategy by zooming on the interplay between Istanbul's garment producers and the so-called shuttle traders (mostly from the Russian Federation and former Soviet Republics). These traders assumed an active role in the emergence of an informal, transnational economy in Laleli (a district in central Istanbul), which in turn caused Istanbul's garments producers to channel some of their operations toward that market, resulting in a change of their strategic orientations. An in-depth analysis of the case of Laleli therefore gives us an opportunity to investigate the exact functioning of the link between poverty and business strategy, which, as this case illustrates, can potentially work in both ways. Additionally, the case study allows us to comment on the particularities of a context that is highly informal as well as transnational in character, and carry not only economic but also social dimensions, with implications for poverty alleviation. How do traders, for instance, establish business ties and learn to trust? Why do the garment producers choose the Laleli market and what is the impact of this choice on their strategic orientations? What kind of formal and informal business networks emerge as we move from small garment producers and shopkeepers in Istanbul to shuttle traders and kiosk managers in Russia? and in what ways, do these business encounters help alleviate poverty? These are the main questions that we will be addressing in the following pages.

The chapter is structured as follows. The next section provides a brief overview of the problem of poverty in Turkey and comments on how informality and poverty have been intertwined in this specific context. The emergence of Laleli as a transnational and informal market is then analyzed in detail in the following section. After providing this contextual information, the chapter zooms into the very first steps in the functioning of this market, by tracking the journey of a typical textile item until its arrival at the shelves of a shopkeeper in Laleli. This is followed in the next section by an examination of the remaining part of the chain, which begins with the contact of the shopkeeper with the shuttle trader and follows the rest of the journey through its move to the cargo companies, to the customs, and finally to its final destination abroad. The implications of the study for the broader literature on the link between poverty and business strategy are discussed in the concluding section, in light of the preceding analysis. Both published and unpublished documents on and about Laleli have been analyzed within the context of the present study, and these analyses are supported by an ongoing ethnographic research on the Laleli market, which started in the year 2002 (see Eder et al. 2002). The authors jointly conducted additional interviews in January 2007 with several shopkeepers in Laleli as well as producers working for the Laleli market, both to update some of the research material and to focus on poverty issues.

Prevalence of Poverty and Informality in Turkey

Measuring and defining poverty in any country has long been problematic, and Turkey is no exception. Though the European Commission's "Joint Report on Social Inclusion" provides some insights in contextualizing poverty, measurement difficulties remain (as cited in http://www.europemsi.org/background_definitions.php retrieved on March 30, 2007):

> People are said to be living in poverty if their income and resources are so inadequate as to preclude them having a standard of living considered acceptable in their society in which they live. Because of their poverty, they may experience multiple disadvantages through unemployment, low income, poor housing, inadequate health care and barriers to life-long learning, culture, sport and recreation facilities. They are often excluded and marginalized from participating in activities (economic and social and cultural) that are the norm of other people, and their access to fundamental rights is restricted.

For instance, with its relatively low levels of food poverty (approximately 2 percent) and its arguably strong social networks, Turkey might not appear, at first glance, as a country with a significant poverty problem. This initial impression, however, is quite misleading when one considers the risk-of-poverty rate, which is defined as 60 percent of median of the equalivized net income of all households. In 2003, 26 percent of the Turkish population was below this line. More striking is the high rate observed among the working population, which amounts to 23 percent, implying that approximately one out of five individuals (among the Turkish citizens who are employed) is a "working poor." This number is threefold the EU-25 average (Adaman and Keyder 2006, 16).

Among the many reasons behind these relatively high risk-of-poverty levels observed in Turkey, the financial crisis of 2000–01 that led to an unprecedented rise in urban unemployment; inability of the economy to create sufficient jobs despite steady economic growth, which is a global trend in the world economy; the restructuring of agriculture in Turkey since the 1990s, which has created significant rural impoverishment; and the utter failure/insufficiency of the welfare state to provide basic services such as decent healthcare and education are often cited as the most fundamental ones (Adaman 2003; Bugra and Keyder 2006; Eder 2003). Furthermore, the image of social networks working as buffer zones to alleviate poverty has also increasingly disappeared in recent years as new urban migrants have been unable to find steady employment and/or bring their family from the countryside (Bugra and Keyder 2003; Keyder 2005).

Under these circumstances, creating informal networks and informal businesses have been among the ways developed to fight poverty. A 2006 national survey, comparing household members with informal traders in Turkey—the shopkeepers, the bazaaris, and street vendors—indicate, for instance, that those who are the most vulnerable have also been the most informal (Carkoglu and Eder 2006). When asked about the length of time they could manage if their income was cut off for some reason, almost 70 percent of the households and 60 percent of the shopkeepers reported that they could survive 30 days or less if their source of income was depleted suddenly. Managing only a month or less after complete income loss appears to be much more prevalent among the bazaaris and street vendors as this percentage skyrockets to more than 80 percent in these groups. This intense economic vulnerability (in the form of an absence of security money or savings) can be one of the important factors that can explain why people prefer, or worse yet, do not have another option but to work in the informal sector (Carkoglu and Eder 2006).

Though poverty is only one form of social exclusion, it feeds into other forms of exclusion such as getting access to basic healthcare and education. Indeed, poverty does emerge as *the* problem and half of the participants in a recent national survey have declared that they felt excluded from society because of the state of their poverty, underscoring how poverty often becomes entangled with the political, social, and cultural as well as spatial dimensions of exclusion (Adaman and Keyder 2006). This multidimensionality of poverty in turn raises serious challenges in terms of formulating appropriate public policies as well as developing effective business strategies for addressing poverty alleviation.

Emergence of a "Shuttle Trading" Center in Laleli

Goods and people have been traveling to, from, and through Istanbul for centuries. As such, there is hardly anything surprising with the current transnational networks that the city seems to have witnessed since the 1990s. In effect, Istanbul is already a city with global links (Keyder 1999). Three aspects of the new wave of transnationalism observed in

Istanbul, however, are notable. One is its informal nature that involves hundreds of predominantly women traders, known as *chelnokis* (shuttles) in Russian (or suitcase traders in Turkish), making repeated trips to Turkey, and second is its size, with significant implications for the Turkish leather and textile industries and their workers. Finally, an additional aspect of the issue that is relevant for our purposes concerns its link with poverty, which was one of the most important factors that triggered this type of trade. Specifically, falling real wages and rising unemployment in Russia in the late 1980s and early 1990s and the resulting increase in poverty brought about developments that paved the way for the emergence of market places that sprung up throughout this country, in an attempt to supply the impoverished masses with cheap goods made available to them, thanks to the shuttle trade (Yükseker 2007, 65). On the Turkish side, Laleli also lured many new migrants into the city looking for jobs and quick cash. The increasingly visible and permanent urban poverty in Istanbul, disappearance of the middle class in the city, and declining manufacturing jobs and employment opportunities (Keyder 2005) rendered the prospect of arbitrage, that is, producing/buying in Turkish liras and selling in dollars in the informal Laleli market very attractive.

Though much smaller in numbers, what started as systematic trips on the part of many Russians to various makeshift harbor bazaars in Turkey's Black Sea coast such as Trabzon and Hopa, gradually shifted to Istanbul and Laleli in particular, becoming more centralized, organized, and diversified. Initially, Soviet citizens would cross the border carrying various items such as small machinery, cameras, and stolen goods from state warehouses. They bartered these goods with leather products and garments. Turkey was not the only destination in this barter trade. Norway, Germany, and Finland were among the favorite bartering sites. While Poles, Czechs, and Hungarians went to Istanbul to trade, Georgians, Azerbaijanis, and Armenians traveled along the Black Sea coast entering the country. By the mid-1990s, however, Russians has stopped bringing goods from their own country, becoming regular shuttle traders in the process. These "tourist traders" initially carried various goods (household products, clothing, electronic goods, etc.) that they bought in Turkey literally in their suitcases and declared them as their personal belongings to avoid customs on their way back home. The transformation of the Laleli district from a sleepy residential area adjacent to the old city, to a bustling shopping district also corresponded with the explosion of trade with the ex-Soviet republics, as suitcase trade or shuttle trade became an abbreviation of all unregistered commerce between Turkey and these republics.

Indeed, over time, this suitcase/shuttle trade became professional-ized, the chelnokis developed long-term informal networks with Laleli shopkeepers, and bulk trading through informal cargo companies and/or tourist operators became common. The outward appearances of Laleli belie the size and importance of this trade: at its peak in 1995, the volume of suitcase trade reached an estimated $10 billion. Even though it has declined to approximately an annual $3 billion since then, it still remains a significant source of hard currency for Turkey. In fact, the extent of this market became first evident when the IMF officials pressured the Turkish Central Bank in 1996 to include shuttle trade estimates in its current account calculations.

The shuttle trade is important for the Russian economy as well, and indeed, represents only one among many important new informal trading networks in the post-Soviet era. Before the August 1998 Ruble crisis, official estimation of Goskomstat on volume of shuttle trade in Russia in the year 1998 was approximately $4.5–5 billion per quarter, and this figure dropped to $2–2.5 billion per quarter after the crisis. The share of Turkey in this overall volume is estimated to be around 40–50 percent (Goskomstat 1999). Even after the Ruble crisis, shuttle trade accounted for 10.3 percent of Russia's foreign trade turnover (Goskomstat 2000). At its peak in 1993–94, an estimated 10–15 million Russians were involved in overall shuttle trade, and in 1999, the turnover of unregistered shuttle trade had reached an estimated $11.5 billion, a figure comparable to the total revenue derived from Russian exports in that year (Goskomstat 1999). With the improve-ment of the Russian economy, thanks largely to the rising oil prices since then, and the Putin government's insistence on increasing customs tariffs as well as on formalizing this trade with prospects for becoming a member of the WTO, these numbers have declined considerably but shuttle trading still remains an important part of livelihood in the peripheries of the post-Soviet region.

As noted above, most of the transactions in shuttle trade occur in U.S. dollars and in cash, and this has been the lure of this market, both for the shopkeepers and the traders. But the suitcase trade clearly does not involve only the shopkeepers and the traders. A whole series of related and supporting businesses has, for instance, sprawled in Laleli, including tourism agencies, hotels, and most importantly cargo com-panies, which feed on the shuttle trade. In the early 1990s, traders transported Turkish goods back home mostly by train, bus, or boat in suitcases, but air transport has now become more widely used. At its peak, Turkish airlines had over 55 passenger flights a week between Turkey and the CIS, Romania, and Bulgaria with a carrying capacity of close to 10,000 (visitors) from those places to Istanbul. In addition, the national airlines of Russia and Ukraine were flying to Istanbul 10 times a week from Moscow, St. Petersburg, and Kiev. Even though, how much of the arrivals from the CIS countries were related to suitcase trading is impossible to estimate, the fact that the entries to Turkey from ex-Soviet Republics have skyrocketed from a mere 40,000 people in 1980 to 2.7 million already provides clues to intensified flows and exchanges (Eder et al. 2002; Kirisci 2005).

Planes, however, are twice as expensive when compared to the main alternative: carrying the goods through tractor-trailers. Trucks and tractor-trailers tend to be rented from the CIS countries. Cargo companies play a crucial role in sustaining this mode of trading. These companies work closely with travel agencies that bring the customers and arrange the hotels for them. Most of the cargo companies also have joint ventures with Russian, Moldavian, and Romanian counterparts. Each partner is responsible for the products until their respective border. The shopkeepers often stated that the 'real money' is being made in the cargo business. The strength of some cargo companies has reached to the extent that they now own their own charter planes. The business is risky, however, as it involves passing customs officials and establishing the necessary networks for 'unproblematic' passage of goods, that is, knowing the right people at the right place. The shopkeepers do not work directly with the cargo companies but simply deliver the goods their client wants, to the cargo company, again designated by the customer. Another related area of activity concerns the warehouses where the customers can leave their goods for $1 a day. The so-called cargo boys, on the other hand, help the customer carry their goods from the shops to the cargo companies, which are conveniently all in Laleli (see figure 7.1).

Hotels in Laleli are also crucial for the shuttle trade. There are some estimated 500 hotels in the region, some subject to regulation from the municipality, some from the Ministry of Tourism. Most hotels work closely with travel agencies in Russia, which in turn tend to have partners in Turkey. (These agencies offer special packages, which include a round-trip ticket to Istanbul and a few nights stay, costing approximately $300.) The hotels have very different rates for these clients. (Some offer as much as 60 percent discount on daily prices.) Most hotels in Laleli have changed their conference rooms to warehouses for the shuttle traders. This allows the customers to leave their goods in the hotel and then transfer them to the cargo company with which the travel agency works. Agencies usually work with two or three hotels in the region.

Figure 7.1   Shuttle traders in Laleli.

Source: Photograph by Mine Eder and Özlem Öz.

It is true that the Laleli market has generated some easy dollars for some of the overnight shopkeepers as well as new prospects for transportation businesses and hotels. In fact, the district became a pathway particularly for some of the new urban migrants to make some money. (Though beyond the scope of this study, it is important to note that the booming of Laleli and the influx of Kurdish shop-keepers coincided with the militarization of the Kurdish conflict in southeastern Turkey, already one of the poorest regions in the country). Many had worked as textile workers and shop clerks and had developed some sort of hands-on experience in the industry. It is also true that the income level of most of the shopkeepers have increased visibly during the first half of the 1990s, as exemplified by the following remarks of an interviewee: "I never used to go and have a vacation in my life or go out in a restaurant before. Now I take my Russian guests/customers to Antalya [a favorite tourist attraction for Russian tourists] or take them out for dinner."

While the story of the embourgeoisement of the shopkeeper is highly appealing, what this dynamic sprawling of new businesses in and around Laleli conceals is the intense volatility and fragility of these informal networks. For many, this boom was only temporary. The fragility became very evident, for instance, during the 1998 Ruble crisis in Russia, which led to the drastic devaluation of Ruble, making all foreign goods very expensive for the shuttle traders. In terms of the numbers, the volume for trade declined from 109,094 tons in 1996 to only 12,095 tons by the June of 1999. Similarly, the number of flights to and from Russian federation and CIS countries dropped from an annual 28,040 flights and more than 2 million passengers in 1997 to 5,301 flights and 383,537 passengers by June of 1999 (LASIAD 2000). The dramatic fall of the volume of the shuttle trade from an annual $8 billion to about $3 billion after the crisis means that more than half of the shopkeepers in Laleli have either gone bankrupt or have lost significant amount of goods and money.

The crisis also brought about some changes in business strategies. Since customers were no longer abundant as it used to be, the shopkeepers had to improve the quality and offer competitive prices. The profit margins declined significantly, pushing the one-timers out of the market. Meanwhile, small and large producer firms that were working on a subcontracting basis with the Laleli shops went under as the shopkeepers were not able to pay for the goods or returned most of them. Furthermore, because of significant collapse of the credit system and the unprecedented rise in nonreturning credits, usury mechanisms, various informal lending and crediting mechanisms along with prostitution are said to have increased. Finally, even though the 1998 crisis was a big blow to patterns of trust between traders and the shopkeepers, those who survived the crisis were able to establish more long-term relationships. In effect, surviving the crises, through devising such methods as granting long-term credits to the traders or agreeing to get no payments until their next trip showed how the informal markets can quickly adjust to the changing circumstances in the external environment.

Another evidence of volatility and fragility of the shuttle trade came during the 1999–2001 IMF program implemented in Turkey. The currency-peg system that the Turkish government adopted resulted in an overvalued currency, in effect, making Laleli goods more expensive in dollar terms. Most shopkeepers complained that they have lost significant amount of business to East Asia, China, and Gulf states during this period. Thus, when the Turkish currency was devaluated in February 2001, the Laleli market appeared to be delighted and witnessed a boom in the aftermath of the crisis. Once again, the vulnerability of this market to any foreign currency fluctuations, where the sellers buy and sell in U.S. dollars, but producers produce in Turkish Lira, is quite evident.

Another factor accounting for the fragility of the Laleli market is linked to the vulnerability of this business to the changes in the Turkish-Russian relations. Problems over the Chechen question and issues related to Blue Stream and other pipeline projects, for instance, are all said to influence the dynamics of trade in Laleli. Finally, Laleli trade is most susceptible to changes in the customs regime in Russia. Despite significant pressures from the Turkish government, for instance, Putin government has issued a decision to limit its shuttle trade with Turkey through applying customs duties and value-added tax for goods that weigh more than 30 kgs (initially 50 kgs) and are worth more than $1,000 (initially $2,000) effective as of 2007 (http://www.kobifinans.com.tr/bilgi_merkezi/0208/14025/8). How this decision will be implemented in practice, however, remains to be seen. The fact that the first government decree to regulate informal trade dates back to December 2003 to be in effect in January 2004, and that the uniform and full implementation on the ground has been impossible since then, with frequent delays and/or relaxations at the customs, suggests radical customs regime changes might be difficult (Russian Federation: Government Decree no: 718) Nevertheless, the increasing constraints and controls, albeit slow, raises significant questions about the long-term sustainability of this type of a transnational market place.

From Workshops to Laleli

Having provided an overview of the emergence of Laleli as a center of shuttle trade, we can now shift our focus to a detailed analysis of the very first steps in its functioning, that is, those concerning production relations. Before proceeding with this analysis, however, we should give some information about the landscape of the relevant economic activities in Istanbul to put Laleli into its context. Istanbul, being the economic capital of Turkey, hosts a huge variety of businesses, textiles and apparel being among the main drivers of its economy. An examination of the geography of this line of activity within Istanbul reveals that retail outlets scattered around the city are fed by numerous producers and workshops concentrated in certain areas of the city, including, for instance, Merter, Ikitelli, Okmeydani, and Caglayan districts in the case of regular items of apparel, and in Tuzla and nearby town of Corlu in the case of leather garments. Among the great variety of retail outlets, concentrations in Osmanbey (textiles/apparel) and Zeytinburnu (leather clothing) have secured a reputation of being high quality, targeting the upper-end of the market. Laleli, on the other hand, has been associated with those outlets that target the lower-end of the market in both product categories, although in recent years there are signs pointing to a change in this respect.

Three distinct types of production relations have been observed in Laleli. The first was in the form of "forward integration" of small textile producers of Istanbul into the Laleli market, which happened in the early 1990s. These small firms were located in various textile districts of Istanbul such as Mahmutpasa and Yeni Bosna. They were mainly targeting the lower-end of the market and shifting their focus rather opportunistically, giving a priority to either Laleli or the domestic market, depending on their relative prospects. From the mid-1990s onward, however, this structure would change drastically, when shuttle traders began to demand higher quality goods and when the textile producers of Istanbul targeting the upper-end of the market (e.g., Osmanbey-based ones) also saw opportunities in Laleli. Shopkeepers themselves, on their part, saw the likely benefits of integrating the production function into their operations, signifying the emergence of the second type of production relations that emerged in Laleli, which took the form of "backward integration" of Laleli shopkeepers into production. They were transforming themselves in such a way that they were now not only retailers or wholesalers but full-scale textile firms. In fact, some Laleli-originated firms later evolved to become large and well-known companies both in national and international markets (e.g., Colin's) (Yükseker 2003). The emergence of the final and the most recent type of relations was triggered by the entry of larger textile/leather garment firms of Istanbul into the Laleli market. Observing that Laleli had its ups and downs, and hence was rather a risky market, the priority of these firms remained in regular export activity. It seems, nevertheless, that they could not resist the high potential of returns offered by Laleli in case the market boomed. The consequences of this move, however, would prove costly for them in the long-run, as will be discussed in the concluding section. Now, we continue with our quest to better understand the nature of production relations in Laleli with the help of two examples: a textile workshop serving the Laleli market and an Osmanbey-based textile store in Laleli.

The Weakest Ring in the Chain: Ahmet's Workshop

Ahmet (the real names of interviewees have been changed) was a yarn merchant in Istanbul in the early 1990s, when he went bankrupt in the aftermath of the 1994 financial crisis in Turkey. In the following seven years, he worked as an ironer in a textile workshop, where he met Sinan who also used to work in the same place. Two friends combined forces to establish a small textile workshop in Okmeydani, a district packed with similar workshops, serving as subcontractors to the firms targeting the upper-end of the market, and located in nearby Osmanbey. One Osmanbey firm that the new-born workshop of Ahmet and Sinan had subcontracting relations with channeled some part of its sales to Laleli, and that's how this small workshop began producing for the Laleli market. Now they exclusively work for this firm.

Ahmet states that it is unthinkable for him to directly produce and sell in the Laleli market, simply because he either does not have the required financial strength or the necessary know-how regarding the functioning of the market. "There are even limits," he says, "to the amount of orders that I can agree to produce, since I work with a given capacity. When the market is booming, when the orders are above the current capacity of my workshop [which employs 10 workers], I need to employ new workers. When the market is down, I unfortunately have to let some of them go." He adds, however, that he tries to resist laying off his workers, who, in the times of crisis, prefer to continue working, sometimes agreeing to a payroll only enough to cover their food-related expenditures, rather than losing their jobs.

Strikingly, the longest time horizon that Ahmet can talk about is "the week," and he considers "not worrying about whether or not he could pay the weekly salaries of his workers" as good business. When asked about what he thinks regarding the fact that the textile items that he produces in his workshop ends up being sold in hard currency in a chain that apparently creates considerable value, Ahmet remains rather silent. "I cannot say anything about that," he says, "but I am lucky that I have a partner firm in Laleli with whom I have a regular, long-term, trust-based relation. Other workshops here are not as lucky." He mentions a friend, a next-door neighbor, who has to close down his workshop from time to time, sometimes for months, when there is a downturn in the market.

What can easily be noticed in the above statements is the vulnerability of not only the workers but also the workshop owners themselves. We argue that this is not only linked to the level of uncertainty in the market and the exposition of the workshops to the resulting risks but also a manifestation of the imbalances in terms of the share captured from the value created in this chain of operations. The consent of the workshops to such a limited share is, in turn, revealing as regards their competitive advantages. They know very well, in other words, that they are not irreplaceable at all, and that there are numerous other workshops their partner firms can turn to, in case they ask for an improvement in their condition. They simply do not have the required resources and capability to upgrade their products and/or technologies and thus to aim for a differentiation strategy. There is not much area for maneuver either, if they would instead try to work on decreasing their costs, given the tough competition (not only from local producers but also from the Chinese competitors) in that part of the market. Their vulnerability, as a result, is very much linked to the limits that they encounter as regards upgrading their competitive advantages, aggravating their overdependence on firms that they have subcontracting relations with.

Connecting the Local and Global: Yakup's Store in Laleli

Yakup's firm started its operations in Laleli in the year 2003. Since it is an Osmanbey-originated firm also engaged in production, this move can be considered as a "step-down" for them, according to Yakup, which reveals the loose reputation of Laleli in the eyes of Osmanbey firms. The firm employs about 100 workers directly, but if you include those in the workshops with which they have regular subcontracting relations, this number rises to about 500. Yakup says that they pay around $10,000 a month as rent for their retail shop in Laleli. Although he quotes a common joke in this business, reading, "produce and sell, make a name; buy and sell, make a profit," he seems content with the decision of his firm to internalize production: "you should have the absolute control over the details of production if you do not want to risk your quality," he stresses.

Yakup further states that his firm (together with others that have made a similar strategic choice) is determined to change the low-quality image of Laleli. In fact, given that the lower-end of the market has already been occupied to a large extent by the Chinese producers, he is of the opinion that they have no other option: "We have no choice but to concentrate on what they cannot do: produce flexibly, in a timely fashion and with a good quality/price ratio." When asked about the extent of transformation observed in Laleli in this regard, he stated that the quality of goods that one could find in Laleli improved considerably over the years. According to him, this was not only introduced by forward-thinking entrepreneurs but was also triggered by a change in the nature of demand: "Previously, our foreign customers were 'hungry,' they would buy anything, but now they also started to demand goods of better quality," he concludes.

It is necessary at this point to underline that this firm was a latecomer to Laleli and represents only one of the differing modes of operation prevailing in this market and that there are a number of other forms, mirroring the case of producers mentioned above. These include those firms that started as small traders in nearby (e.g., Mahmutpasa) districts and made an opportunistic and early move to Laleli, and typically not involved in production, or their spin-off firms. It is not uncommon for this latter type of firms to have gone bankrupt several times throughout their business lives in Laleli. Yet another mode of operation in Laleli includes those firms that improved their businesses substantially over the years by making very good used of the opportunities that the Laleli market provided. One leather clothing firm that we interviewed for this study, for instance, enlarged its operations in the district to the extent that they now have four retail stores in Laleli, another one in Zeytinburnu, and one tannery (production unit) in Corlu. This happened "thanks to the opportunities that the crises provided" in the words of one of the owners of the firm, who further states confidently that they are now a well-known brand in the Russian market. He adds that the lower-end of the market in leather clothing business is now served by the Chinese and Pakistani producers, and that was one of the main triggers of his firm's move toward the upper-end of the market: "We were in a way forced to that," he says, "you cannot be creative enough in finding remedies, unless you are under real competitive pressure."

This real competitive pressure, however, has not been equally easy for others to confront. Many firms in Laleli that could not adjust to the changing circumstances got eliminated in the course of time, and this is not unexpected in theoretical terms. Specifically, as mentioned in the beginning of this text, it has been underlined in the literature that only some of the entrepreneurs that start new ventures end up being successful in their endeavors (Karnani 2006), posing a question mark regarding the relevance of promoting entrepreneurship as a major strategy for alleviating poverty. The presence of those who "made it," in other words, does not change the fact, that there are numerous others who did not.

From Laleli to the Final Destination Abroad: Tracing the Journey of Shuttle Traders

The information in this section is based on International Research Exchange (IREX) project 2002, and the interviews were conducted by the Russian partner in the project, Professor Andrei Yakovlev (Eder et al. 2002). Though the recent oil boom in the Russian economy with its glitzy shops and haute couture establishments makes it hard to believe, the birth of shuttle trading corresponds with the intense contraction of the Russian economy in the early 1990s (some 20 percent during 1991–93) as mentioned above, which brought severe financial difficulties for the average families. People quitting their defense jobs, women who used to work in now-closed or bankrupt industries, public servants not getting paid—in short, people with diverse occupational groups began to engage in shuttle trading. As such, unemployment, poverty, or the threat of poverty were the most important push factors at the beginning of this shuttle trade. As noted above, the first shuttle traders (who were mostly women), like the Soviet customers, were inexperienced and unscrupulous with regards to quality; they, as a result, mostly bought cheap and low quality products. Turkey was among the favorite destinations for this initial type of demand, along with Poland and China.

Though beyond the scope of this chapter, it is important to note that shuttle trading was not the only industry that these post-Soviet women got into in the 1990s. The domestic-care and sex industries in Turkey also witnessed an unprecedented inflow of irregular women migrants from these former Soviet republics. In fact, some of the start-up capital for shuttle trading is said to be accumulated through prostitution (Yükseker 2003). This also explains the lingering prejudice against these shuttle traders by equating them with the so-called Natashas, a pejorative term used for sex workers coming from the region. Icduygu (2006, 11) provides a broad sectoral breakdown of these irregular migrants. Accordingly, Moldavian and Bulgarian women worked in domestic work, Rumanians, Moldavians, Russians, and Ukrainians in the sex and entertainment industry, still Moldavian and Rumanian women in textiles, and Iranian, Iraqi, Moldavian, and Rumanian in the construction industry. Some of these migrant women also work in Laleli shops informally as clerks or shop assistants. They are favored by the shopkeepers because of their language skills and familiarity with the customers and consumer tastes.

The initial traders started the trade with as little as $2,000 worth of merchandise. A medium-size trader would have $10,000–20,000 worth of goods to be sold often in more than one sale point, and maximum amount is estimated to be $50,000 (Melnichenko, Bolonini, and Zavatta 1997, 4). At its peak, professional traders made as many as 20 trips per year for shuttle trading. Proximity of Turkey, the easier entry to the country thanks to the convenience of the sticker visa issued at the border, the clustered nature of Laleli with its hotels and cargo companies, the attractive price/ quality ratio, and a wide selection of items to purchase were all cited among the reasons favoring Istanbul when compared to other destinations. Not surprisingly, a significant amount of partnerships and a degree of trust have emerged through this trade to facilitate small-scale transactions undertaken with little excess capital. A typical transaction involved the Russian partner faxing the order and sending half the cash for the merchandise by boat. The rest of the money arrives by the return boat after the merchandise has been sold.

As this trade became more professionalized and organized, cargo companies took over the transportation of goods. So a typical shuttle trade transaction would involve a shuttle trader, who is overwhelmingly female, to contact a tourism agency in her hometown. The agencies often work jointly with cargo companies (sometimes they are one and the same). The reservations are then done for a few days with a Laleli hotel, just enough to complete shopping. The shuttle trader then flies into Istanbul, transported into her hotel, and starts shopping. The shopkeepers have either received the orders from this shuttle trader in advance or will push their subcontractors to meet the deadline for producing the amount of clothing or goods demanded by the shopkeeper. These goods are then packaged by the cargo companies (or by the traders themselves depending on the volume). The shopkeeper is mainly responsible for delivering the demanded goods. In order to ensure timely delivery, he/she often works with more than several subcontractors. Once again, developing working relationship with the subcontractors proves to be vital. The cargo company then delivers the good either directly to the open market or to the requested shop at the trader's hometown.

Meanwhile, just like their counterparts in the Laleli district, these traders also had to struggle with the low-quality image of their goods as the demand became more and more sophisticated. While China and South Korea started to cater to the lower-end of the market, with the high-end served by Italy and some other European countries, Turkish goods gradually became priced out in the market, which not only explains the decline in the number of chelnokis traveling to Istanbul, but also underscores the dual nature of shuttle trading. Those with little capital, specializing at the lower-end of the market, were going to the Far East and were selling their goods mostly at open bazaars with rented stalls, others with the power of the purse were expanding to Europe and selling their goods in regular shops, in effect, formalizing their economic transactions. Even the saleswomen thought it was not prestigious to wear stuff from the open-air market.

Nevertheless, shuttle trading has been an effective strategy for a significant number of post-Soviet women to make a living and survive the rather violent transition to capitalism. Most of these women narrate the difficult origins of their start-ups, how they scrambled for initial money, borrowing from friends and relatives, how they could not find jobs in line with their education, and how they learned this commerce "by doing." Others talk about the difficulties of transporting goods prior to the arrival of the cargo companies, how they had to travel by boat for days, how they had to deal with the police and the customs officials. These women substituted, in effect, their time and labor with capital and know-how as regards formal trading activities by frequently traveling long distances, sometimes in harsh conditions. One shuttle trader, for instance, describes a journey she took as follows: "Once I took a boat across the Black Sea. That was a continuous suffering, although cheap. We sailed and slept on the floor for 10 days." Upon completing such a journey, these shuttle traders then have to face equally harsh conditions on the market: "I stand on the market and sell the goods myself. . . . Each time you bring new goods, you worry a lot thinking that it might not sell. Market is a cruel thing, if you go bankrupt, nobody will help. Everybody thinks about himself/ herself." Under these circumstances, in the words of a trader, "survives the strongest," while the less skillful and inadept are forced to leave the business. Even though the cargo companies have since taken over transportation and arranging customs, much to the relief of many of the chelnokis, the repeated trips and the volatility of the markets continued to be a source of constant concern. "People lost in one month all what they have earned in one year after the 1998 crisis," noted one chelnoki, "though the bankruptcies were not as many as those in Turkey, many on the Russian side also went out of business or stopped trading for a while." Another shuttle trader, rather disappointed with her first genuine encounter with the market, finds its functioning rather arbitrary: "A lot depends on chance," she says, "luck, conditions and the availability of capital are crucial. . . . Future is undetermined. We live by the single day." But, "We will continue doing this until we find an alternative," says another trader, revealing not only that they currently lack any real alternatives but also that they do not see any way out as regards their present conditions.

Although, as the Russian economy booms and domestic production increases, shuttle trading is expected to die down completely, albeit gradually, we see more optimism on the Turkish side regarding the future of this type of trade: "We will find ways to survive in this market" explained the owner of a firm in Laleli; "when the Putin government increased customs, we had to divide up our customers' orders into smaller bulks and land them in smaller airports where inspections are not as strict. They still don't know how to import formally, they don't trust their government. Until this fact changes, we will find a way to get our goods into Russia."

Concluding Remarks: Consequences of an Entrepreneurial Escape from Poverty

In this chapter, we have examined an informal and transnational market, Laleli, with the ultimate purpose of scrutinizing the interplay between business strategy and poverty. Several issues of key importance in our analysis stand out in this regard: the link between informality, transnationality, and poverty; the dynamic relationship between poverty and business strategy; different manifestations of poverty and their respective degrees of vulnerability; and finally some of the likely consequences of an "entrepreneurial solution" to the condition of poverty. These are discussed in detail below.

We have seen in this chapter that the reactions of individuals to increased levels of poverty or the threat of poverty (the triggering factors may be related to, say, a failure or insufficiency of public social protection mechanisms) might force them to get engaged not only in informal but in transborder economic activities as well. We have also seen that such an undertaking might bring about a temporary relief to some, but not all, of these entrepreneurs who have to try hard and find a solution to their condition. It is clear, for instance, that as an informal, totally unregistered market, Laleli offered a temporary income boost for many of the shopkeepers, formal textile workers, clerks, or new migrants. The rising demand from Soviet customers for almost any mass consumption goods at the initial stages of this trade generated significant amount of wealth for both the chelnokis and the shopkeepers in Laleli. Some moved on and expanded their businesses, moved into production, and some opened new shops, others took to early retirement after some lucrative lump-sum transactions. Not all of the businesses, however, were as lucky. The collapse of this market—particularly after the 1998 Ruble crisis, which led to a series of bankruptcies—closing of the shops, lost goods, unreturned payments, and a significant drop in the number of chelnokis underscored the uncertainty and volatility of these markets. Furthermore, since almost nothing was registered, none of the goods, credits, or money could be reclaimed. Such crises demonstrate that the significance of the so-called informal networks and entrepreneurial trust should not be exaggerated. Though building trust and networking is evidently crucial in developing this kind of trade, such networks can easily be broken and has clearly been broken, in times of economic hardships. Laleli being a microcosm of a transnational informal marketplace, shows how volatile, uncertain such informal economic transactions are, and proves that such informal business strategies can only provide a temporary and partial solution to the more fundamental and structural problems of poverty. Besides, it should be underlined that the linkages between informality and poverty raise a very serious vicious cycle, particularly with regards to the public policy. With 50 percent of its working population employed in the informal sector, for example, the Turkish economy suffers from significant revenue loss, which in turn undermines the ability of the state to provide basic services. With only the formal jobs covered in the social security system, many are left extremely vulnerable to the ups and downs of the markets and fragility/uncertainty of the informal business and employment.

Not only did shuttle traders and small-scale Istanbul manufacturers/suppliers not pay taxes "but they also contributed to the creation of a 'bad reputation' of Turkish products as being of low quality" (Yükseker 2007, 65). This issue is of paramount importance as it illustrates that the link between poverty and business strategy is a dynamic one. The case of Laleli shows that individual entrepreneurs' (e.g., Russian shuttle traders') reaction to the conditions prevailing in a given location might open up new avenues in terms of possible business strategies that can be adopted by firms (e.g., Laleli firms) located in a totally different region of the world. The resulting transformation in the latter firms' strategic orientations however, is not always progressive. This can be exemplified by the experience of Istanbul's leather garment manufacturers. Specifically, we see that in the early years of the Laleli market, the established leather clothing producers of Istanbul were mainly targeting the high-quality segments in Western Europe and were not showing interest in Laleli. Over time, however, seeing the enormous potential of this market, they channeled some of their sales to Laleli, which inevitably brought a change in terms of their strategic orientations. They were now producing and selling for customers who required low-cost products and were much less demanding when it comes to quality. Although the sacrifice of quality meant easy sales in the beginning, and the charm of an easy life was hard to resist, this brought about some unintended consequences in the form of poor image for their goods, which later would prove difficult to counter (Öz 2004). Furthermore, starting from the late 1990s, the Laleli market began to be stratified, reflecting the changing character of demand in their target markets, which was evolving toward better quality goods. This meant that apart from the difficulty of reestablishing the neglected contacts with their European customers, leather clothing firms now had to improve their image in their shuttle trade markets as well, since they heard that some shuttle traders began removing the "made in Turkey" labels from their products. Besides, they would soon discover that it was impossible for them to compete with the Chinese, Indian, and Pakistani leather garment producers in the price-sensitive segments. Their opportunistic shift to an easy life, in other words, proved rather costly for them in the long run. What this translates to in theoretical terms, is that, when the market conditions changed in such a way that the preferences of the customers evolved toward the upper end of the market, they found themselves "stuck-in-the-middle" (Porter 1985). Following the path-dependency and lock-in paradigm (Arthur 1985), for some entrepreneurs it even meant that the particular path that they opportunistically chose to follow was rather irreversible, revealing the hidden traps in the process of strategizing.

Another conclusion is that there are different forms and thus manifestations of poverty, which also exhibit differing degrees of vulnerability at any given time, in that, as the position of some actors strengthens, some others may be losing ground. If one walks through the streets of Laleli, s/he can easily observe different levels of poverty and vulnerability. From big and small shops to stalls selling various clothing items out in the open in front of these shops, from mega-mafia-looking cargo companies to cargo carrying boys, from fancy, air-conditioned hotels to dingy looking ones, from parking lots where new migrants conjugate with hopes of finding jobs to curbsides where goods constantly get loaded and unloaded, from shop clerks shouting in Russian to attract potential customers to weary-looking chelnokis overlooking the packaging of their goods, Laleli does offer a micro-cosm of all shades of poverty and uncertainty. It is the sporadic, almost arbitrary nature of this economic landscape that gives one the impression that all of this can disappear with a blink of an eye: the shop would not be there when you return, Ahmet's workshop having long gone bankrupt, the stalls would have all but gone, the shop clerk would have been deported for working without work permit, new migrants rounded up by the police for overstaying their visa. It is this level of uncertainty, or what one can call "the violence of uncertainty" that appears to temporarily replace poverty in the case of Laleli. As such, this district of informal transnational market place is a far cry from being an alternative to lasting, sustainable poverty alleviation programs and solid social policies.

Finally, it must be clear that the link between poverty and busi-ness strategy is a complicated one which requires closer scrutiny and reflection. It would be rather naive, in other words, if one hastily concludes that formation of new entrepreneurial ventures and networks will automatically help alleviate poverty. Besides, "although small entrepreneurs in the suitcase trade network can generate very high rates of turnover, they usually undertake high risks since none of them control the top level of the chain, namely the creation and propagation of fashion" (Yükseker 2007, 69). Indeed, rapidly changing demand, consumer tastes, fashion designs coupled with competitive pressures both at the lower and higher end of the market, underscore the difficulties of formulating sus-tainable business strategies. Transforming the poor into entrepre-neurs may also bring some unintended consequences as discussed in this chapter, which has revealed that actions of those who are forced to be entrepreneurs as a result of increased levels of poverty may not only produce "heart-warming" outcomes regarding the poor "who made it," as suggested by some in the emerging litera-ture focusing on this key issue (see Khawari 2004). It is equally possible that the very same set of forces and the very same environ-mental conditions may also entail some "heart-breaking" out-comes. We have also seen in this chapter that it is by no means guaranteed that even successful entrepreneurial ventures will carry satisfactory benefits for all parties involved. There are always those on the edges with little spill-over effect from the wealth created. Furthermore, integration of small entrepreneurs/employees into a well-functioning system (such as Laleli) does not mean that this position is sustainable. Just the reverse, the degree of vulnerability at the beginning and at the end of the chain in our case example is striking, and the difficulty of breaking this negative loop is rather obvious. That is exactly where the systemic nature of the problem and the necessity of government action in the form of a targeted social policy to correct the imbalances inherent in the prevailing system become most evident.

Acknowledgment

Özlem Öz would like to thank TUBA for their financial support.

References

Adaman F., A. Carkoglu, R. Erzan, A. Filiztekin, B. Ozkaynak, S. Sayan, and S. Ulgen. 2006. BALKANDIDE Study on Social Dimension in the Candidate Countries—Bulgaria, Romania, Croatia, and Turkey: Country Report: Turkey. http://ec.europa.eu/employment_social/social_situation/docs/balkandide_tr_country_report_en.pdf (accessed December 5, 2007).

Adaman F. and C. Keyder. 2006. Poverty and Social Exclusion in the Slum Areas of Large Cities in Turkey. A research report prepared for the European Commission, Employment, Social Affairs and Equal Opportunities.

Arthur, W.B. 1985. *Competing Technologies and Lock-in by Historical Events: The Dynamics of Choice under Increasing Returns.* CEPR Technical Paper No. 43. Stanford: Stanford University.

Blowfield, M. 2005. Corporate Social Responsibility: Reinventing the Meaning of Development. *International Affairs* 81(3): 515–524.

Bugra A. and C. Keyder. 2003. *New Poverty and Changing Welfare Regime in Turkey.* Ankara: UNDP.

———. 2006. The Turkish Welfare Regime in Transformation. *Journal of European Social Policy* 16(3): 211–228.

Carkoglu A. and M. Eder. 2006. Urban Informality and Economic Vulnerability in Turkey. Unpublished article being revised for *World Development.*

Darrell, H. 2005. The Fortune at the Bottom of the Pyramid. *Supply Management* 10(3): 35.

Eder M. 2003. Political Economy of Agricultural Liberalization in Turkey. In *La Turquie e le Developpement,* ed. A. Insel. Paris: L'Harmattan. pp. 211–245.

Eder M., A. Carkoglu, A. Yakovlev, and K. Chaudry. 2002. Redefining Contagion: Political Economy of Suitcase Trade between Turkey and Russia. Unpublished final IREX Research Project Report.

Goskomstat. 1999. *The Russian Statistical Yearbook*. Moscow.

———. 2000. *The Russian Statistical Yearbook*. Moscow.

Hoque, S. 2004. Micro-credit and Reduction of Poverty in Bangladesh. *Journal of Contemporary Asia* 34(1): 2–32.

Icduygu, A. 2006. *Labor Dimensions of Irregular Migration in Turkey.* Research Report, Florence: European University Institute RCAS.

Islam, T. 2007. *Microcredit and Poverty Alleviation*. Aldershot: Ashgate.

Karnani, A. 2006. Fortune at the Bottom of the Pyramid: A Mirage; How the Private Sector Can Help Alleviate Poverty? Working Paper no. 1035. University of Michigan Ross School of Business.

Keyder, C. 1999. The Setting. In *Istanbul between Global and the Local*, ed. C. Keyder, 3–28. Lanham, MD: Rowman and Littlefield.

———. Globalization and Social Exclusion in Istanbul. *International Journal of Urban and Regional Research* 29(1): 124–134.

Khawari, A. 2004. Microfinance: Does it Hold its Promises? A Survey of Recent Literature. Discussion Paper no. 276. Hamburg Institute of International Economics.

Kirisci, K. 2005. A Friendlier Schengen Visa System as a Tool of Soft Power: The Experience of Turkey. *European Journal of Migration and Law* 7: 343–367.

LASIAD Laleli Industrialists and Businessmen Association. 2000. Unpublished information leaflet, Istanbul.

Melnichenko T., A. Bolonini, and R. Zavatta. 1997. Russian Shuttle Trade: General Characteristics and Its Interconnection with the Italian Market. Unpublished research paper. Economisti Associati.

Morduch, J. 1998. Does Microfinance Really Help the Poor? New Evidence from Flagship Programs from Bangladesh. Harvard Institute of International Development and Hoover Institution, Stanford University. http://www.princeton.edu/~rpds/downloads/morduch_microfinance_poor.pdf (accessed December 5, 2007).

Öz, Ö. 2004. *Clusters and Competitive Advantage: The Turkish Experience.* London: Palgrave MacMillan.

Porter, M.E. 1985. *Competitive Advantage: Creating and Advancing Superior Performance*. New York: The Free Press.

Prahalad, C.K. 2005. *The Fortune at the Bottom of the Pyramid: Eradicating Poverty through Profits*. Upper Saddle River, NJ: Wharton School Publishing.

Rankin, K.N. 2001. Governing Development: Neoliberalism, Microcredit, and Rational Economic Women. *Economy and Society* 30(1): 18–37.

Sen, A. 1999. *Development as Freedom*, Oxford: Oxford University Press.

Senses, F. 2001. *Küresellesmenin Öteki Yüzü Yoksulluk*. Istanbul: Iletisim.

Singer, A. 2006. Business Strategy and Poverty Alleviation. *Journal of Business Ethics* 66: 225–231.

Walsh, J.P., J.C. Kress, and K.W. Beyerchen. 2005. Book Review Essay: Promises and Perils at the Bottom of the Pyramid. *Administrative Science Quarterly* 50(3): 473–482.

World Bank. 2003. *Turkey: Poverty and Coping after Crises.* Washington DC: World Bank. http://www-wds.worldbank.org/servlet/WDSContentServer/IW3P/IB/2003/08/20/000160016_20030820130639/Rendered/PDF/2418 50TR0SR.pdf (accessed December 5, 2007).

———. 2006. *World Development Indicators 06.* Washington DC: World Bank. http://devdata.worldbank.org/wdi2006/contents/cover.htm (accessed December 5, 2007).

Yükseker, D. 2003. *Laleli-Moskova Mekigi: Kayitdisi Ticaret ve Cinsiyet Iliskileri.* Istanbul: Iletisim.

———. 2007. Shuttling Goods, Weaving Consumer Tastes: Informal Trade between Turkey and Russia. *International Journal of Urban and Regional Research* 31(1): 60–72.

Chapter Eight

Alleviating Poverty Using Microfranchising Models: Case Studies and a Critique

Lisa Jones Christensen

Microcredit—Brief Overview

Over 30 years ago, Muhammad Yunus founded the Grameen Bank in Bangladesh with just $27 and the idea that desperately poor, working rural women were credit-worthy (Yunus 1997). Yunus found that women almost universally used the credit to expand their fledgling businesses, and they would pay back the loans with proceeds from these businesses. Yunus thus developed the idea that even with no collateral, these women should be granted small loans at competitive interest rates with frequent payback cycles. This concept, that small loans (usually less than $100) should be granted to the previously "unbankable," came to be called microcredit (Unitus 2007). Early on, practitioners such as Yunus realized that microcredit borrowers have payback rates as high as 95 percent (Felder-Kuzu 2005). These payback rates allow the lending institutions to survive, expand, and provide loans to additional borrowers. Concurrent to the work of Yunus in Bangladesh in the early 1970s, other social innovators developed similar practices in other countries (consider ACCION and its early work in Brazil or the subsequent work of John Hatch and the growth of village banking [ACCION 2007; FINCA International 2007]). Thus, the microcredit movement was born.

To fully understand microcredit in its current incarnation, it is important to clarify that these small (or micro) loans are guaranteed by social capital or social collateral—as groups of borrowers are collectively responsible for repayment and individual borrowers must vouch for (and occasionally "cover" for) each other. With this format, borrowers pay back their loans in weekly or biweekly meetings. Thus, by design, payments are small enough to not be overwhelming and the meetings are frequent enough that people maintain responsibility to each other. Women are the primary targets for these loans because they tend to pay back the loans faster and they typically spend a higher percentage of earnings on the family and on business-related investments than do men (Microcredit Summit 2007).

Another important aspect of microcredit is that the loans are subject to competitive interest rates. The average interest rates typically run close to 4–5 percent per month, but once annualized, the 48–60 percent rate may seem high to some (CGAP 2002). Determining "appropriate" interest rates is a controversial topic within the field, and a full discussion of interest rates is outside the scope of this chapter. What remains critical to clarify is that these rates are standard to the practice and they are highly competitive when compared to the alternative sources and costs of capital in these environments. Specifically, these interest rates are necessary to cover the costs of administering many small loans to many different borrowers. Also, the average rates for alternative credit (usually from moneylenders) can be as high as 180 percent per day, or 1800 percent per year (CGAP 2002).

Overall, these tiny loans are enough for hardworking microentrepreneurs to start or expand small businesses. They are typically used to finance endeavors as small and varied as: weaving baskets, raising chickens, or buying wholesale products to sell in a market. It is now understood that income from these businesses provide better food, housing, healthcare, and education for entire families, and most important, additional income provides hope for a better future.

Microfinance—Brief Overview

The interest in microcredit from commercial, educational, and nongovernment organizations (NGOs) has grown significantly since its inception in the 1970s; and the interest is now focused on more than just the microcredit loans. When people refer to a full range of financial services for those in poverty, they typically adopt the term "microfinance." The term refers more generally to the professionalized microcredit industry (there are now over 3,000 organizations delivering loans to an estimated 113 million clients [Microcredit Summit 2006]), as well as to the extension of services beyond the granting of loans. More specifically, microfinance refers to the services that are or can be bundled with microcredit, such as microinsurance, microhousing loans, savings products, deposit services, transfer services, and others (Asian Development Bank 2007).

Issues about terminology aside, it is critical to clarify that the concept and practice of microcredit has expanded since it was first introduced. Since inception, microcredit has grown into an industry (microfinance) with additional products and with increasing commercial interest (there are now U.S. and international microcredit and microfinance investment funds as well as U.S. and international investment-grade microfinance-related bonds). It has also grown into an industry with significant reach and effect.

In terms of the success rate of microcredit and/or microfinance products in alleviating poverty, results of the work over time indicate that microcredit and the related microfinance movement are proven effective in poverty alleviation. Some statistics show that recipients of microloans lift themselves and their families above the poverty line within 12–14 loan cycles (Bulletin on the Eradication of Poverty 2004), and certainly within one generation (Khandker 1998).

Overall, the growth of the microcredit and the microfinance movement has been marked by several milestones, and some of the most recent include: 1997 marked the first Microcredit Summit in Washington DC; 2005 was declared the International Year of Microfinance by the United Nations; 2005 also marked the period where over 113 million clients were reached (Microcredit Summit 2006); and 2006 heralded the year where Muhammad Yunus was granted the Nobel Peace Prize for his "efforts in promoting economic and social development from below."

Microfranchise—Brief Overview

Personal experience and research on methodology reveals that the practice of giving microloans and other microfinance products is most often based on assumptions that 1) recipients are microentreprenuers who already operate (or who know how to operate) viable businesses, 2) that they know *how* to expand these businesses to enable themselves to manage larger loans, and/or 3) that they have the interest and the ability to do so. However, many borrowers (or thwarted borrowers) do not fit this description. Instead, there are people on both sides of two extremes—on one side, there are those who want to scale faster than currently allowed by the loan size and meeting frequency constraints of current microcredit models. On another side are some loan recipients who simply want to stabilize themselves and their businesses (meaning they do not want to grow their businesses); some do not have the skills or temperament to invent and develop a business (they are not typical entrepreneurs—instead they are enterprising people who simply want loans); or still others are interested in work, but they are not aspiring owners or investors (Gibson 2007).

Thus, even with the presence of microcredit/microfinance as a tool to enable microbusinesses, there still exists a need for different business-related interventions that can 1) more quickly lead to scale for those who have more aggressive interests in such expansion, 2) that can provide multiple jobs rapidly—in order to create infrastructure and opportunity for those who may want stable and rewarding work as employees, but who cannot or do not want to be owners, and/or 3) that can prescreen opportunities for people so that they can overcome the "creative barrier" of finding and vetting an appropriate local business (Gibson 2007).

Microfranchising is a phenomenon that begins to address this need for small and medium enterprises that provide an outlet for the truly entrepreneurial, while still providing jobs and a potential livelihood for those who desperately want to work but who are not interested in creating their own ventures. Specifically, microfranchising refers to "a small business that can easily be replicated by following proven mentoring, marketing, and operational concepts found in formal franchises, where the overall objective is to promote economic development by creating sound replicable business models that can be managed easily by entrepreneurs at the base of the pyramid" (Small Fortunes 2007). To simplify, microfranchising refers to the development and promotion (by sale) of smaller businesses that are affordable to enter and affordable to replicate for poor people in the developing world.

Relationships among and between Microcredit, Microfinance, and Microfranchising

Before moving on to illustrate different microfranchising models, it is important to clarify interrelationships (or lack thereof) between and among the practice of offering microcredit, offering microfinance options, and/or promoting microfranchising. Essentially, microcredit was an initial social innovation designed to use business techniques (loans with interest) to help microentrepreneurs build better and more profitable businesses. As borrowers' needs expanded and as organizational competition increased, microcredit-related organizations responded by offering additional services and products—which are referred to in aggregate as microfinance. Thus, the relationship between microcredit and microfinance is primarily one of scale. However, the relationship between these two and microfranchising is not as clear. At a minimum, microfranchising and the other terms simply share the use of the word "micro" and a similarity of focus on people in the developing world. At a maximum, microfranchising *relies* on microcredit and microfinance for growth and expansion. Both extremes of thought about the relationships are found in the microfranchising field, and the cases outlined below were chosen in part to highlight the different views on this subject. These issues are more fully explored within the case studies that follow a discussion of the varieties of microfranchising models.

Varieties of Microfranchising Models

Typically, people tend to reference a Western-style restaurant-related model when they consider the concept of a franchise—yet this analogy only partially applies to the concept of a microfranchise. With the standard Western franchise model, an interested party (the new franchisee) applies for ownership, learns stipulations, pays a purchasing cost as well as licensing fees, and then runs the newly acquired business according to the rules and stipulations (and usually with the marketing support) of the parent company (the franchisor) (Justis and Judd 2003).

With this model, there is a clear franchisor and franchisee; the boundaries between the two are delineated and somewhat fixed; the relationship between the two is relatively permanent; and there are few variations on the model. The analog in a microfranchise *can* be similar, but is not always so.

For example, with microfranchising, an NGO (rather than a commercial company) could decide to suggest and provide a microfranchise opportunity to its clients, and the NGO would thus cultivate and replicate a franchise business—ultimately offering the opportunity for its clients to purchase the franchise and receive training and ongoing support. In this format, the relationship between the NGO and the client is most similar to the relationship between the traditional commercial franchisor and franchisee. However, as stated above, with microfranchising, there are more options than this first example implies.

Specifically, there are situations where an NGO may want to develop and provide successful business models to its clients but the

NGO has no interest in providing *continuing* support or ongoing training (Gibson 2007). This more simplified "provide-suggestions-only" approach is viable in a microfranchising model but not found in the more traditional franchising model.

Other microfranchising alternatives to the traditional model include (but are not limited to): cases where independent microfranchise owners sell to others to thus become informal microfranchisors; cases where NGOs create a business from scratch and then replicate and sell it; situations where NGOs invest in a struggling business and help the business grow to a microfranchise level managed by others; or situations where NGOs utilize a sliding scale of ownership (the microequity method—this occurs when the NGO very intentionally and very slowly transfers a viable business into the hands of a microfranchisor). Also, it is possible (but less likely) that a multinational company (MNC), rather than an NGO, could do the sponsoring, mentoring, or promotion.

Clearly, one way to characterize a microfranchise is by what type of agency sponsors it (MNC or NGO), and another way (not yet covered above) is to determine whether the origin of the business idea being promoted is indigenous/local or is imported from abroad. Such distinctions could help researchers trace the provenance of successful and unsuccessful ventures, and may help explain such issues as growth rates, turnover rates, and other important concerns. Table 8.1 incorporates these two dimensions into a 2×2 structure, and then lists different microfranchise operations (described later in this chapter) that illustrate each categorical type.

Given the many variations in microfranchise types described above, it remains critical to distill what all of the variations may have in common. The feature that characterizes all of them (and differentiates

Table 8.1 Organizing framework for analysis of microfranchise opportunities

Origin of Business Idea (Local or Imported)	*Microfranchise Sponsor (MNC or NGO)*	
	MNC	*NGO*
Imported	Type: MNC-sponsored: Imported (E.g., Scojo, Bata)	Type: NGO-sponsored: Imported (E.g., Grameen Village Phone Direct)
Local	Type: MNC-sponsored: Local (E.g., PuR (in some countries))	Type: NGO-sponsored: Local (E.g., Cellular City)

them from the traditional franchise approach) is that the objective is to use *any one* of the many options to provide appropriately scaled turnkey operations to small-scale entrepreneurs in developing countries. The traditional approach is usually larger and focused on a higher income entrepreneur in a more developed situation.

One way to illustrate the variety of approaches to microfranchises is through specific case-based explorations of different types of microfranchises. The similarities and the differences illuminate the scale and scope (as well as the limits) of the microfranchise model.

Microfranchise Case Studies

The following case examples feature key aspects of the microfranchise phenomenon, and highlight both MNC-sponsored organizations as well as NGO-sponsored organizations. Where possible, the cases attempt to provide information on the role of microcredit or microfinance, the cost of entry, the potential for profit, and the current "reach" of each organization.

Case #1 Scojo Foundation

Type: MNC-Sponsored (Large-Sized with Original Microfinance Involvement)

One of the foremost examples of a microfranchising model is the work being done in several developing countries by the Scojo Foundation. The Scojo Foundation, founded in 2001, is focused on broadening access to affordable reading glasses in the developing world—and the foundation intends to achieve this goal by enabling related microfranchises. Almost 1.6 billion people in the developing world need reading glasses, and at least 700 million of the world's poorest suffer from blurry "up close" vision (presbyopia) (Scojo Foundation 2007). This condition hinders the ability to work and/or severely limits productivity—yet only 5 percent of people in need have access to the solution, which can come in the form of nonprescription, low-cost reading glasses. The Scojo Foundation uses microfranchising to address this development problem. Specifically, the foundation identifies, equips, and trains motivated men or women as "vision entrepreneurs" who can conduct vision screenings, sell affordable reading glasses, and then refer more advanced cases to reputable clinics. Vision entrepreneurs receive training, support, and inventory in the form of their own "business in a bag"—a sales kit that contains everything required for sales, marketing, vision screening, and data collection. Scojo first began offering these kits in Guatemala, El Salvador, and India, and plans for expansion into Bangladesh, Mexico, South Asia, and parts of Africa are either underway or are soon to be announced ("Pyramid Power" 2007).

The economics behind the success of these microfranchises is found in the fact that each pair of glasses that Scojo provides costs about $1 to make and deliver, and the franchisee pays $2–$3 per pair and sells them for 3$–5$ (or more) per pair. The specifics behind the model include: a typical inventory consisting of a display case, eye charts, a uniform shirt, repair kits, a badge, signage for a home or business, and about 20 pairs of reading glasses (Gibson and Fairbourne 2004).

Initially, Scojo provided microcredit loans for the purchase of equipment (typical start-up costs are approximately $120), but Scojo representatives soon learned that they were becoming a loan administration agency instead of microfranchisors at scale (Gibson and Fairbourne 2004). Now, Scojo typically operates by either providing the initial setup for free (this is rare) or they offer the setup on a consignment basis (postsale). This means that the women can pay for the products with profits from their first sales of the products for which they must pay. This arrangement also means that there is no up-front cost to the women. Scojo management has found that the consignment model is more effective than the loan model because if a microfranchisee ever elects to stop working, she can simply turn in her inventory and then owe nothing to Scojo (Notes from Microfinance Learning Lab 2005).

Some basic facts about the Scojo microfranchise model include: the typical inventory of one entrepreneur is 20–30 pairs of glasses; one star performer in El Salvador earned $1,500 in one week; one microfranchise can have from 50–1,000 people in the market area; and district sales promoters can manage up to 15 microfranchises (Notes from Microfinance Learning Lab 2005). To ensure commitment from the vision entrepreneurs, Scojo requires that they sell a minimum of 10 pairs per week. It is important to mention that women do not always stay with these businesses for the long-term—as management shares that they have up to a 50 percent annual turnover in the microfranchise ranks (Notes from Microfinance Learning Lab 2005).

One way that the Scojo Foundation has stayed successful and grown significantly despite this potential for high turnover is that management is constantly focused on continuous improvement, and eagerly seeks innovative ideas directly from the microfranchisees. One example of the constant improvement is evidenced in the fact that the foundation is exploring adding a very low-cost ($0.10) lens (this lens is the size of a credit card) to the women's inventory. This addition could optically magnify objects to help a person with presbyopia see with clarity, and could add a very low-cost option to the vision kits. (Notes from Microfinance Learning Lab 2005).

Scojo has sold at least 50,000 pairs as of early 2007, and they plan to sell one million pairs by 2010 ("Pyramid Power" 2007). There are now more than 600 vision entrepreneurs trained and operating businesses in the developing world. The foundation is supported by Scojo Vision LLC, which helps with purchasing power for the glasses and which also donates 5 percent of its profits to the Scojo Foundation, thus ensuring its steady growth. This link to a supportive corporation is what prompted the designation as "MNC sponsored".

Clearly, Scojo represents one way that microfranchising can be used to reach many people quickly and this scale can be achieved in part because very poor people can enter into business without paying a hefty entry fee. This very strength hints at a potential related weakness, in that, it does not tend to support multiple jobs for multiple employees (the model has "scale" but perhaps less "scope").

Another example of an MNC-backed microfranchise (Vodacom, outlined below) illustrates a slightly different approach to the microfranchise model, and one that has a more immediate potential to create jobs for multiple participants.

Case #2 Vodafone and Vodacom Phone Services for South Africa

Type: MNC-Sponsored (Medium-Sized without Microfinance Involvement)

The Vodacom "phone shops" in rural South Africa provide another example of a microfranchise opportunity sponsored by a large multinational company (Vodafone). Originally started in 1994, the Community Services program was designed to enable local entrepreneurs from disadvantaged communities to own and operate phone shop franchises (Christensen, Reck, and Wood 2007). At a cost of about $3,500 a local entrepreneur can purchase a refurbished shipping container fully converted into a turnkey branded business. The business comes complete with five phone lines and the support materials required to open a phone shop where locals enter and pay for communication services on a per-minute basis (Christensen, Reck, and wood 2007).

New owners are responsible for the initial financial investment, for selecting and defending the location of the phone shop, for obtaining all electrical and land ownership permissions, as well as for the cost of transporting the container. Profit margins are relatively fixed, with owners earning roughly 33 percent of the per-minute fees charged for phone use (Christensen, Reck, and Wood 2007). Despite the low margins and the low incomes of most prospective customers, results indicate that phone shop owners can generate average revenues (in early 2003 dollars) of at least $1,200 per month (Christensen, Reck, and Wood 2007). Most shops create some additional jobs in the community, and a shop with 10 phone lines typically requires the hiring of at least two on-site employees per shift. Currently, there are over 1,800 owners and over 5,000 phone shops, and they deliver an estimated 85 million minutes of outgoing call time per month.

In terms of impact, since its inception, the microfranchise project has created more than 20,000 jobs and the phone shops have also grown local communities; a side benefit of the project is that related businesses tend to move nearby the phone shop containers (Vodafone 2007). The microfranchise system is also helping empower black entrepreneurs and women, as nearly 40 percent of franchises are owned by women (Vodafone 2007).

Given this information, this case example adds value to the discussion of microfranchising because its results suggest some second-order effects that can stem from the building of microfranchises. Namely, related businesses may emerge and may attempt to colocate, new jobs can be created, and/or seeds of social change can emerge when microfranchises are built and running. In particular, the latter can occur when members of a previously marginalized social sector advance for themselves while simultaneously serving as role models for others. These benefits of microfranchising are not often discussed, but perhaps deserve to enter the literature more fully.

Unlike the Scojo microfranchise or the Vodacom Phone Shop microfranchise, the Cellular City microfranchise is newer and currently operates on a smaller scale. Thus, it has concomitantly received less press. However, Cellular City is an important example of how non-U.S. entrepreneurs can be the *original* source of replicable ideas for use in microfranchising. In contrast to the Scojo and Vodafone examples, where an international foundation saw and met a development need by using the microfranchise model, Cellular City provides an example of how a Filipino entrepreneur (ultimately working with and through a Philippine-based NGO) was able to incubate a viable business model for others to replicate in a microfranchise capacity.

Case #3 Cellular City

Type: NGO-Sponsored (Small-Sized without Microfinance Involvement)

The Cellular City microfranchise was launched with the help of the Academy for Creating Enterprise (ACE or "the Academy"). The Academy is a nonprofit educational training center and NGO located in Cebu, Philippines. The strategy of the Academy is to provide intense business training with an emphasis on entrepreneurship (they offer both eight-week courses and one-week short courses). Their stated goal in relation to microfranchising is to identify high-performance microenterprises started by graduates, distill the best performers, and then develop approximately five main business opportunities to offer for sale and replication to other Academy graduates (Notes from Microfinance Learning Lab 2005). The Cellular City stores are one tangible result of this strategic focus.

Cellular City (started in 2002), is an example of an exemplary franchise with 34 stores in operation as of April, 2007—25 of the stores are owned by 12 Academy graduates (Personal communication with Stephen Gibson, founder of ACE, April 23, 2007). Cellular City is a retail franchise where the products include multiple brands of new and reconditioned mobile phones, prepaid phone cards, and accessories (and services including repairs) (Gibson and Fairbourne 2004). Start-up costs for a Cellular City franchise are higher than those discussed in previous case descriptions. Specifically, the cost is close to $8,000–$10,000 with a $2,000 franchise fee included in this figure. Representatives from the Academy report that owners of these microfranchises earn between $50 to $100 per day (net income), which is about 10 to 20 times greater than the Filipino average wage (Notes from Microfinance Learning Lab 2005). Another aspect of their success (which also differentiates their impact from that of Scojo or Vodacom) is the fact that each microfranchise location tends to employ from three to seven (or more) additional employees who earn better than the local minimum wage (Gibson, personal communication, April 23, 2007).

Cellular City microfranchisees typically fund their purchase with money from family and friends (often other graduates of the Academy), or with funds from remittances (Email correspondence with Ronald Alban, graduate of ACE and owner of 25 percent of Cellular City, April 24, 2007). The Academy does not confound its mission by providing funds; instead, it operates on the belief that when it offers knowledge, superior graduates can use this to secure funding. The Academy has also found that in their situation "lenders can't be mentors" (Alban, email communication, April 24, 2007). Thus, its management intentionally does not offer microcredit loans or other financial services in relation to the microfranchise opportunities they endorse.

Two of the most recent developments with the Cellular City franchise are 1) recent success and high levels of interest have led to a new "spin off" repair business that is being launched as a stand alone microfranchise operation and 2) there has been an *intentional* slowing of the growth rate because the main microfranchisors want to ensure that they are fully responsive to the needs and innovative requests of current and future microfranchisees. Both developments seem to indicate that Cellular City and the work of the Academy are moving forward in a positive direction, where growth is both intentional and managed.

The latest information on microfranchising from Academy representatives indicates that they are working on offering/replicating bake shop businesses with entrance costs closer to $2,000. They are also working with graduates to promote other opportunities that may have entrance costs closer to $200 (Gibson, phone correspondence, April 23, 2007).

The example of Cellular City indicates that powerful business models and microfranchise examples can originate in and from non-Western individuals and NGOs. These models can have a significant effect on local and regional economies (recall that each franchise creates up to 10 jobs for others and also has the potential for second-order role-model example effects). Thus, this case suggests that similar examples need to be discovered, investigated, publicized, and perhaps replicated.

Thus far, the cases discussed illustrate how non-locally-based foundations and NGOs (Scojo or Vodafone) or an indigenous NGO (ACE) have catalyzed large- and small-scale microfranchises, respectively. All examples focused on developing-country entrepreneurs who either paid for the microfranchise post hoc (from sales receipts) or who obtained original funding from sources *not* related to microcredit. In fact, in the case of the Scojo Foundation and the Academy, the organizations explicitly *abandoned* or avoid the practice of bundling microcredit with the expansion of their franchises. The Academy also explicitly chose to separate themselves from the granting of credit for business projects.

In contrast to these examples, the case of Bata Shoes and the Rural Sales Program in Bangladesh (and the Grameen Village Phone Direct program—further below) illustrate how microcredit groups can be fundamentally tied to the identification, training, and even funding of microfranchisors.

Case #4 Bata Shoes and CARE Canada

Type: NGO-Sponsored (Small-to-Medium-Sized with Microfinance Involvement)

In the case of Bata/CARE, in early 2004, over 70 women participating in women's self-help groups in Bangladesh were sponsored, trained, and supported in their personal and business growth by microcredit programs from CARE Bangladesh and CARE Canada (Personal correspondence with Jesse Moore, formerly of CARE Enterprise Partners, March 1, 2007). At this time, these women were typically loan recipients participating in basic microcredit training. Importantly, they were not guided toward any particular business model. Over time, when approached by representatives of the Bata Shoe Company (an international shoe manufacturer with operations from 4,600 retail stores scattered across 5 continents and 50 countries [Bata 2007a]), CARE agreed to partner with Bata to promote sales of low-cost sandals in Bangladesh. The terms of the early partnership hinted at the birth of a new microfranchising opportunity.

Specifically, the arrangement was for certain self-help groups to form a cooperative business unit (CBU), and the CBU would select a leader. This CBU leader would interact with Bata and would interface between the women (the future sales force and potential franchisee) and Bata (the product source and potential franchisor). Bata was to provide trade credit, training support, point of purchase materials, and timely delivery of a limited set of retail offerings (usually versions

of popular and low-cost sandals for men, women, and children).
CARE was to provide a credit guarantee and training and support
services to the self-help groups (Bata 2007b). Essentially, while Bata
was interested in working with these very poor women in their capacity as a sales force, they needed CARE to initially "vet" the women
and the partnership idea.

The first pilot program (which could be considered as beta testing of
these shoe-selling microfranchises) was run in 2005 with 50 women
(Bata 2007b). The average cost for a woman to buy into the business was
relatively low, and interest in participating in the microfranchise was
quite high—ultimately, women were chosen based on how they had performed in earlier projects (as the women were selected from among those
who had been with CARE for four years as part of a Rural Maintenance
Program that included several days per month of microenterprise
training (Moore, personal correspondence, March 1, 2007).

The average sale price of a shoe in the business portfolio was $1 (there
was also some demand for higher-priced shoes due to the perceived
quality), and women typically earned upward of $0.20 per sale (Moore,
personal correspondence, March 1, 2007). Over time, the partnerships
(and the women) were deemed successful, and the program was officially
expanded in May 2006 to include several hundred more women, with
plans to launch with 1,000 women forthcoming (Bata 2007b).

The Bata/CARE case describes one fledgling way that microcredit
organizations can and do play a role in the growth, funding, and
expansion of some types of microfranchises. However, while the story
may be inspiring for groups considering expansion into microfranchising through similar routes, it nonetheless remains the story of a
project that is relatively small in scale and scope—and which may stay
that way in the near future.

In contrast, the case of the Village Phone Direct microfranchise
opportunity illustrates the role that microcredit institutions can play in
the growth of microfranchises, while also illustrating that such
involvement can be designed to rapidly reach scale.

Case # 5 Village Phone Direct

Type: NGO-Sponsored (Large-Sized with Microfinance Involvement)

The Village Phone Direct program is sponsored by the Technology
Center at the Grameen Foundation USA, and it is entirely different

from (although inspired by) the Grameen Village Phone model that
has received considerable press to date. For those not familiar with
Grameen Village Phone, it refers to a country-wide joint venture
program of the Grameen Bank and Telenor where "village phone
ladies" in Bangladesh buy cell phones and air time from the venture
and then sell air time (usage) to others on a per-minute basis at a profit
(Grameenphone 2007). Grameen Phone has more than 10 million sub-
scribers in a country with about 15 million telephone users—and in
2001, the phones were allowing women to make a profit of close to
$100 per month (Cohen 2001). Grameen Foundation USA, a related
U.S.-based NGO, intentionally planned to build on the success of the
highly regional Grameen Phone program by instituting a Village
Phone Replication program in many countries. This program has been
successful in Uganda, Cameroon, and Rwanda (Grameen Foundation
2007). However, the successes of the replication model also caused
representatives of the NGO to realize that the model, in that form, was
not able to scale quickly enough to meet the very high demand.

Thus, Grameen Foundation USA developed a new way to spread
communication technology by using microfranchising—and this new
program was announced in December of 2006. The full launch is still
underway, and its aims and structure are fully outlined below. This
new microfranchising program is called Village Phone Direct (VPD)
and it was designed from the outset to 1) embrace the phrase
microfranchise and 2) to work in tandem with microfinance institutions (MFIs) all over the world.

Specifically, VPD allows any microfinance institution to directly
and independently develop a Village Phone product for their clients.
Unlike the Phone Replication model, the VPD program does not
require a national or institutional infrastructure. Thus, it can scale
more quickly than a Village Phone program and it is particularly
suited to launch in rural areas. It uses existing mobile communications
products and does not require the full engagement of a telecommunications company. Thus the microfinance institutions can directly
implement the program, define the marketing strategy, and control all
aspects of implementation (Grameen Foundation 2007).

The Technology Center at Grameen Foundation USA has worked
with Nokia and Skymast to make a Village Phone Equipment Kit
available. Microfinance clients can purchase their kit through their
microfinance institution, and the kit includes a Nokia mobile phone
(new and not refurbished), a Skymast booster antennae, a recharging
solution, and custom cables to connect all components. Local customization allows for MFIs to select the telecommunications provider

and local marketing strategy (including signage) that suits regional needs (Grameen Foundation 2007).

Both the price and the contents of the kit can vary significantly depending upon the country, the level of supporting infrastructure (which affects whether booster antennas and/or battery chargers are needed or not), the support from the partner telecommunications company, and the level of marketing support that is included. Thus, the kits can be as inexpensive as $50 and range up to $300 (Emma Le Dû, Grameen Technology Center, personal communication, April 23, 2007). Also, with the Village Phone Direct business model, it is important to clarify that no MFI (and by extension, no microfranchisee) is required to use the Nokia phone or the Skymast antenna (or any other inventory or products). Instead, MFIs and others are free to identify and source all phone kit contents. They are also free to create any partnerships that are best suited to their technology needs and regional specifications.

The targets for returns for the microfranchisee are that he or she be able to run the business without ever losing money or experiencing penalties related to their microloans. Thus, payback times are unique and are closely tied to the loan type. The plan is that most people will be able to repay the loan for the kit within four to twelve months. After that, the profits become entirely unrelated to any loans and the venture can become purely a profit center (Emma Le Dû, personal communication, April 23, 2007). As the program is currently launching, there is a suggested emphasis on the idea that this model may be best suited for microentrepreneurs who already run a business. The assumption is that people who are in a position to attract clients can make money faster by supplying these "captive" potential customers with additional services, rather than having to attract new ones.

The program is intentionally marketed to MFIs, but representatives recognize that microfinance institutions have an inherent competitive advantage in rural markets given their networks, their community relationships, and the ability to provide financing to the interested microfranchisees. However, representatives also realize that the spread of the program is a pull rather than a push model, and it is highly likely that telecommunication firms and other types of NGOs may also become interested in advancing the Village Phone Direct model in some way. All potential enablers of the microfranchise are welcome to participate, and participation is intended to be primarily through the use of a customizable instruction/operation manual as well as through an informative and highly interactive Web site (Emma Le Dû, personal communication, April 23, 2007).

While it is still too early to evaluate the success of this project, it is not too early to clarify the Grameen Technology Center plans for the project: pilots are currently running in the Philippines, and other countries are planned for rollout in 2007 (Emma Le Dû, personal communication, April 23, 2007). There is also a goal to have a presence on each continent by 2008.

Up to this point, all the cases have involved either sponsorship/support from a multinational or sponsorship by an NGO, and each had varying degrees of involvement (or noninvolvement) with microcredit. I close the case studies with a final look at a hybrid sponsorship model—one where both an MNC and an NGO work together to promote the microfranchise. Just as with the first case, the following example of the Procter and Gamble and Population Services International partnership is also focused on a business that is relatively low cost and easy to enter, particularly for people who are extremely poor.

Case #6 Procter and Gamble (P&G) PuR Water Purification Sachets

Type: MNC- and NGO-Sponsored (Medium-Sized with or without Microfinance Involvement)

This case description represents a microfranchising opportunity that is jointly promoted by a multinational corporation and an international nongovernment social marketing organization. Specifically, Procter and Gamble and Population Services International (PSI) (or other NGO partners depending on the country) jointly work to promote the PuR water purification sachets for sale for individual household use in developing countries (Hanson and Powell 2007).

The PuR sachets are small packets that contain a compound that performs the same functions as are performed at scale in a regional water treatment plant in the United States. The compound is premeasured to be mixed with 10 liters of water (the water can be in any state—from fully black and turbid to apparently clear but still contaminated), the mixture must be stirred for 5 minutes, allowed to flocculate (the pollutants bind to iron and other ingredients included in the sachet), and then the mixture must be filtered into a new container through a T-shirt or any other piece of material to ensure that all particulates are removed. The remains left at the bottom of the original container must be disposed of in such a way as to avoid their consumption. The treated water can sit in a household for several days and retain its purity and freshness for that entire period. During product demonstrations and in daily use, the PuR product appears miraculous when it visibly alters the appearance (and taste and quality) of brackish, turbid, black water to clear, clean, beautiful, and good-tasting water. PuR is able to remove arsenic, DDT, and other bacteria that cause diarrhea and other problems in children and in adults with compromised immune systems (P&G Health Sciences Institute 2007).

Procter and Gamble is interested in spreading the availability and usage of the PuR sachets, and PSI is interested in the same goal—with an extra emphasis on their part in securing behavioral change in individuals and families related to time taken to treat and safeguard their water supply. Thus, the two organizations have formed a partnership that uses a cost recovery model to enable both the spread of the product in developing countries *and* the continuation of their respective organizations.

The cost recovery model is directly related to a microfranchise opportunity. Specifically, Procter and Gamble manufactures the product and, thanks to strong support from the Retired Officers Program (and other parts of the organization, including the PuR U.S. brand and the Children's Safe Drinking Water program), P&G can offer the product to PSI at cost (approximately $0.035) (Personal correspondence with Dr. Greg Allgood, Director of the Children's Safe Drinking Water Program at Proctor and Gamble, April 2, 2007). PSI can provide the cost to in-country employees and affiliates while incurring approximately an additional $0.03–$0.05 of cost (from taxes, shipping, custom fees, handling, etc.) (Dr. Greg Allgood, personal correspondence, April 2, 2007). PSI can then supply a local microfranchisee with varying quantities of the PuR sachets at this final cost of close to $0.06. The microfranchisee can add about another $0.03 per sachet and ultimately he or she sells the product for approximately $0.10 Representatives from Procter and Gamble suggest that the final price should be comparable to the price of an egg in that country.

Most families spend money weekly on this product, and the microfranchisee can make an income from the product if he or she promotes it regularly to a steady stream of repeat customers. As with the Village Phone Direct model, this PuR sachet microfranchise opportunity works best when the microfranchisee already operates an existing business with an extant pull for foot traffic. Typically, small shop owners and corner vendors sell this product with the most success. It can also be bundled with emergency supplies (such as batteries) to reach additional customers concerned about preparing for frequent weather-related disasters, and this joint packaging promotion has launched in the Dominican Republic with some success for the microfranchisees (Dr. Greg Allgood, personal correspondence, April 2, 2007).

While there is no formal program in place to bundle this opportunity with microfinancing, there is also no explicit desire or plan to *avoid* the introduction or involvement of microfinance. In fact, Procter and Gamble representatives remain open to discussions about all types of creative ways to enable more reach for the product and more habit change for families in developing countries who are plagued with unsafe and unsanitary water. Thus, unlike some of the other products described in previous case examples, this business model can be characterized as either microfinance positive or microfinance neutral.

While the PuR water purification sachet offers significant public health benefits as well as the potential for significant commercial benefits for microfranchisees, it also differs from previous case examples in that it is a product/franchise opportunity that cannot support a microfranchisee on its own (e.g., without the presence of complementary products to augment income). Given this fact, the true value in the case lies in the fact that the PuR product/sales opportunity uniquely exemplifies a joint effort by a multinational and an NGO to promote a product via the microfranchise (and unique cost recovery) model.

The PuR sachet sales opportunity has launched in several countries, and its success is still being monitored and measured. Thus far, it has augmented the incomes of many hundreds of microenterprises, and it represents yet another example of how the microfranchise model for developing countries embraces much more creative and unique aspects than the current franchise model in the developed world does.

Comments: Microfranchising and the Role of Microfinance

Clearly, the diversity of microfranchise business model options described above indicates that there is no overarching trend regarding the ideal role for microcredit or microfinance in the development of the microfranchise model. Some microfranchise models depend on microfinance for success and others have incorporated microfinance and then subsequently abandoned the tie. Still other organizations remain neutral on the subject. It is not the intent of this chapter to endorse any particular approach, but rather to share the options and to suggest that any organization considering microfranchising should explore the option of including microcredit; should carefully consider their organizational stance; and should be very explicit about the final organizational decision—because the inclusion (or exclusion) of microcredit can be a key element in a microfranchise organization's growth and replication strategy (for more information on the role of microcredit with microfranchising, see [Hatch 2007]).

Microfranchising: Critique and Research Questions

Clearly, microfranchising as a field is still in its infancy. Further, researchers and practitioners agree (and even insist) that the term encompasses a wide range of business opportunities (e.g., NGO-sponsored, NGO-suggested, NGO-nutured; or MNC-endorsed, MNC-sponsored, MNC-nutured, among others)—a state that can only slow the creation of a clear identity and agenda for this new field. However, after describing and analyzing myriad examples, including those addressed in cases above, it appears that the most critical questions for the field are not yet being addressed in the literature. Thus, this point of "critique" also becomes a departure point for an exploration into the questions that face practitioners and researchers interested in this topic.

Some critical questions include: what are the individual characteristics of successful microfranchisors and microfranchisees? Further, (and related to this chapter) which characteristics are related to success or failure with different microfranchise models? Does microfranchising (or do microfranchisors) differentiate between managers and entrepreneurs? Do they need to do so in order for the microfranchises to succeed? How much do we know about how business replication works in developing economies with weaker rules of law and where literacy and education are not "givens"? Has the field gathered the generalizable learnings? If so, where? Is the need for innovation in the field a need for more business models or for more innovative ways of teaching and training new recruits (or something else entirely)?

While there remain many more questions, I ask a closing question focused on the enterprises rather than on the individuals running them: how are we to evaluate the success or failure of a microfranchise? Is the answer related to number of employees? To rapidity of replication? To longevity of existence? To access to funding? To something else entirely?

I suggest that as this new field emerges to define itself, researchers and practitioners need to address these questions quickly and well in order to sustain the long-term interest and the valuable attention this potentially far-reaching social innovation deserves.

The cases illustrate that microfranchising offers several different—but fully efficacious—ways to alleviate poverty at many levels of society. What remains, then, is to work to alleviate confusion in the field itself. Working together, researchers and practitioners can accomplish this task. The results will have worldwide benefits for those who want to lift themselves and their families from poverty.

References

ACCION International. 2007. Our History. http://www.accion.org/about_our_history.asp (accessed December 5, 2007).

Asian Development Bank. 2007. Microfinance Development Strategy. http://www.adb.org/Documents/Policies/Microfinance/microfinance0100.asp?p=policies (accessed December 5, 2007).

Bata. 2007a. About Us. http://www.bata.com/about_us/bata_today.php (accessed December 5, 2007).

———. 2007b. CARE in Bangladesh. www.bata.ca/about_us/care_in_bangladesh.php (accessed December 5, 2007).

Bulletin on the Eradication of Poverty. 2004. http://www.un.org/esa/socdev/poverty/documents/boep_11_2004_EN.pdf (accessed December 5, 2007).

CGAP. 2002. Occasional Paper No. 1: Microcredit Interest Rates. pp. 1–12.

Cohen, N. 2001. *What Works: Grameen Telecom*. World Resources Institute Digital Dividends Case Study. World Resources Institute.

Felder-Kuzu, Naoko. 2005. *Making sense: Microfinance and Microfinance Investments*. Hamburg, Germany: Mermann Verlag GmbH., p. 29.

FINCA International. 2007. Finca's History. http://www.villagebanking.org/site/c.erKPI2PCIoE/b.2604291/k.99B5/FINCAs_History.htm (accessed December 5, 2007).

Gibson, S. 2007. Microfranchising: The Next Step on the Development Ladder. In *Microfranchising: Creating Wealth at the Bottom of the Pyramid*, ed. J. Fairbourne, S. Gibson, and G. Dyer. 235–239. Northampton, Massachusettes: Edward Elgar Publishing.

Gibson, S. and J. Fairbourne. 2004. *Where There Are No Jobs* vol. 4: *The MicroFranchise Handbook*. Academy for Creating Enterprise, Provo, UT.

Grameenphone. 2007. About Us. http://www.grameenphone.com/index.php?id=64 (accessed December 5, 2007).

Grameen Foundation. 2007. Frequently Asked Questions about Village Phone Direct. http://www.grameenfoundation.org/what_we_do/technology_programs/village_phone_direct/faq_village_phone_direct/ #howisvpddifferent (accessed December 5, 2007).

Hanson, M. and K. Powell. 2006a. Procter and Gamble and Population Services International (PSI): Social Marketing for Safe Water INSEAD case study. Fontainebleau, France: INSEAD.

———. 2006b. Procter and Gamble PuR Purifier of Water (A&B): Developing the Product and Taking It to Market INSEAD case study. Fontainbleau, France: INSEAD.

Hatch, J. 2007. Opportunities for Partnership: How Microfinance and Microfranchising Complement Each Other. In *Microfranchising*, ed. Fairbourne, Gibson and Dyer. Northampton, Massachusettes: Edward Elgar Publishing.

Jones Christensen, L., J. Reck, and B. Wood. 2007. Vodacom Community Services: Rural Telephone Access for South Africa. In *Microfranchising*, ed. Fairbourne, Gibson and Dyer. Northampton, Massachusettes: Edward Elgar Publishing.

Justis, Robert T. and Richard J. Judd. 2003. *Franchising*. 3rd ed. Ohio: Thomson Custom Publishing.

Khandker, Shahidur R. 1998. *Fighting Poverty with Microcredit: Experience in Bangladesh*. Published for the World Bank. New York: Oxford University Press.

Microcredit Summit. 2006. The State of the Microcredit Campaign Report 2006. http://www.microcreditsummit.org/pubs/reports/socr/2006.htm (accessed December 5, 2007).

———. 2007. Why Target Women? http://www.microcreditsummit.org/involve/page1.htm#Whygive (accessed December 5, 2007).

Notes from Microfinance Learning Lab. 2005. September 15, 2005. http://www.nextbillion.net/blogs/2006/01/09/microfinance-and-microfranchise-a-perfect-marriage (accessed December 5, 2007).

P&G Health Sciences Institute. 2007. Safe Drinking Water. http://www.pghsi.com/pghsi/safewater/ (accessed December 5, 2007).

Pyramid Power. 2007. *Economist*. December 5, 2007, p. 60.

Scojo Foundation. 2007. Mission and Vision. http://www.scojofoundation.org/2_1_mission.html (accessed December 5, 2007).

Small Fortunes. 2007. Glossary. http://www.kbyutv.org/smallfortunes/glossary/ (accessed December 5, 2007).

Unitus. 2007. Poverty and Microfinance. http://www.unitus.com/sections/poverty/poverty_main.asp (accessed December 5, 2007).

Vodafone. 2007. Case Studies. http://www.vodafone.com/start/responsibility/publications_faqs/case_studies.html (accessed December 5, 2007).

Yunus, M. 1997. Empowerment of the Poor: Eliminating the Apartheid Practiced by Financial Institutions. *Humanist* 57 (4): 25–28.

Yunus, M. and A. Jolis. 2003. *Banker to the Poor: Micro-Lending and the Battle against World Poverty*. New York: Perseus Books.

Chapter Nine

Using Business to Create a More Vibrant Craft Sector

Jan Hack Katz

Introduction

Every society develops products to deal with the mundane aspects of life: preparing food, creating a living space, adorning the body, and so on. Some of these products are primarily utilitarian while others carry strong aesthetic components. As museum catalogs generally argue, however, both utilitarian and artistic items are informed by the cultures in which they were developed. From this creative process, then, has come an array of culturally informed craftsmen who use their specialized skills to generate relatively high incomes serving their local communities.

Unfortunately, globalization has eliminated the traditional local markets for many of these artisans, as consumers turn to mass-produced goods that are typically less expensive and also often, a valued sign of modernity. The likelihood of reversing this displacement of traditional, locally marketed craftwork is limited, and so, it is imperative that alternative business models be found to save these relatively high-income positions and avert the creation of a new impoverished group.

One solution has been to bring craft items to global markets and several groups have sprung up to enable this trade. The largest of these groups (Aid to Artisans and Ten Thousand Villages, for example) support large number of artisans, but its benefits are limited because of its very honorable focus on employment generation with local cultural authenticity, rather than on the full range of management functions. As case studies presented here show, by expanding management activities to include scale-driven sourcing, improved human resource allocation, and innovative marketing, the benefits could be expanded substantially.

Displacement of the Craft Sector

In recent years, artisans[1] serving local markets have been displaced by increasing competition from cheaper goods imported into even relatively isolated communities (Scrase 2003). Mass-produced plastic bowls are replacing pottery and mass-produced textiles are replacing local weaves, either eliminating demand or at least severely depressing prices. In the past, artisans might have been able to lower prices somewhat, but this is now difficult because of rising input prices. Rapidly growing economies, such as China, have greatly increased production of textile, apparel, and personal and home accessories and gobbled up supplies of key artisan inputs, such as skins and hides, woods, and certain types of metals (Scrase 2003). In Colombia, rising clay prices have led the major commercial ceramics producer, Corona, to import clay—possible for a large company, but not for a small potter. Higher input prices also raise the inventory maintenance costs of artisans who typically have limited working capital, making profit even more elusive.

Displacement has also occurred as elite artisans' traditional patrons have been lost as in the Taureg culture of Niger (Davis 1999). The impoverishment of ethnic nobility due to geographic and social displacement led support for artisans to decline precipitously. Some workers found alternative outlets with the new economic elites (primarily expatriates) and in the tourist market, but others were displaced. Even those with continued sales were often forced to adapt, to "mass-production of exaggeratedly exotic tribal sculpture, tools, and handicrafts . . ." (p. 485), which some critics view as the elimination of true artisanal work.

Sadly, some social improvement efforts that have the best of intentions also lead to artisan displacement. Efforts to reduce child labor, for example, have created pressure to move craftsmen into factory-like settings, which are easier to monitor, depriving them of the traditional home-work option. In the Indian carpet industry, for example, there are more than 200,000 home looms in Uttar Pradesh, Bihar, and Madhya Pradesh alone and oversight of this geographically dispersed group is financially impossible. The Rugmark certification scheme, for example, is purported to certify that rugs are child-labor free, but has only eight inspectors to inspect more than 18,000 associated home looms (Arova 1997). Valid certification can only occur if workers come together into production rooms that are comprehensively monitored. But this eliminates the opportunity for artisans to work on looms as a second job, after their agricultural tasks, for example, which is a common practice now. If demand drops in the absence of valid certification, the home option will no longer be available and artisans will be displaced.

Interestingly, Greenwald and Stiglitz (2006) have argued that it is not domestic industrialization that displaces craft workers. Rather, domestic industrialization can have spillover effects that increase income in crafts and agriculture. For example, industrialization allows the local government to increase revenues because the concentrated economic growth of industrial firms is easier to tax than fragmented, geographically dispersed craft and agricultural producers. In Ecuador, traditional weavers who temporarily migrated to large-scale urban textile mills brought home new techniques that were integrated into traditional fabrics to create new hybrid forms that sold well in trade markets (Korovkin 1998). With this increased revenue, governments can invest in research and development and infrastructure that support the craft sector. The Colombian government does indeed have several programs—an artisan support program within ProExport, the trade authority, and Artesanias de Colombia, a retail outlet for craft goods that are paid for almost entirely by taxes on industry and agribusiness (e.g., cut flowers). This argument is consistent with the displacement literature, which tends to focus on mass-produced imported goods as the primary vector for craft sector pressure. There are cases, however, in which domestic industrialization has harmed artisans. Scrase (2003), for example, cites the example of the Indonesian textile industry in which development of a domestic commercial, mass production system created approximately 80,000 industrial jobs, but led to the loss of approximately 410,000 jobs for artisans involved in weaving, dyeing, and so on.

The Costs of the Craft Sector Displacement

Economic Losses

As mentioned, craftsmen have relatively high wages due to the return on their craft-based expertise. A study across 11 states in the United States found that the household income of craftspeople was 26 percent higher than the median household income, ranging from 14 percent higher in North Carolina to 54 percent in Georgia (Coda Survey 2001). If they are displaced, job alternatives are typically limited because skills are not often transferable and artisans are forced into the unskilled labor force at a significantly lower wage. Communities therefore lose relatively high wage earners and instead have yet another person added to the unskilled workforce that is typically in oversupply. The craftsman, therefore, clearly loses.

Offering less expensive alternatives to craft-made goods, however, benefits others. Lower prices for imported goods create an "income effect," making consumers better off by allowing them to lower household expenses and so, have more disposable income. As well, retailers gain profits from the new sales. As there are both winners and losers as artisans are displaced, the economic benefit (loss) to the community as a whole is difficult to estimate.

The net benefit or loss to the community is determined by what happens with the extra money available to consumers and retailers. By importing goods, some of the community's wealth leaves. If cash freed up with these cheaper goods is used to increase local productive capacity at a greater rate than what is lost, then the community can be better off. This is particularly true if the new productive capacity creates exports, goods sent to other communities either nearby or far away, because this draws new income into the community. If the extra money, however, is spent on buying more imported goods, people may feel that the economy is improving because they immediately have a better lifestyle, but ultimately the local economy will diminish and the community will be worse off.

Cultural Loss

As mentioned earlier, craft sector work generally embodies some aspect of indigenous culture—materials, design, or technique, though there is significant debate over what constitutes "authentic" culture (Davis 1999). Some argue that only completely traditional aesthetics and processes are authentic while others see the demand to remain static as paternalist, allowing consumers to feel confident superiority to an "earlier stage of human culture" (Clifford 1988, 228). With both definitions, craft work is a means to the maintenance of physical culture and as Scott (1985) noted, it is particularly important as a means for marginalized workers and citizens to retain their cultural identity. Displacement of artisans, then, can have a significant negative impact on communities due to loss of cultural touchstones.

There are also cases, however, where even severely inauthentic artisanal activities have prevented cultural loss. This is probably best illustrated by the tourist-focused activities of the Miccosukee Tribe of Florida (United States). This group was struggling to survive in the early twentieth century until they, with the help of outsiders, developed inauthentic arts, such as alligator wrestling, creating exciting "attractions" for travelers who were beginning to visit Florida in large numbers. These artificial tourist arts drew income to the community—allowing them to support their authentic lands, language, and lifestyle that was primarily kept from outsiders until the late twentieth century. In this way, the small Miccosukee community was able to maintain a profitable, inauthentic outsider face that allowed the protection of the authentic insider cultural reality (West 1998). In another case, the weavers of Otavalo, Ecuador, adapted their traditional textiles in color, style, and fiber content to satisfy tourist and trade markets, enabling maintenance and evolution of their community culture (Korovkin 1998).

In both cases, through the production of authentic artifacts and wholly artificial crafts, cultures have been maintained. In the absence of the skill maintenance and/or income production, this is far less likely.

Gender Equity Costs

The craft sector is a rare case of work in which both women and men participate, though often in different niches. Women are heavily involved in textile and apparel production and in pottery (cf. Trade and Investment Division 2005) Some have argued that women are the craft producers and men the traders (Scrase 2003) while others have found the men to be the producers and the women the traders (Mintz 1971). In fact, women's participation in the craft sector is so well discussed that it has drawn the ire of some analysts who argue that women should be considered for all sectors (Garwood 2003). Nonetheless, even critics agree that the craft sector provides a positive opportunity for women.

The opportunity to produce at home is one of the reasons that craftwork so appeals to women. Though potentially exploitive (cf. Wilkinson-Weber 2004), home-based work does provide income opportunities where women are unable to mix freely with people outside their own family. As well, when they must care for children, home work provides the necessary flexibility and proximity.

Many national development initiatives in the past two decades have focused on creating gender equity in the employment sphere due to the intergenerational benefits of having women employed. If opportunities for craft production are reduced, viable employment for women, particularly those who are most economically at risk because of their inability to find other public jobs, declines and sets back those many development efforts.

The Difficulty in Reorienting the Craft Sector

The potential market for craft goods outside of their traditional geographic areas has indeed grown in recent years with increasing international travel and interest in other cultures. Consumers in industrialized countries are more interested in purchasing items that embody foreign cultural forms and symbolize both as an exotic experience and as a means to signal their "unique" aesthetic (Nash 1993). On the other hand, most consumers want colors, shapes, and sizes that reflect current styles and they often seek fully or partially utilitarian versions of traditional objects that can be more easily embedded in industrialized countries' surroundings. Several problems exist in the realignment of the local craft sector, therefore, to serve international markets in a way that will benefit the craft producer:

- Limits on working capital
- Lack of access to distribution systems
- Difficulty in understanding consumer preferences in terms of aesthetics
- Restricted communication channels that prevent efforts to expand demand
- Inability to match personal skills with market requirements and so, access the most profitable niche
- Inadequate knowledge of basic management skills

Fortunately for many artisans, a range of organizations has arisen to provide outlets for traditional crafts both in the home market, among tourists, expatriates, and local elites, and in foreign markets. Though these do not solve all of the relevant problems, in many cases, they have provided partial solutions and employment for millions worldwide.

Outlets within national market have been created by small-scale, local traders who saw the opportunity to supply tourists with mementos to relatively large-scale government efforts that seek to move income to poorer areas to reduce social unrest and to use traditional crafts as a means of reasserting a national identity as the case of Colombia, below, will show. As well, as Davis (1999) has found in

Niger, wealthy expatriates sometimes seek out artisans and become their patrons: creating a system similar to the traditional nobility-dependent artisanal system, though with an interest in using the arts to experience indigenous culture rather than as the traditional signal of status.

Sales in international markets have also been driven by a wide range of agents. Mass-market retailers Target, for example, has annual Global Bazaar Collection that includes painted trays from Peru, decorated furniture from Thailand, and block print quilts from India in 2007. The Web retailer Overstock.com has a Worldstock collection that they stress supports female craft workers worldwide.

Aside from these efforts that are primarily directed toward filling a market need or simply providing employment, a number of not-for-profit efforts have sprung up with the intention of moving more of the income generated to the artisans themselves. Now placed under the umbrella of the fair trade movement, these Alternative Trade Organizations (ATOs) have been building over the past 50 years. Ten Thousand Villages, for example, which is supported by the Mennonite Central Committee, has eased the task of less-industrialized country artisans who were unable to access higher profit foreign markets. (Imhoff 1998). These ATOs provide artisans with relatively direct access to markets in an effort to generate higher earning by eliminating traditional middlemen. According to Littrell and Dickson, ATOs return 33–45 percent of the retail price to artisans, compared to 10 percent from traditional for-profit retailers (Littrell and Dickson 1997).

Both ATOs and for-profit small-scale and mass marketers have eliminated a number of barriers faced by craft workers. Many provide insights into consumer tastes, whether that comes in the form of the relatively informal suggestions of Hausa traders in Niger who buy from Taureg artisans to sell in the tourist markets (Davis 1999) or in the very formal training of artisanal communities provided by groups such as Aid to Artisans (www.aidtoartisans.org). Perhaps most important, these groups provide distribution channels to relatively wealthy, large-scale markets.

Unfortunately, they have created some new issues. Because craft workers worldwide are competing for a piece of this exotic goods market, they face cost pressures much like any other for-profit business. This is particularly a problem with mass retailers, which, on top of cost pressures, require very large production runs, substantial design and quality consistency, and now, often proof of appropriate labor conditions. This necessitates significant working capital and a variety of control systems, which has led to craftwork that is more similar to factory-based mass apparel production. Factory owners deskill artisanal tasks to allow for consistent mass production, shifting employment to workers with limited skill. Most of the profit therefore accrues to factory owners while workers' wages reflect other low skill occupations.

ATOs can be significantly more flexible with work conditions because consumers have a reasonably naïve tendency to believe that they provide oversight that ensures good conditions. Further, ATO material often stresses the social value of flexible employment of women, cutting off questions as to the likelihood of children participating in home production or the difficulty in monitoring potential subcontracting to other suppliers. As well, ATO consumers tend to value the "authentic" nature of the goods and so, are willing to accept imperfections and variations across items. As noted, then, the financial return to artisans (assuming no subcontracting is actually taking place) is far better than that provided by mass market situations. Still, as for almost all goods, there is a downward sloping demand curve and price competition exists. Expansion of markets would relieve some of the pressure, but while online and bricks-and-mortar retail outlets of ATOs have increased the size of the market, most groups have limited marketing skills and their brands have relatively low awareness and the broad array of items carried makes it difficult to gain premium prices through more refined niche marketing.

In recent years, more for-profit businesses have become integrated into the network of NGOs and government agencies that support the craft sectors. Relying on business knowledge, these businesses have developed innovative strategies and tactics to mediate barriers faced by artisans. By looking at two systems in which for-profit businesses have participated—a hybrid NGO/for-profit organization in South Africa, and a government-business network in Colombia, these innovative solutions can be drawn out.

Sociopolitical and Economic Background for the Case Studies

Colombia and South Africa provide strong bases for studies of artisans because both have maintained relatively strong indigenous economies due to the limited investment interest of foreign firms. Colombia, with its longstanding history of civilian violence, has seen little foreign direct investment. Though South Africa had substantial foreign investment through the late 1970s, much of this withdrew due to the political pressure surrounding apartheid. Domestic control of the economy, while primarily affecting industrial firms, also seems to have encouraged substantial innovation in craft industries. Both countries offer a wide range of crafts—in South Africa because of the ethnically diverse population and in Colombia, because the variation in climate and ecosystems creates very different regional traditions.

As well, innovation and maintenance of the South African and Colombian craft sectors are also likely due to both governments' view supporting the craft sector as a means of reducing societal inequities that exacerbate national, social, and political instability. As a result, the two countries have developed development programs that have a positive impact on craft based sectors.

The systems that have encouraged craft sector development differ substantially, however. South Africa's primary economic concern is in redressing the injustices of the former apartheid regime. One major initiative has been Black Economic Empowerment (BEE) legislation, passed with the intent of putting more of the economy in the hands of previously disadvantaged groups. Among other things, it encourages businesses to source goods and service from companies owned by these disadvantaged groups. As a result, corporations have an incentive to become involved in purchasing locally produced crafts as a means of raising their BEE ratings.

The Colombian government's economic development activities, on the other hand, rely heavily on government efforts to increase the effectiveness of export industries. Most of this effort goes to more typical commodity businesses (e.g., cut flowers, sugars, oils) or industrial manufacturing (e.g., textiles, apparel, metal products). At the same time, however, the government recognizes the need to bring money to indigenous groups that typically live in relatively isolated areas and are caught up in the national political turmoil and violence. Given the wide range of crafts that were and are traditional in these communities, the government also chose to include a craft-oriented initiative designed to increase the opportunities available to artisans nationwide.

Interestingly, the role played by tourism also differs strongly across the countries. With its long history of domestic violence, Colombia, with the exception of Cartagena, has not traditionally been considered a tourist destination by most. South Africa, on the other hand, is a well-developed tourist destination with its exotic animal parks and beaches. In South Africa then, there is a significant tourist art market while in Colombia, most goods must be sold to local consumers or exported.

These very different national economic development policies and tourism contexts have created very different conditions for craft sector realignment. By selecting one case study from each, we can therefore see two systems—one that creates domestic sales opportunities to the business sector and tourists and the other that focuses on sales to elite locals and foreign customers. In both cases, government intervention is not designed to solve the problem, but it does create national structures that support business solutions to those.

Case 1: Out-of-the-Box, South Africa

Out-of-the-Box is a relatively new organization established in a legal form available in South Africa, but not in all countries. It is a public service organization that takes donations, but plans to distribute excess profits to "owners" when those profits are created. Essentially, this allows the organization to evolve over time from a partially donor-funded organization to a regular, independent, for-profit business.

The organizational goal was to create an outlet for craft producers in South Africa because of the limited options available. While the large tourist market should create substantial opportunities for sales, South Africa actively enforces a vendor licensing system and supplies far fewer licenses than artisans request. As a result, very few artisans are able to interact with tourists either directly or through informal workers, something you would see in most other less-industrialized countries.

Rather than focusing on the tourist or export markets, however, the founder, Nina Venjakob, understood changes in domestic market pressures and identified a novel and profitable niche—the corporate gift market. Corporate gifts are relatively price-insensitive and the companies purchase in large quantities, making sales relatively efficient. But this also means that individual artisans are unable to supply the market because of insufficient scale. At a time when most South African companies were buying imported commercially produced gifts, Black Economic Empowerment legislation and the business, union, and government were supporting "Proudly South African" campaign, which encouraged domestic manufacturing and created incentives for companies to source corporate gifts locally.

Out-of-the-Box would offer all crafts techniques that were traditionally South African and customized for the corporate client. To do this, Venjakob developed a network of independent artisans around the country—bead workers, metal crafters, apparel producers, and so on—with the understanding that they could continue to work on their own craft, but that she would also offer them contract orders, for which she would supply the materials, designs, and transportation to customers. Deadlines were critical because the corporate market requires timeliness, and as a result, Venjakob had to build overcapacity into the system to ensure that orders could be filled.

This network system permitted workers the flexibility they often sought in craft work: they could choose the orders in which they wanted to participate and the quantities they wanted to supply in the given timespan. Also, workers could be quite isolated because all coordination with suppliers and customers was done by Venjakob, and though workers might be geographically concentrated due to a certain artisanal tradition, they did not have to be.

The flexibility for artisans came at a price, however, because artisans were not guaranteed work. On the other hand, artisans quickly sorted themselves into those that wanted to participate on a relatively full-time basis and those who sought only occasional work. As well, as independent businesses, the artisans were not provided with any healthcare or work interruption benefits.

The initial Out-of-the-Box system then eliminated several of the barriers to sales faced by South African artisans. Venjakob created the links to customers, worked with them to develop appropriate designs, bought materials for craft workers, which ensured consistent quality, but also used scale to reduce costs and eliminated the need for working capital, and provided transportation for finished goods to the market. With a relatively simple service operation then, this virtual craft company was able to increase sales for artisans significantly by identifying a strong niche market and essentially providing corporate staff functions without much real involvement in production.

While the system worked reasonably well, it had its limitations. Initially, artisans were not given additional training and because many were illiterate, they had trouble checking their own work to produce corporate logos consistently. A large order for beaded pens with a corporate logo, for example, could not be delivered because many of the pens were delivered with the letters of the company name upside-down, backward, and transposed. Additionally, as orders grew, it was difficult to attract sufficient artisans to supply in a timely manner. This forced Venjakob to rethink the model and transform it into a more complete service support system that maintained the benefits of independent artisans while increasing system effectiveness.

The first addition with the new system was training. While Out-of-the-Box produced items that were informed by South African cultures, Venjakob's focus had never been on cultural "authenticity," but rather on employment/income generation. As a result, she was not troubled by creating a training program that taught people entirely new skills or upgrading skills that were not necessarily part of their traditional culture. Many of the trainees would be displaced workers from other fields who had an affinity to craft work.

Though not directly linked to craft skills, literacy training was seen as critical to success. Because most of the artisans were working in relatively isolated locations, continuous quality control was not feasible and so, each artisan had to be responsible for monitoring their own production. Through early interactions, it became clear that artisans were very capable of doing complex geometric patterns consistently, but letters, which are often not symmetric in any direction, were very difficult for the artisans to replicate. The first, class then, was basic literacy.

To generate a sufficient pool of artisans, Out-of-the-Box also planned skill-based classes. The classes, however, required a location and it had to include a diverse array of services, including childcare, because many of the artisans had preschool aged children, and housing, because many came from a distance to learn the craft. Once a facility was found, the question was how to use it most intensively to lower the overhead costs per sale. It was through this that the team recognized that their site was conveniently located to the Johannesburg airport in to which a high percentage of tourist flew. Because the city itself has relatively few tourist sites, the training location could be developed into a tourist destination to observe traditional craft production. With that, a sales showroom could be created and products of the network artisans could be offered.

The training program, coupled with the showroom, would enable Out-of-the-Box to improve on two other dimensions—output consistency and money paid to artisans—through better artisan sorting. Because the corporate customers demanded a wide range of crafts as gifts, training was offered in a wide variety of crafts and this portfolio of offerings permitted better matching of artisans to crafts. During classes, it became clear that some people were just not capable of producing adequate quality work. Clearly, the organization could not allow them into the artisan network of that craft for quality control reasons and if they continued with that craft, the craft workers would have trouble selling the goods on their own due to poor quality. Instead, teachers were told that they should encourage students to move across crafts to find the one that best suited their interests and skill levels. This self-sorting is rarely possible in an NGO-artisan systems because they tend not to offer a portfolio of skills in a given location. With sorting, however, artisans were able to match to a skill that would generate the best return for them.

The showroom created an opportunity for the highest quality artisans. Corporate gifts required adequate, but not excellent artisans, to produce large quantities consistently. As a result, the niche provided more income for artisans who would not normally get a skill-based premium. It did not, however, have a means to generate a very high return for excellence. With the tourist market, the highest quality artisans could be featured and their items sold individually, with a higher profit per item. By pairing the corporate gift and tourists market, then, the system was able to gain a higher than normal return for adequate artisans and provide a higher profit outlet for excellent artisans.

The Out-of-the-Box case shows that pressures that are typically confronted by for-profit organizations, but not by most NGOs and government agencies, can lead to innovative responses to the needs of the craft sector. Competitive pressures, for example, led to the identification of the corporate gift niche market; cost pressures forced the identification of additional profit streams, such as the development of a tourist attraction at the training facility. Pressures for consistency and lower prices led to the system for pooled material sourcing. Quality control issues led to the recognition of different skill levels among artisans and the plan to better match workers' capabilities with the craft and with the market that paid best for the skill level.

As often happens, the strategic and tactical innovations were created as Out-of-the-Box sought methods to relieve market pressures rather than in a planned manner. As well, change was a continuous process at Out-of-the-Box because as one innovation occurred, such as the training program, it created pressures and opportunities that led to more innovations. While this process can be artificially induced in not-for-profit organizations, both government and nongovernmental, they typically are not. Market-oriented for-profit organizations, therefore, will provide an important means to increase efficiency and effectiveness of the craft sector.

Case 2: The Colombian Government-Business Network

The initial improvement of the craft industry in Colombia was driven by the national government, which placed an artisan focused division within the Ministry of Commerce, Industry, and Tourism export agency. This work was supported by capital from The Alliance for Progress, a U.S. aid program founded during the Kennedy administration that channeled money to Latin America. The Colombian agency identified traditional crafts and developed means to bring them to the market, including exhibitions aimed at foreign wholesale customers and domestic sales outlets, which is typical of government craft programs. The positioning of this effort, however, was unusual.

Rather than emphasizing mass-market low-cost items, Colombia chose to focus on very high quality, elite designs at a premium price. Wood carvers were not encouraged to produce huge numbers of inferior carvings, but instead to produce fewer fine pieces of furniture or decorative accessories. This system made sense because of the minuscule tourist market, eliminating the potential to sell massive amounts of low-quality mementos. Most products had to be sold in the domestic market or via export. To maximize income, a decision was made to focus on the elite domestic market because Colombia has a reasonably large wealthy population. More important, those elites who have chosen to stay through all of the violence have a deep sense of nationalism. As a result, buying items that are influenced by local culture was consistent with elite consumers' interests.

The government employed designers who worked with indigenous communities to create hybrid crafts that were consistent with tradition, but that reflected the needs of modern consumers. The amount of adaptation varied with the item. Woven grass urns that were traditionally used to store liquid and solid foods remained more or less as traditional, though they were sold as household decorating accessories. Designs for furniture, however, were influenced much more by modern styles, color preferences, and efforts at product differentiation.

Artesanías de Colombia stores were opened in elite neighborhoods to offer artisanal goods produced in the government supported programs. The stores offered a range of items, though primarily focusing on household goods. They were strategically well focused, offering a price point that appealed to very wealthy customers, but not the wealthiest group. This niche was particularly appropriate for Colombia because it was sufficiently large to generate sales, but would attract people with more mid-range incomes and make them aspire to own this type of item.[2] Without the need to profit, the government stores could showcase goods, gain customer awareness, and generate interest for the goods among a wider income range with less immediate pressure for sales. As sales and product interest increased, however, for-profit businesses did enter the market.

Within a two-block area of one Artesanías de Colombia store in the elite Northern district of Bogotá, there are at least four additional stores focusing on indigenous crafts for the domestic market. Galleria Cano, which initially sold only pre-Colombian influenced jewelry, positions itself for consumers who are even wealthier than the Artesanías group, while Arté is slightly below the Artesanías price point and Xué sells to the more modest consumer. As an example, traditional hand-woven hammocks are available at Artesanías de Colombia for $125, while Galleria Cano carries elaborately woven hammocks with crochet embellishments for $350 to $700 and Xué carries more coarsely woven, but still handmade hammocks for $45. These other retail stores provided markets for a wider variety of goods as well—from clothing to musical instruments. So the government, to a great extent, is responsible for the initial domestic market development for refined artisanal goods, but then for-profit retailers entered to satisfy other market niches.

Other businesses sprang up to satisfy foreign customers. Marietta was founded to sell to foreigners who came to Colombia to work for NGOs, foreign governments and companies. When Marietta was founded more than a decade ago, most foreigners did not leave their hotels, except to go to work, due to security concerns.[3] To sell to this segment, Marietta developed alliances with hotels that allowed the company to display craft items to these consumers. The company has built tall glass cabinets and placed these near hotel front desks. The cabinets are filled with colorful, local crafts and whenever a guest comes to the front desk, he or she sees the items for sale. All one has to do is, select an item from the cabinet and ask the front desk staff to add the cost of the item to his/her bill and the sale is made. For foreign business people who need to take gifts home, this method of purchase is convenient and easy.

As the market grew and competition advanced, innovation became the hallmark of the sector. While design changes in furniture occurred as international styles moved, more rapid innovation occurred with other products, such as jewelry. Jewelry is a very large market in Colombia because women dress well and like to accessorize. While some of the jewelry sold is expensive gold or silver, most women do not wear very expensive jewelry in public for security reasons. As a result, it is relatively easy for artisans to enter the market because they do not need the working capital to afford gold, silver, and expensive stones.

As jewelry artisans developed, so too did distribution systems, because government agencies allowed and supported a wide range of public forums for sales—mobile craft fares follow a regular schedule of locations in the cities, some relatively derelict buildings in the city center are devoted to craft sales with artisans' booths and a variety of temporary pedestrian malls and weekly fairs are set up, where craft sellers are allowed to exhibit.[4] This creates intense competition, but rather than compete on price, the Colombian jewelry sector, in part due to the intervention of the government design team, focuses on innovation. The form of the innovation is interesting however, pushed by cost control and sustainability. Cost control arose because many of the artisans had very little working capital and most of the consumers could not afford to buy high-priced jewelry. Sustainability came from the national pride in the country as one of the world's most varied ecosystems and also initially from NGOs that were trying to protect critical ecosystems by finding incentives for locals to protect the environment.

As a result of these pressures, artisans began to use what would generally be described as garbage to create beautiful jewelry. For example, Colombia has both Atlantic and Pacific coasts and fishing is a major industry. In processing the catch, massive amounts of fish scales and bones are produced. In Colombia, a technique was developed to clean, dye, and dry the scales, making them look like luminous flower petals that can be easily strung. Fish vertebrae are cleaned and dyed or painted making them look like turned-wood beads that could be arranged into graduated chandelier-style earrings and necklaces. Melon and pumpkin seeds, which also have no other use, are dyed or left in their natural state and used for necklaces, bracelets, and earrings. New nuts, beans, and other natural materials are integrated into jewelry production each year. The cost of the original materials is zero or near zero and processing costs are very low because of the volumes processed; so, artisans are able to purchase a wide variety of materials and mix and match them in innovative and interesting ways.

In the Colombian system, the government began the process of artisan development, but stayed relatively limited in its efforts, allowing for-profit business to enter into production and retailing. With these entrants, competition rose and retailers began to integrate backward to provide design assistance to artisans and help with logistics, both domestically and internationally. New producers were able to take advantage of institutions created and their own wave of innovation in an effort to lower costs and increase product differentiation. As a result, the Colombian craft sector is extremely vibrant and provides employment for a wide range of artisans.

An Addendum: Problems with Commercialization

Unfortunately, the development of larger and more profitable markets for artisans is not wholly without negative effects. The demand for

larger quantities of embroidered textiles led to massive changes in the
chikan production in Lucknow (India), including the recruitment of
large numbers of embroiderers from outside of the community.
Pressure for volume resulted in an acceptance of those with limited
skills causing a diminution in both quality and variety (Wilkinson-
Weber 2004). Even those with extensive skills began to focus on the
most popular stitches in order to increase output (Scrase 2003). This
recruitment of outsiders, narrowing of skills, and quality decline could
harm rather than help culture if it is done without reasonably explicit
community discussion, as occurred in the cases of the Miccosukee
alligator wrestlers and Otavalo weavers, mentioned above, who all
used inauthentic arts to preserve their culture.

Economic dependence on tourism and export-directed craft production is also troubling because demand from these markets can be
highly variable. Particularly in the current climate of world political
violence, massive shifts in travel are common. As tourists worried
about instability in the Middle East, tourism in Petra (Jordan) has
been declining since 2000 from several thousand per day to generally
fewer than 1,000 per day. Though the site has better and worse
months, declines can be dramatic. Tourist arrivals in October and
November 2006 were 24.6 percent lower than in these months in
2005 (Dajani 2006) leading to a significant impact on the embroidery
workers, glassmakers, and other artisans who sell their work at
Jordan's primary tourist attraction.

In addition, change in consumer preferences in foreign markets
can lead to massive booms and busts in demand. When tourism to
Central America expanded in the 1980s and 1990s, demand for
brightly colored Guatemalan textiles boomed, but after a few years,
styles changed and demand dropped, leaving many artisans with
inventory that could not easily be sold (Imhoff 1998). In the absence
of a portfolio of potential markets—some of which, like the corporate
gift market mentioned in the cases, are relatively stable—and an
innovative capacity—which allows traditional techniques to evolve
with changes in fashion and customer interest—this variation in
demand can be as destructive to communities as the original artisan
displacement.

There are also potential environmental costs to craft expansion
for global markets. When traditional crafts are based on a limited
resource, expansion of production may cause serious ecological harm.
Ironwood (tree) carving, for example, was traditionally practiced by
the Seri ethnic group of Sonora, Mexico. As their traditional craft
gained a wider audience, ironwood in their area was depleted. The Seri

went further afield for ironwood and non-Seri carvers began to offer products, ultimately leading to very significant pressure on Mexican ironwood stands (Imhoff 1998). Concern with limited resources should be a part of the strategic plan of artisanal-based businesses. In the ironwood case, it was primarily the carving style and not the ironwood itself that made the goods attractive to the markets and so, an alternative and more plentiful wood could have been found. As mentioned, environmental concern is part of artisan development in Colombia, where evolution of traditional seed and nut jewelry has helped to save endangered plants, such as the palm-producing tagua nuts (also known as vegetable ivory) and has developed products using a range of inexpensive and sustainable inputs, from melon seeds to navy beans.

More radical theorists have argued that the entire premise that leads us to consider linking artisans from less industrialized countries to consumers in industrialized countries is faulty (c.f. Stephen 1993). Their argument, put simply, is that the link places the artisans in a position of dependency to cultures with very different values and attitudes leading to the destruction of authentic culture and an end to appropriate political discussion of the injustice of economic disparity. As well, the marketing efforts create a romanticized and stereotypic view of the producers and producing nations that divert attention from the truly deep problems confronted by these poor societies. This misleading image can be seen on the Web sites of major alternative trade organizations, where close-up pictures of smiling artisans' faces cover the still-marginal nature of most of their incomes.

While this criticism has a clear element of truth, it should be pointed out that the dependence of artisans on elites and the resultant fragile position of the artisans is for the most part as old as the arts themselves. While crafts did serve utilitarian purposes, the greatest artisans were often devoted to the service of elite patrons (Davis 1999). In the case of the Otavalo (Ecuador) weavers, an ancient weaving tradition was first upgraded by Inca conquerors, who introduced llamas and specialized workshops to the region in order to serve the royal court and then by the Spanish conquistadors, who introduced sheep (wool) and treadle looms to the region to supply the demands of the Spanish Crown as well as consumers in colonial mining centers (Korovkin 1998). While the exploitation associated with this production and the economic decline that accompanied the loss of markets created problems that should not be underestimated, the resultant textile industry also created one of the most vibrant communities in modern Ecuador.

A Last Thought—Intellectual Property Protection

Regardless of what is done to support artisans worldwide, there remains the potential for their profitable positions to be eliminated by low-cost, mass producers. A major move now is to provide some form of intellectual property protection for traditional art forms. If colors can be protected in the United States because of their tight association with specific companies[5] then it would seem reasonable that traditional designs and other aesthetic content could be legally protected intellectual property.

Notes

1. In this paper, the words craft worker and artisan are used interchangeably. Distinctions can be made based on the aesthetic and personalized content of the output, but in the context described here, no clear distinction can really be made.
2. As in most Latin American countries, consumers aspire to appear wealthier than they are—the American Wal-Mart niche of being proudly working class, does not really exist.
3. Over the past decade, most areas of Colombia are now much safer and foreigners do leave their hotels for restaurants, bars, and nightclubs, but they are still not likely to walk into craft stores because they are not part of that consumer segment.
4. Many government initiatives in Colombia have been devoted to increasing security and quality of life and so, any activity that brings people out in a fun environment is encouraged. Every Sunday and holiday, for example, the city of Bogotá shuts an approximately 100 km. ring of roads and for the Cyclovia, when any human-powered vehicle with wheels (and some runners and walkers) take to the roads for fun and exercise. The craft fairs and weekly street festivals are alternative means to draw out crowds.
5. Owens Corning was allowed to register the specific pink used in its insulation as part of its trademark in the 1980s and federal courts have supported color protection by companies in *Qualitex v. Jacobson Products*, 514 U.S. 159 (1995) and *Fabrication Enters. v. Hygenic Corp.*, 64 F.3d 53 (2d Cir. 1995).

References

Arova, Vasantha. 1997. *Carpet Exporters Delegation Opposes Blanket Ban.* India-West, 23(7): 427.

Clifford, James. 1988. *The Predicament of Culture: Twentieth Century Ethnography, Literature and Art*. Cambridge, MA: Harvard University Press.

CODA Survey. 2001. Growing Appalachian Economies through Craft, cited on Appalachian Regional Commission Online Resource Center. www.arc.gov/index.do (accessed December 5, 2007).

Dajani, Dalya. 2006. 31,926 Tourists Visited Petra Last Month. *Jordan Times*, December 15. http://www.jordanembassyus.org/12152006002.htm (accessed December 5, 2007).

Davis, Elizabeth. 1999. Metamorphosis in the Culture Market of Niger. *American Anthropologist* 101(3): 485–501.

Garwood, Shae. 2003. Tied in Knots: The Complex and Troubled Relationship among Women, Aid, and Development. *Iris* 46, Spring/Summer: 31–39.

Greenwald, Bruce and Joseph Stiglitz. 2006. Helping Infant Economies Grow: Foundations of Trade Policies for Developing Countries. *AEA Papers and Proceedings: New Developments in Macroeconomics* 96(2): 141–146.

Imhoff, Dan. 1998. Artisans in the Global Bazaar. *Whole Earth* 94, Fall: 76–81.

Korovkin, Tanya. 1998. Commodity Production and Ethnic Culture: Otavalo, Northern Ecuador. *Economic Development and Cultural Change* 47(1): 125–154.

Littrell, Mary and Marsha Dickson. 1997. *Alternative Trading Organizations: Shifting Paradigm in a Culture of Social Responsibility. Human Organization* 56(3): 344–353.

Mintz, Sidney. 1971. Men, Women, and Trade. *Comparative Studies in Society and History* 13(3): 247.

Nash, June. 1993. Introduction: Traditional Arts and Changing Markets in Middle America. In *Crafts in the World Market: The Impact of Global Exchange on Middle American Artisans*, ed. J. Nash, 1–3. Albany, NY: SUNY Press.

Scott, James. 1985. *Weapons of the Weak: Everyday Forms of Peasant Resistance*. New Haven, CT: Yale University Press.

Scrase, Timothy J. 2003. Precarious Production: Globalization and Artisan Labour in the Third World. *Third World Quarterly* 24(3): 449–461.

Stephen, Lynn. 1993. Weaving in the Fast Lane: Class, Ethnicity and Gender in Zapotec Craft Commercialization. In *Crafts in the World Market*, ed. Nash, 25–57.

Trade and Investment Division, United Nations Economic and Social Commission for Asia and the Pacific. 2005. Developing Women Entrepreneurs in South Asia: Issues, Initiatives and Experiences, December 29, reference number: ST/ESCAP/2401.

West, Patsy. 1998. *The Enduring Seminoles: From Alligator Wrestling to Ecotourism*. Gainsville, FL: University Press of Florida.

Wilkinson-Weber, Clara. 2004. Women, Work and the Imagination of Craft in South Asia. *Contemporary South Asia* 13(3): 287.

Chapter Ten

Doing Well by Doing Good—Strategizing for the Bottom of the Pyramid in India

Wolfgang Amann and
Shiban Khan

Introduction

Unilever's name in India was Hindustan Lever (HLL). Project Shakti was one of the seven new initiatives to tap the vast pool of potential customers in non-urban India (Amann, Steger, and Ionescu-Somers 2006a, Ionescu-Somers, Steger, and Amann 2006). Shakti meant "strength" or "power" and was an ambitious plan to stimulate new demand at the lower end of the market by creating a self-sustaining cycle of business growth through people growth. HLL planned to develop a win-win partnership with rural self-help groups (SHGs) by helping them access microcredit, buy HLL products, and sell them in their villages. If successful, the initiative would create hundreds of jobs, train new entrepreneurs, and extend HLL's distribution reach to the most inaccessible of India's rural villages. Penetrating the informal sector in this way was a potentially risky endeavor; furthermore, was it really the company's role to develop rural areas? At that time, the management had been concerned about potential channel conflicts with the existing, successful distribution network. Coordinating with governmental and NGO partners would be a key success factor, but this also brought its own complexities. Training mostly illiterate women in sales and promotion techniques was a major challenge, although the payback in terms of new markets and wealth creation was potentially enormous. Like many new ventures and innovative sustainability projects, Shakti was clearly not risk-free.

Unilever in 2007: The Multilocal Multinational

In 2007, Unilever, an Anglo-Dutch multinational, held a formidable position as a global giant in food, home, and personal care products. It had a total of 1,600 brands. Some of them showed substantial brand value, such as Knorr, Rexona, Langnese, Dove, Lipton, and Hellmann's. But Unilever was poised to scrap many of the less-promising ones in a "path-to-growth" strategy that would concentrate innovation and development on a portfolio of 400 core brands. A Fortune 500 transnational company with a worldwide turnover of €40+billion, Unilever operated in 150 countries and had over 220,000 employees.

Unilever and Local Communities

Back in the nineteenth century, one of the company founders, William Hesketh Lever, built a reputation as a social reformer, promoting a shorter workday, employee savings plans, and health benefits for his employees. He laid the foundation stone for the strong corporate responsibility leadership that later became inherent in Unilever's culture. By 2005, Unilever had evolved into what it called a "multilocal multinational." Its management held the view that the company's long-term sustainability depended on looking after consumer needs and improving local communities' quality of life. Being an integral part of local communities and markets gave Unilever invaluable perspectives; it could anticipate market opportunities, develop strategies and levels of investment tailored to particular needs, and anticipate changes in consumer tastes. Unilever produced global brands, but it knew there was no such thing as a global consumer.

Unilever's "Gateway to India"

When Unilever first became engaged in India in the 1930s, the opportunity to conquer unexplored markets was enormous. The company broke ground by establishing the first edible oil, soap, and personal product companies in India: The Hindustan Vanaspati Manufacturing Company (edible oil), Lever Brothers India Limited (soaps), and United Traders (personal products) were all founded between 1931 and 1935. The three Unilever companies merged in 1956 to form Hindustan Lever Ltd (HLL).

By the 1990s, HLL represented Unilever's business in India entirely. Given its long-standing presence in India, it had become a uniquely Indian company and was perceived by Indian people as a local company and not a multinational. The company made painstaking efforts to become implanted in the people's hearts and minds by showing that it cared about local communities. Its corporate mission statement noted "to succeed requires the highest standards of corporate behavior toward our employees, consumers and the societies in which we live." HLL had several ongoing projects that focused on rural development, education, health, community welfare, resource conservation, sustainable development, and national heritage in art and culture.

By 2007, HLL was one of India's largest fast-moving consumer goods company—with market leadership in home and personal care products—and one of India's seven biggest exporters. HLL operated over 100 manufacturing facilities across the country, together with several third-party manufacturing arrangements. It was one of the most desired employees for Indian graduates in management and marketing. A job at HLL would endow them with a unique starting position and experience for their careers.

The HLL Distribution Network

In 2007, India was one of the fastest-growing economies in the world, with a population of more than one billion, which could clearly drive large sales volumes. It was therefore a key target for Unilever's global strategy for growth. HLL's potential distribution outreach in India was 3,800 towns and 627,000 villages. However, of the total number of villages, the existing distribution network only reached 300,000. HLL's dilemma was how to extend this into the 327,000 smaller villages in inaccessible rural areas.

HLL already had one of the widest and most efficient distribution networks for consumer products in India; in fact, this was recognized as one of its key strengths. HLL's products were distributed through a network of about 7,500 redistribution stockists (RS) who sold to shops in urban areas and villages with more than 2,000 people that could be reached by vehicle. Its supply chain was supported by a satellite-based communication system, the first of its kind in the fast-moving consumer goods industry. This sophisticated network with its voice and data communication facilities linked more than 200 locations all over the country, including the head office, branch offices, factories, depots, and the key redistribution stockists. This was a tried and tested model.

However, penetrating new markets would be a challenge, not only because of their inaccessibility, but also because the consumers needed to be educated in both personal and oral hygiene matters—HLL products would be entirely new to the lifestyle of these rural communities.

Operation Streamline

In 1997, HLL had already launched Operation Streamline as one of its growth engine initiatives to penetrate rural markets that could not be reached by vehicle. With the help of local stockists, distribution was extended to villages with fewer than 2,000 people, thus doubling the rural reach. Through this new conduit, goods were distributed from the HLL agents to the redistributors, who then passed them to "Star Sellers" in local communities. In turn, the Star Sellers sold the brands to retail outlets, selling everything from detergents to personal products.

However, HLL wanted to penetrate these local communities even further and work deep within the villages. A profound knowledge of Indian rural communities would give HLL an unbeatable market advantage. One ingenious solution was to work with the rural SHGs.

Self-Help Groups and Microfinance

In the early 1970s, access to credit was a major problem for the poor in India, as well as in many other developing countries. The poor did not have access to own capital to purchase land, housing, and other assets, and banks were reluctant to lend even very small sums without any tangible security. The only solution for many Indians below the poverty line was to borrow from a moneylender at extortion rates. The poor were under particular financial pressure to borrow from moneylenders at times of births and weddings, when inviting the whole village to celebrate these events was a social tradition and expectation.

A solution had been found to counteract the power of the moneylender in rural Indian areas. The successful Grameen Bank initiative, launched in Bangladesh in 1976, had more than proved that commercial banking for the poor without collateral was not a pipe dream. The Grameen Bank was set up by Nobel laureate Professor Muhammad Yunus, head of the Rural Economics Program at the University of Chittagong. This action research project examined the possibility of designing a credit delivery system to provide banking services targeted at the rural poor. The initiative proved that it was possible to:

- Encourage banks to extend their facilities to the rural poor
- Eliminate the use of moneylenders in rural communities
- Create self-employment opportunities for the unemployed rural poor
- Create and organize an effective savings system, which people (mainly women) from the poorest households could easily manage themselves.

The Grameen Bank initiative set up, organized, and trained homogenous affinity groups of between 12 to 20 women below the poverty line (families earning less than Rs.750 per month; Rs.55 equal roughly €1) in local communities. Members of these SHGs were encouraged to meet and save regularly and to pool the savings in a group savings account, thereby giving them access to credit based on group savings and allowing the group to use the interest gained for group projects. Members of the group could take out loans for consumption (a wedding, birth in the family) and production requirements (purchase of animals or grinding mills), as well as for financing microenterprises such as cycle rentals/repairs, retail outlets, or tea stalls. Peer pressure proved to be an extraordinarily powerful mechanism to ensure that debtors made their repayments.

The 95 percent repayment rates that Grameen experienced were more than the banking community could have dared to hope for, since this had never been achieved in normal commercial operations. In the 1980s, the Indian government started vigorously promoting economy at the grass roots level all over India, working with NGOs to create more and more SHGs. By 2000, India had a rich tradition of financial SHGs. Making credit available for microenterprise had had surprising results, stirring as it did the innate entrepreneurial spirit within the country. The creation of sustainable livelihoods was the basis of the microcredit schemes. In fact, microfinance—as it was called—became increasingly important in the development process as a tool for alleviating poverty.

A Macro Opportunity Based
on a Micro Model

HLL's growth strategy was to ask SHGs to operate as rural direct-to-home teams of saleswomen, who would accomplish several tasks by raising awareness and educating people about HLL products as well as selling the products directly within their communities. The idea was for the women to not only act as salespeople, but also as veritable brand promoters, often physically demonstrating products, such as shampoo, by offering hair washes at religious festivals, or at the *haat*, the local village market, or by performing hand washing experiments to compare washing with soap to simply washing with water.

Apart from selling, the women would work on changing people's mindsets—for example, convincing them that a simple wash with water did not guarantee hygiene, or that shampoo could be used as a grooming product for the hair instead of just using soap to clean it. These rural consumers did not have access to television or radio, but the Star Sellers, by demonstrating and promoting HLL products at the *haat*, made up for this lack of audiovisual brand advertising.

HLL's challenge then was to test whether this organized, potential major direct sales force available in the local communities could help achieve HLL's business strategy objectives of "meeting the everyday needs of people everywhere" while creating wealth in the community. The existence of a ready-made network of SHGs was a great opportunity. HLL established a committed project team to help them plan a strategy to achieve this. HLL had the credibility to work with banks and convince them that the company could give local women a meaningful income-generation activity. The new microentrepreneurs would thus be able to access microcredit and use it to stimulate both demand and consumption at the local level. This could be a win-win situation that would modify the traditional microcredit model, but without making the model overly complex. Because their products could clearly offer health benefits, HLL established partnerships with UNESCO and NGOs, working with small theater groups to stage dramas that helped to build the local rural people's health awareness.

In fact, HLL had recognized that lending the local population a helping hand rather than giving a handout would meet its own business strategy and provide opportunities for new distribution channels for its products, as well as contribute to a more stable and prosperous society. HLL felt that if microcredit were available to local people, it would be possible to build and develop established SHG networks to become direct-to-home HLL distributors in rural markets. This would help create desperately needed new jobs and lead to an improvement in the living standards and general wealth and prosperity in India. However, for HLL, this new direct sales model signified a major change from its traditional model of formal sector distribution channels and professional sales representatives—and carried with it an inevitable element of risk.

A pilot initiative was set up in the Nalgonda district of Andhra Pradesh in November 2000, with 50 SHGs in 50 villages with between 1,000 and 2,000 inhabitants participating. A kick-off meeting on November 28, 2000 began with a few sparse attendees, but as the morning progressed, women who had traveled long distances began to arrive. A discussion involving 150 women, all members of SHGs who ran microcredit operations, ensued.

The initiative was facilitated by the DRDA in Nalgonda—a body under the authority of the Andhra Pradesh government with a mandate to promote and develop SHGs. As P. Shylinapo, representative of the DRDA at that time remarked:

> The women were looking for ways of capitalizing on their savings. The idea of buying HLL products at cost and making a profit on sales was exciting to them. They also realized that the direct sales training provided would serve them well.

Together with an organization called MART (Marketing and Research Team)—a consulting agency specializing in rural marketing and microbusiness promotion in rural areas—the DRDA worked toward promoting microenterprises in the district of Nalgonda. MART was responsible for coordinating the HLL-SHG business partnership and would also provide formal training on microentrepreneurship to the direct-to-home sellers. Once fine-tuned, the model would be scaled upward to cover more than 150,000 villages in India.

Making it with MACTs

As part of the Shakti Project, HLL also worked with Mutually Aided Cooperative and Thrift Societies (MACTs) in Nalgonda District. The MACTs were federations of 20 SHGs with up to 400 members that elected a representative committee to facilitate decision-making. The MACTs often acted as financing agents for SHGs and, given their membership volume, were in a position to offer a higher level of loan.

They also made decisions on investments to benefit the community, for example, investing in a school or setting up a supermarket. These MACTs were fostered by the same NGOs that earlier had been conduits for finance and advisory services to SHGs. The NGOs later handed over supervision of the MACTs to the SHGs themselves that could clearly better identify with the basic issues and problems facing their members.

In a bid to encourage fledgling entrepreneurs, the Indian government gave incentives to successful MACTs, sometimes donating infrastructure, such as buildings, to facilitate further development. The MACTs in Nalgonda opened 14 supermarkets (called "bazaars") across the district in order to further encourage entrepreneurship amongst the members. HLL even envisaged that the MACTs would become distribution stockists for the SHGs. This would keep the distribution costs low and allow HLL to create a parallel commercial system to the Star Seller system.

For HLL, the challenge of maintaining a different price for the rural consumer when he or she purchased from the SHG sales representative was more important than the scalability of this model. However, HLL also knew that having two channels of the same company competing on price would, unless carefully managed, have its problems. Undermining local retailers would not be a solution, as this would be a real threat to the initiative's success.

The First Reality Check

By the beginning of 2002, the project team had already reached the entire Nalgonda district and exceeded 400 villages with no signs of this momentum slowing down. This project had the potential of giving the company a lasting superior understanding of rural consumers, which would ensure the sales and marketing team's favorable position in the future. HLL was succeeding in profiling itself as a sustainability leader. Shakti also attracted the media's attention. The risk to the company's credibility if the project should fail was high indeed.

As many sustainability ideas need adaptation in the implementation phase, Shakti was in serious trouble, providing the women with little earnings, a major reason why they were dropping out of the scheme. HLL did, however, learn more about the situation deep in the villages. Vijaylaxmi, to name just one example, from the village of Aregudem, near Hyderabad, was one of the new direct-to-home sellers. She often hosted her SHG group's meetings, in which she took a leadership role, at her home. She kept the HLL products neatly stored in an annexed corner of her sitting room. Pratik, the marketing manager of HLL, commented:

> When I started with this project, I thought that the problem of training these women was practically insurmountable. Many seemed timid, and none had ever done anything like this before. For example, it is quite amazing to see how confident Vijayalaxmi has become, given the practice.

Vijayalaxmi, however, commented:

> I am delighted to have had this training, but the amount of income generated from this is almost not worth the effort: between Rs 100 and Rs 150 a month. Given a choice, I would prefer HLL to set up a production unit in our area that would give jobs to our children and us.

In another village, the local schoolteacher's wife also sold HLL products, with the products clearly on display for any visitor who cared to pass by. She said:

> It all started off well in November, but now that we are in May and it is harvest time, people do not have time to think about HLL products. And neither do I have the time to travel very far to find new customers or to stock up at the MACT. The only way of doing it is to go on foot.

The fluctuation in SHG sales throughout the year was an element of concern for HLL. With these fluctuations in sales and low level of transactions, it was difficult to see how HLL could scale up quickly. There had to be strong rational reasons for rural villagers to purchase from SHGs, and this meant putting the SHG margins under pressure so that the group could compete with the local retailer. Increasing the overall number of individual transactions was indeed a true challenge. There was also a stigma attached to door-to-door selling, so the women waited until the SHG got together to sell the products. Besides, there was no transport for door-to-door selling—it had to be done on foot.

Glimpses of Hope

The good news was that a few months into the experiment, the retailers had not noticed a decrease in their business as a result of the SHGs' new involvement in selling HLL products, but it was an important aspect to monitor. Although the retailers had not as yet objected, most probably due to the low level of transactions, what would happen if the transactions increased? The overall impact on HLL sales was undoubtedly positive. The consumption of HLL brands in the district had increased by 17 percent in six months. Simultaneously, the local consumers showed a dramatic increase in awareness of several brands previously almost unknown to them. For example, awareness of Red Label Tea had increased from 0 percent to 35 percent.

Continuing with this momentum presented a challenge, since the SHG women, who devoted only part of their time to selling HLL products (and also wove or farmed the rest of the day), did not have the time to do the type of brand awareness building and hygiene education that the Star Sellers could do in the traditional system.

Changing the System or Giving it Time to Take Off?

It was clear to HLL that the success of the model depended on being able to create a significant enough earning for the women so as to retain their interest and grow through their involvement and effort. The strategy for overcoming the obstacles and ideas for increasing the women's earnings meant that one or both of the following steps had to be taken: 1) increase overall sales, and 2) increase margins.

Working on the sales side, an analysis of the low sales showed that selling directly to consumers was a difficult proposition and was taking time to become established. The reasons for this were the following:

- Consumers were used to purchasing from retailers and there needed to be a good reason for them to change
- Consumers preferred to go to retailers because of the range of products that they stocked
- Reluctance on the part of the Social Entrepreneur to go and sell at consumers' homes.

It was clear that the bulk of purchases in the village took place at retail shops. Yet, the model as it stood then did not allow sales to the retail trade, because the MACTs, as an intermediary, received 3 percent. This prevented the SHGs from selling to the retail trade. As a concept, MACTs were not prevalent in most parts of the country—there were some MACTs in Andhra Pradesh (where the project was launched)—for this reason it did not make sense to keep them as part of the broader Shakti model. Removal of the MACTs could result in an additional margin being available for the SEs, which could increase their earnings as well, since they could theoretically earn a higher margin on the same turnover.

By 2007, Shakti had already been extended to about 50,000 villages in 12 states—Andhra Pradesh, Chattisgarh, Gujarat, Karnataka, Madhya Pradesh, Maharashtra, Orissa, Punjab, Rajasthan, Tamil Nadu, Uttar Pradesh, and West Bengal. Shakti already had about 13,000 women entrepreneurs, reaching no less than 50,000 villages and 15 million people in rural areas, in its fold. Shakti was thus undoubtedly creating opportunities for rural women to improve their living conditions and, most likely, their self-esteem, while changing their families' overall standard of living for the better.

Alterations to the supply model were, however, deemed necessary. HLL indeed modified it so that the rural distributor could sell directly to the SHGs. This freed them of the MACTs' margins of 3 percent and enabled the SHGs to sell to the retail trade as well, which boosted their overall sales significantly, ensured that retention rates climbed, and gave them a breathing space to start creating a direct customer base in the village. No conflict of interest was involved, because it meant that the retailers would not have to travel to purchase stock, and that the SE was there to service them. The retailers did not suffer capital and capital cost problems by having to buy in bulk and many among them actually had no other sources of supply.

Further changes took place: The stocks were no longer sent from the Cash & Forwarding Agent (C&FA) but from the rural distributor (RD). This ensured faster and more frequent servicing of orders. Small orders, such as the SEs would typically place, were easily serviced by the RD, while it was a huge issue at the C&FA that was only used to servicing bulk orders. Furthermore, no SHG Fed/NGO was involved in the process. The stocks were directly sent to the SHG Group/individual (products were delivered to the SE's doorstep by the rural distributor) and cash was paid on delivery to the rural distributor. The bank linkage was set up by HLL as it also facilitated the loan process.

As home-to-home selling posed a serious challenge to the initiative, HLL started a very large home-to-home campaign that was anchored by a company representative. He or she took the SE along and approached the homes. The fact that the company representative was doing home-to-home sales was a crucial step, as it ensured the legitimization of the activity in the eyes of both the SEs and the village community. The HLL team were pleasantly surprised to see that after the first few home visits, the SEs were very enthusiastic to participate and took it on. The ice had been broken, and the SE was "on her way." To this day, HLL makes sure that its rep does home calls as a part of his daily routine, since it helps the SE break through.

Over the months, HLL realized that the then current level of interaction with and supervision of the rural sales promoters was clearly too high. HLL wanted to reduce the supervisory visits from two to one a month.

The key motivator for the women was obviously profit, and this made giving recognition important. HLL had therefore developed a reward recognition program (i.e., a consumer silver card holder as a form of recognition). There would be several grades of entrepreneurs who would be entitled to different benefits. HLL also felt there was still too much slack in the system, which had to become more cost effective and efficient. Consequently, HLL decided to drive the recruiting and training aspects much harder. Economies of scale were essential. The resulting challenge thus resided in increasing the contribution from home sales. HLL presented a number of brand-centric activities to enhance brand loyalty and increase the number of homes reached. HLL established a new target of 80 homes per village per person, as well as an incentive system to encourage brand loyalty.

Economically, HLL had recently experienced challenging times in the form of intense local competition. But the project objectives were not abandoned, nor were the levels of investment decreased. This included financial resources, as also top management attention. There had been tremendous support for the initiative from the top management. In fact, the investment had increased 20-fold from what it had been in 2001. The local population was very supportive of Project Shakti as well.

Never Resting on its Laurels

Shakti Vani and iShakti were new initiatives, among others, that were subsequently added. They had both significantly increased the Shakti footprint in the communities. Shakti Vani was a communication program that spread awareness of best practices in health and hygiene. Local women were appointed as Vanis, and trained in matters relating to health and hygiene. They used specially designed communication material, such as pictorial literature, and spread awareness at SHG meetings, school contact programs, and other social fora.

iShakti spread education modules among the children of the village and gave the community, particularly the youth, an opportunity to learn to use a computer. The monthly income that an SHG representative could expect had greatly increased from about Rs.150 to about Rs.750 per month in average. This represented nothing less than a doubling of their household earnings and far more than they could possibly achieve through any other vocation in their villages. As other opportunities did not abound for women, the SEs were quite happy.

When the project extended from Andhra Pradesh to 12 other states, the SHGs received varying degrees of support from the different state governments. Where the support was limited, HLL had developed a direct contact model for recruitment that involved directly reaching out to women in villages and presenting a proposition for a stable, low-risk income for them. HLL also had the support of local NGOs for their proposition.

In turn, HLL also benefited, possibly creating a true win-win situation: HLL obtained a vehicle that increased its distribution reach by over 50 percent—an additional 50,000 villages were now covered. The project covered more than 1 million homes every month—a phenomenal outreach for a brand that had been and continued to be interested in doing trials or communicating with a large rural audience. HLL had a rather unique one-to-one, interactive communication channel that built brands in media-poor villages. HLL succeeded in building significant goodwill amongst the community due to it providing opportunities to earn a livelihood as well as the communication programs such as Shakti Vani/iShakti. There were substantial market share and consumption gains in the villages. HLL's studies have shown that there was a 17 percent increase in the consumption of HLL products across various categories in the Shakti villages. To date, this was achieved through regular HLL brands being sold through this channel. No customized products had been specially developed, creating further future opportunities.

While HLL at that moment had more than 13,000 SEs covering over 50,000 villages and reaching 15 million people, the project dynamism would rather accelerate than slow down. HLL had a daring vision for 2010. By then, HLL envisaged 100,000 SEs covering 500,000 villages and benefiting 500 million people.

Lessons Learned from HLL's Project Shakti

In India, Unilever innovated a new sustainability strategy. Hindustan Lever also fully integrated sustainability into its growth strategy. Several lessons can be learned from this success story.

Localizing Sustainability Strategies

HLL's strategy was so successful because it cleverly incorporated local idiosyncrasies. It understood that women in India had no other training or promising job opportunities, which prevented them from changing their roles in their households, villages, and society. By providing them with unique income possibilities and education, the women became thankful, loyal program participants, creating true win-win situations. HLL also relied on common practice and the availability of microcredits to largely finance the distribution system. Such local particularities should not be understood as a complexifier, but as an opportunity to create meaningful local sustainability strategies.

Applying Network Thinking to Sustainability Strategies

The main success pattern to be learned from HLL's growth strategy in India is based on network thinking. Networks between entrepreneurs throughout the system are the best means of ensuring that each element in the network maximizes the opportunities (Buchanan 2003). HLL managers not only got committed network members on board, they also trained network members and empowered them. The company thus created a system that allowed this committed sales force to build trust and use these relationships of trust on a local level. Once relationships have been built for the distribution of products, growth becomes easier when the product offer is expanded and consumption increases. Customers then build brand loyalty.

Such networks also match the complexity in HLL's targeted area. As little is known about the actual demand of diverse regions, only a decentralized system is open enough to learn what is needed. The networks had to be based on the trial and error principle, as no manager in the far away HLL headquarters could possibly anticipate which products would work best—practically none of the HLL products had originally been known in these remote village.

Networks have to rely on exclusivity though. Consequently, HLL succeeded in ensuring that the self-employed women only distribute HLL products and visibly benefit from increased sales. In the past, strategizing efforts often suffered from a lack of clarity: should a company be the first mover or fast follower? Applying network thinking actually helps to answer this question. If companies are able to build exclusive networks and a distribution system that cannot be copied easily, there are undoubted first-mover advantages. Not only does HLL have good products, but it also has a unique network in place with households in villages satisfying their consumer goods needs with the help of their trusted Shakti friend. This is a system that no competitor could break easily. Public product demonstrations at weekly markets make customers even more familiar with HLL products. The organization has built a unique competitive advantage with tremendous sustainability impact, using a modern logic to develop a dynamic, exclusive, and scalable network.

Anticipating Adversity

Strategizing's current reality is quite sobering. According to our research into strategizing efforts' success, companies struggle by and large (Amann and Tovistga 2007). More than 80 percent of strategies are not implemented as planned. Of the smaller, new strategic initiatives, 90 percent fail as well. Only 1 in 300,000 ideas lead to a product, of which 98 percent are not profitable. In larger companies, 95 percent of employees do not even know what their company strategy is. How can they then trigger the right action steps if the need arises? These figures are an accurate description of reality, although there is a truly global talent pool available to companies. Consulting companies provide services to anybody willing to cover their fees. Company-internal strategists, the CEO, or board members usually represent a positive selection of people as well. However, all this is no longer enough in today's challenging environments. HLL experienced the same pattern. A well-designed idea almost failed in the implementation process—at least initially. Unanticipated events and behaviors cause adversity and would do so again in the future. Examples include 1) the stigma attached to door-to-door sales, 2) women dropping out during harvesting season as they have to help in their village, or 3) the MACTs being a good idea, but offering practically no added value in return for their 3 percent margin. Any great sustainability idea is thus likely to experience a "valley of tears" before adaptations eventually lead this idea to success. Such learning is not failure though, it just eventually ensures the sustainability strategy's success. Dealing with adversity is part of the sustainability strategizing process.

Dealing with Complexity in
Sustainable Strategizing

Many sustainability strategies comprise environmental contributions as a key element. HLL's strategy was successful in increasing the household income of the country's poorest of the poor. It provided training opportunities for women who would otherwise have been ignored. This in turn allowed HLL to prosper. Dealing with complexity represents yet another crucial element in successful sustainability strategies. HLL first focused on the financial and social dimension. By trying to integrate an environmental dimension from the very beginning—most likely in vain—would have rendered the project too complex. There were no easy solutions, no low-hanging fruits. The same stakeholder dialogue would have been necessary to organize recycling or garbage collection, but would have overwhelmed the project managers in the early stages of the project. This is especially true, as neither the project's success, nor its scale was by any means certain. By omitting the environmental dimension and, thus, decreasing the complexity was a key success factor for HLL's Project Shakti. Furthermore, in general, simplicity is a formula for well-functioning, sustainability strategies. Similar thoughts apply when dealing with the ambiguity—another complexity driver. Is it really in the women's and India's best interest to have Western patterns of consumption perhaps imposed on them? If society survived without consumer goods such as HLL shampoo and toothpaste for centuries, is a shift toward them really the indisputable way forward? The list of Project Shakti's shortcomings is by no means short, but substantial income for the country's poorest, an improvement in hygienic conditions, providing hungry people with food, and providing training and jobs inarguably enhance HLL's social footprint in India. The women participating in Project Shakti most certainly agree. Ambiguity is part of every sustainability project, it should not be ignored, but accepted.

Conclusion

HLL teaches several crucial lessons on sustainable strategizing. The field of sustainability needs companies that will come up with innovative, localized solutions. These solutions have to be scalable so that their functioning patterns can be multiplied. Complexity should not overwhelm and cannot be ignored, but has to be dealt with. Somewhere in the strategizing process, simplifiers are required. Starting with a good idea—which may not be the perfect one yet—and subsequently improving it as HLL did, is of greater value than lengthily and in vain attempting the best option possible. HLL developed a sustainable strategy and helped 13,000 women and households, covering over 50,000 villages and reaching 15 million people. By 2010, these numbers should have increased to 100,000 self-employed women covering 500,000 villages and benefiting 500 million people. HLL thus sets the standards that are required to create dynamics at the Bottom of the Pyramid in India—and elsewhere. The HLL example should inspire companies to come up with equally effective initiatives in other settings. Good can always be done better!

References

Amann, W., and U. Steger, and A. Ionescu-Somers. 2006a. Delivering the Desired Results. IMD Case Study.

———. 2006b. The Reality Check. IMD Case Study.

Amann, W. and G. Tovistga. 2007. The Future of Strategizing. *Henley Management Perspectives* 3, 2007: 10–13.

Buchanan, M. 2003. *Nexus: Small Worlds and the Groundbreaking Theory of Networks*. New York: W.W. Norton.

Ionescu-Somers, A., U. Steger, and W. Amann. 2006. Hindustan Lever A—Leaping a Millennium. IMD Case Study.

Chapter Eleven

Marketing in Subsistence Marketplaces

Madhu Viswanathan, Srinivas Sridharan,
and Robin Ritchie

Introduction

Management research has recently begun to shed new light on the role
and nature of business innovations targeted at subsistence marketplaces
(Viswanathan and Rosa 2007), the four billion poor that have also been
referred to as constituting the Bottom of the Pyramid (Prahalad 2005).
The notion that ways might be found for business to effectively serve the
needs of subsistence markets is gaining increasing currency, and holds
promise for both firms and consumers. For firms, it constitutes potential
access to a vast, undertapped market for products and services. For
subsistence consumers, it includes the promise of affordable access to
products hitherto unaffordable or unavailable. Although gaining
momentum, this viewpoint still faces many challenges, including the
central question of whether business really can help to overcome the
problem of poverty. We contend that the best way to begin to address
such issues is to develop deep understanding of the lives of individuals
living in subsistence conditions. This paves the way for a bottom-up,
grounded understanding of the potential for business to contribute to
economic and social development among the poor. Our subsistence
marketplaces perspective is a bottom up approach to understanding
buyer, seller, and marketplace behavior that complements mid-level
business strategy approaches, such as the base of the pyramid approach,
and macro-level economic approaches to studying business and poverty
that currently exist in the literature.

Our emphasis in this chapter is on outlining principles of marketing
innovation that have the potential to improve business and social
performance in subsistence markets. These insights are based on an
understanding of subsistence marketplaces in India that emerged from

a combination of sources: 1) a six-year research program that has used observational, qualitative, and quantitative research to understand buyers, sellers, and marketplaces, 2) analysis of business practices, as described in recent literature on subsistence marketplaces or the Bottom of the Pyramid, 3) a social initiative that has been providing consumer and entrepreneurial literacy education (Viswanathan, Gajendiran, and Venkatesan 2007; www.marketplaceliteracy.org), and 4) a teaching initiative in which students have worked with companies to develop products and business plans that are specifically tailored to the needs of subsistence contexts (http://www.business.uiuc.edu/~madhuv/submktcoursemainpage.html). Although space constraints preclude a detailed account of these sources here, such descriptions are available online or upon request.

Our approach in this chapter does not purport to be exhaustive; rather, it seeks to highlight a number of ways that research and practice in marketing can benefit from an approach that differs from those developed for conventional markets. To illustrate these differences, we cite business examples where alternative approaches have been particularly successful. Our findings emphasize the need to view individuals living in subsistence marketplaces as both producers and consumers, as well as the value of a deep understanding of buyer and seller behavior when devising marketing strategies. Our perspective is also guided by the importance for businesses of enhancing individual and community welfare, conserving natural resources, and reducing negative impact on the environment, in addition to achieving financial objectives, although space constraints limit detailed discussion of some of these important elements. Though our conclusions are limited by the specific context in which we conducted our research, they provide a starting point for an important and overdue discussion on ways that new marketing models might be created to enable firms to function effectively in subsistence environments.

The Nature of Subsistence Marketplaces

Our discussion begins with an overview of the defining characteristics of subsistence marketplaces in India. We consider both the market as a whole and the individuals—both buyers and sellers—that comprise it, so as to address both the psychological and sociological factors that influence marketplace behavior (see figure 11.1). These analyses provide the conceptual foundation for our subsequent discussion of alternative marketing approaches for subsistence markets.

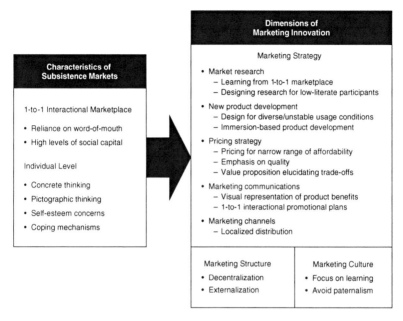

Figure 11.1 Marketing in subsistence marketplaces.

Marketplace Characteristic— The 1-to-1 Interactional Subsistence Marketplace

Among the most visible characteristics of subsistence marketplaces are the severe constraints on traditional economic resources, and the consequent uncertainty and lack of control for consumers over many aspects of day-to-day life. However, another important but often over-looked quality of such environments is their 1-to-1 interactional nature—the pervasive and highly social one-on-one relationships that exist among buyers and sellers, and among individuals in general (Viswanathan 2007; see figure 11.1).

The personal nature of marketplace interactions in subsistence environments results largely from the interdependence that character-izes life in resource-poor settings. Since incomes are modest and unstable, and low literacy is commonplace, individuals are frequently compelled to rely on others for help in times of need. Moreover, because buyers and sellers often come from similar economic strata and thus undergo similar adversities, and buyers may have at least some experience as a vendor, marketplace dealings are characterized by considerable empathy. This has a number of consequences. For one thing, offerings are regularly customized, with price, quality, and quantity adjusted to account for the personal circumstances of both buyer and seller. In addition, thanks to highly frequent communications among individuals, word-of-mouth is a heavily relied upon source of information for buyer and seller alike. It serves both to limit unscrupulous practices and to condition individuals to be guarded about their transactions (e.g., keeping price discounts discreet). All this stands in stark contrast to typical situations in developed markets, where consumers' marketplace interactions typically consist of detached exchanges with anonymous employees of chain stores.

For businesses seeking to serve subsistence contexts, the importance of these differences is that the relationship between buyers and sellers in these environments extends well beyond their marketplace roles. As a result, economic exchange may be treated as an extension of everyday personal interaction, rather than being divorced from it. This important insight can provide a basis for new marketing approaches, because it acknowledges social relationships as a community-owned resource that might be harnessed to add value for that community through market exchanges. Such an approach has considerable appeal, as its underlying philosophy is one of building on the strengths of subsistence markets rather than dwelling on perceived weaknesses. Some authors have argued that strategies that fall into the former category will tend to outperform those that fall into the latter (London and Hart 2004; Ritchie and Sridharan 2007) in creating both business and social value.

From a theoretical standpoint, 1-to-1 interactions are valuable because they contribute to the creation of "social capital"—the ability of individuals to secure benefits by virtue of their membership in social networks or other social structures (Portes 1998). Scholars have long viewed social capital as an asset that can aid economic activity, particularly in poor regions (see Iyer, Kitson, and Toh 2005 for an overview). Moreover, its specific potential as a marketing resource has also been highlighted in the literature (Frenzen and Davis 1990; Ritchie and Sridharan 2007). We elaborate on this notion in this chapter by providing specific examples of ways that social capital can help enhance the value of product offerings to subsistence contexts.

Although our discussion treats social capital as a means of creating benefits for buyers and sellers, it is worth noting that the marketplace consequences of social capital are not necessarily uniformly positive or constructive. For instance, although flexible payment plans made possible through relationships are generally advantageous, unscrupulous sellers can abuse the arrangement to set astronomical interest rates. Similarly, when the outcome of price negotiation is perceived to be too disadvantageous, sellers may manipulate the accuracy of product weighing as a countermove. On the buyer side, meanwhile, there are similar examples of consumers using the advantage of their social networks to disparage sellers by engaging in excessively negative word-of-mouth. All of this suggests that, even as they look to harness the power of social capital, businesses must be mindful of the potential for such power to be abused.

Individual Characteristics—Literacy and Income in Subsistence Marketplaces

Whereas marketplace-level phenomena are important considerations when serving subsistence contexts, it is also helpful to consider characteristics of individual consumers. Particularly relevant are low literacy, low income, and the consequences that arise from their joint occurrence (see figure 11.1). Research on literacy in the United States provides an interesting starting point for understanding these effects. Perhaps most striking is the difficulty experienced by functionally illiterate consumers when faced with abstractions—labeled concrete thinking (Viswanathan, Rosa, and Harris 2005). A related predilection is pictographic thinking—the tendency to view brand names and prices as images in a scene rather than symbols, and think about product quantities by picturing them rather than using available symbolic information. Functionally illiterate consumers develop several coping mechanisms to deal with these limitations, including depending on others, or buying one item at a time from a menu. Central to their marketplace interactions is a need to maintain self-esteem in public settings that could potentially "expose" their low literacy.

Research we conducted in India suggests that concrete thinking and pictographic thinking are also common in subsistence marketplaces, as are coping mechanisms to compensate for individual shortcomings in marketplace proficiency. Self-esteem issues are also widespread, with low literacy leading to fear of interaction, inability to ask or answer questions in conversation, avoidance of unknown products and unfamiliar pricing schemes, and feelings of futility in making enquiries or demands. Low literacy may thus hinder consumers from evaluating quality and lead them to accept products as is. Even when they do assess quality, the process may often be one of trial and error due to low literacy levels. Another consequence of low literacy is that individuals may compensate for shortcomings by resorting to coping strategies, such as pattern matching when they are unable to read the name of a medicine or a bus number, or depending on their children to read or compute when they cannot. When coupled with severe income constraints, low literacy and associated difficulties with abstraction may also lead to a short-term orientation characterized by lack of planning for future needs.

As the preceding discussion suggests, subsistence consumers struggle with many of the same challenges faced by low-literate consumers in the United States. However, the 1-to-1 interactional marketplace appears to afford some unique advantages that can enhance coping ability. For example, the experience of buying generic unpackaged products gives consumers considerable practice at judging products. Similarly, constant interaction with sellers and fellow shoppers hones consumers' ability to leverage the knowledge of others when deciding which products to buy, where to purchase, and how to get a bargain. This contrasts sharply with the situation in the United States, where making wise purchases essentially involves carefully monitoring store flyers, scrutinizing package information, familiarizing oneself with store policies, and using technology to add up bills. Subsistence consumers also have an opportunity to hone their marketplace skills by acting as sellers, a common occurrence in some contexts such as India. The vendor skills of bargaining, counting, and completing transactions, and the perspective-taking that is associated with them, are all directly relevant to the individual's role as consumer. A final factor that helps to enhance consumer skills in subsistence markets is, ironically, severe income constraints that often lead to careful planning out of sheer necessity. When the decision often involves something as basic and immediate as the next meal, careful purchase and consumption habits usually develop, with discounts and "free" promotions carefully pursued and unnecessary purchases eschewed.

These marketplace-level and individual-level characteristics are important in that they differentiate subsistence environments substantially from relatively resource-rich markets that most businesses are used to dealing with. This understanding of buyer, seller, and marketplace behavior has important implications for business practices in general and marketing practices in particular. Next, we illustrate some implications in three domains—marketing strategy, marketing structure, and marketing culture.

Marketing Strategy

Day, Weitz, and Wensley (1990) conceptualize marketing strategy as marketing activities and decisions that are pertinent to the generation and sustenance of competitive advantage by firms. In this section, we describe five elements that are central to this function—market research, product development, pricing, promotion, and distribution—and discuss how they should be approached differently in subsistence markets in order to create business and social value (see figure 11.1).

Market Research

Market research is generally acknowledged to be a key component of a firm's marketing strategy, since it provides much of the information that guides the marketing activities of the firm (Malhotra 2001). In developed markets, such research is conducted by a large, thriving industry that has built up an impressive array of tools and techniques to elicit consumer and market information for the benefit of competitive players. However, in subsistence contexts, market research remains in its infancy, leading to a consequent lack of knowledge regarding appropriate best practices. At a minimum, it seems clear that many of the tools and techniques found to be useful in resource-rich and literate contexts are unlikely to be as effective here.

An important element of market research is the concept testing that enables companies to refine products before launching them on a large scale. Conventional market wisdom relies heavily on attribute-based approaches to product design, employing methods to identify an optimal combination of relevant attributes. However, low-literate consumers tend to think of products holistically, making it difficult for them to express their preferences along abstract attributes. A more effective approach for subsistence markets would therefore be to present the product in a more tangible way. Customer-ready prototypes can be helpful in this regard, since they enable low-literate consumers to experience the product and develop an overall sense of preference.

Product testing in subsistence contexts should also be adapted to account for the concrete reasoning and pictographic thinking of low-literate consumers, as well as their lack of experience as participants in market research. These characteristics suggest a need for more realistic product testing situations, using concrete, visual stimuli rather than abstract tasks. And because low-literate consumers focus primarily on experiential attributes, product testing should represent the product in as close to real form as possible. Field-testing and observations of products *in situ*, which tend to do this as a matter of course, are highly effective but not always possible. As a practical alternative in our broader research program, we developed a task in which participants sort sheets of paper containing pictorial representations of a product whose various versions differed on several attributes; appearance (different colors), cost (using currency notes), convenience of availability (using pictures of shops located nearby versus far away), familiarity of the vendor, availability of credit for purchase, and whether the product was advertised on television. The sorting task itself provided a means of eliciting responses without overburdening the respondent with an abstract task of completing ratings on different attributes. By the same logic, other forms of market research are also likely to benefit from the use of more concrete, realistic stimuli. Instead of cueing respondents with a list of brand names, for instance, questionnaires are likely to produce more valid findings if they feature images of actual product packages.

Market research exercises aimed at eliciting consumer information should also recognize that self-esteem plays a central role in the decision-making of subsistence consumers, and can compound problems of low literacy and unfamiliarity with market research. This argues for in-person administration of surveys and other data-gathering exercises, since these methods are more effective in building personal rapport and eliciting trust from participants. In addition, when used in conjunction with a relatively unstructured data collection approach, personally administered methods may help to alleviate some of the test-taking anxiety triggered by low literacy. Conventional, structured approaches, which require respondents to rate products from memory using numbered or labeled response scales (such as numbered seven-point scales), can be abstract and thus anxiety-inducing for individuals with low literacy and numeracy skills. In our own research, personal interviews have been effective in collecting such data. When employing seven-point scales, we have used a two-stage process that begins by asking respondents whether they are neutral, positively, or negatively inclined toward the target (or alternatively, neutral, in agreement with or in disagreement with particular statements), and then ask for further discrimination within the positive or the negative side of the scale to determine their overall favorability/agreement on the scale.

Other pertinent considerations when conducting marketing research in subsistence contexts include the length and language of procedures. Generally speaking, participants should be able to relate to the tasks they complete and have at least a general understanding of the purpose of the research, lest the abstract nature of the task result in inaccurate responses. To avoid placing unreasonable cognitive demands on the respondent, language and procedures should be straightforward, and surveys, if used, should be of reasonable length. In our experience, long interviews are possible, but only if they feature interesting tasks that respondents can relate to, include a sufficient number of planned breaks, and use empathetic interviewers who are capable of developing a genuine rapport with participants.

In addition to the above, the fundamentally social nature of the 1-to-1 interactional marketplace suggests that researchers would do well to think in terms of collectives (i.e., groups, communities, etc.) rather than individuals, and conduct their research on that basis. One approach is to test market, since this makes it possible to capture the effects of natural social networks and most of the vagaries of the broader market. Researchers would then be able to monitor word-of-mouth, with special attention given to the views of local opinion leaders such as retailers, community organizers, and leaders of local self-help groups. In situations where a test market is not possible, research methods such as focus groups can be used to mimic the sorts of processes that occur naturally in the marketplace.

A final key issue is that market researchers need to develop a deep understanding of the contexts in which subsistence individuals survive, buy, and consume products. While this is true of market research in any context, its importance is accentuated in these settings where market researchers often lack familiarity and personal connection with the individuals whose lives are being studied. Moreover, deep understanding of life circumstances may be a precursor to designing products that are likely to be used in varied contexts while being included in the restrictive set of products that subsistence individuals can afford to consider.

New Product Development

New product development is an aspect of marketing strategy that has received substantial attention in the literature (Wind and Mahajan 1997). The process involves formulating business and marketing strategy, understanding customer desires within targeted markets, and generating product concepts that meet those desires better than competitive products (Srinivasan, Lovejoy, and Beach 1997). In this section, we discuss the uniqueness of the subsistence context with respect to new product development, and suggest ways that marketers can respond.

From power cuts to water shortages, consumers in subsistence markets grapple with substantial unpredictability in their daily lives. When new products are developed for these markets, it thus makes sense to test them using procedures that can capture this variability in environmental conditions. Such an approach runs counter to the norm for product development processes in developed markets, which are typically designed to produce efficient solutions for specific usage scenarios. In subsistence markets, consumers must often demonstrate considerable ingenuity to cope with extreme resource constraints. In such instances, product development techniques that assume a narrow set of usage conditions can be an impediment to the successful development of new products. Understanding the various ways in which subsistence consumers might need to use the product can enable the marketer to avoid situations where an apparently value-added feature actually detracts from the overall utility of the product. Prahalad (2005) highlights the often hostile conditions under which products have to perform in subsistence markets, illustrating the point with examples such as salt that is iodized using an innovative process that ensures it is retained in food, rather than lost, during the cooking processes typically used by consumers in these environments.

The above discussion of unpredictability of usage context is merely a specific aspect of the more general and basic notion that product design in subsistence contexts must be driven by a deep understanding of consumer needs and the environment in which the product will be used—an understanding that is currently lacking when it comes to subsistence and poverty contexts. Indeed, genuine appreciation of the challenges faced by consumers in high-poverty, low-literacy environments is likely to be difficult for typical product development teams, which tend to be composed of highly specialized, relatively resource-rich individuals. This argues for a grounded approach in which every step of the product development process includes immersion in the field, and separation between engineering tests and market tests of a product may become blurred. Examples of such processes exist in high-technology industries—an environment in which uncertainty is also quite common—where cross-functional product development teams and lead user teams have been a hallmark of a number of product successes (Sethi, Smith, and Park 2001). There is reason to believe that similar systems might be effective in conceiving new product concepts for subsistence environments.[1] Product design should also take into consideration the need to conserve natural resources and the potential ecological impact of products, such as through use of recyclable materials, and through local manufacture of elements.

Considerable research has addressed the issue of boosting the creativity of product design processes and making ideation more effective. Analogical thinking merits special attention in this regard, since it appears to be a basic mechanism underlying tasks where people transfer information from familiar, existing categories and use it in the construction of new product ideas (Dahl and Moreau 2002). What may be needed for subsistence marketplaces is a similar approach, with inputs from nonprofit organizations, small vendors and retailers, and self-help group leaders. Finally, contrary to assumptions that only product functionality matters to subsistence consumers, our experience suggests that product aesthetics and visual aspects of product design play an important role as well. This suggests a similarity with developed market consumers in terms of the importance they have been found to attach to aesthetic considerations while evaluating new product designs (Veryzer and Hutchinson 1998).

Pricing Strategy

As the only marketing mix element that directly influences the inflow of resources rather than their outlay, pricing is among the most critical aspects of a firm's marketing strategy (Monroe 2002; Kotler 1999). For managers involved in setting and managing prices for products marketed to subsistence markets, several important implications arise from careful consideration of the nature of these markets.

Perhaps the most important of these is that the extreme resource constraints faced by subsistence consumers imply a very narrow range of acceptable price levels. Our observations suggest that, even if a consumer is inclined to consider quality when appraising product value, low income and low literacy can result in a feeling of futility when shopping—that is, the sense that a particular quality level is all one can expect for that price. However, even within these narrow price levels, subsistence consumers still seek out higher quality and are willing to pay higher prices to trade up. In this regard, Prahalad (2005) notes the need for quality products at affordable price levels (Dawar and Chattopadhyay 2002) to serve the needs of discerning subsistence customers. Although this may seem counterintuitive, it can be understood by recognizing the centrality of specific consumption events to subsistence consumers' daily life, the severe resource constraints they face, and the consequent consideration of a very narrow set of necessary products. For instance, since paying a slightly higher price often enables an individual to obtain better quality rice (a staple food in South India), the importance of what may be the only square meal of the day can prompt consumers to pay more for an upgraded product. Pricing managers should recognize that this tendency may exist across a variety of product categories, including expensive, high-technology products that have traditionally been seen as out of reach for subsistence consumers. For instance, an interesting consequence of the recent boom in the telecommunications industry in India is that rural fishermen and fisherwomen, even those that are extremely poor, have come to rely on mobile telephones. They use these devices while working at sea, in order to communicate estimated catch sizes and negotiate prices with fish buyers and wholesalers back on land. Such communication demands a high quality phone capable of supporting the fisherman's livelihood-generating activity; as a result, many are willing to pay more for better quality.

A second critical pricing consideration stems from what subsistence consumers account for when appraising a product's value. In the United States, consumers often consider saving of time and effort in the "give" component (what they give up) when considering a product's value (Zeithaml 1988). In contrast, the lack of monetary resources in subsistence markets makes it difficult for consumers in those environments to think beyond price. This is compounded by low literacy, and a tendency to struggle with abstractions. The result is that subsistence consumers tend to consider price as the sole determinant of the give component when determining good product value.

In light of the monetary and time constraints faced by subsistence consumers, the preceding discussion suggests that firms must carefully consider the value proposition of their offering when setting pricing strategies. For instance, by recognizing instances where quality is highly valued, even though consumers are able to afford only products within a very narrow price range, firms can create a win-win outcome by offering higher quality options and pricing them at an appropriate premium. On the other hand, subsistence consumers often focus heavily on monetary cost when assessing the give component of product value, while ignoring potential saving of time and effort. For example, they may go to great lengths to pay less for product purchases, even at great risk to their health, or seek to reduce family expenses by skimping on important medical services. However, time is a precious commodity for subsistence individuals for a variety of reasons, such as the need to constantly seek out livelihood opportunities or the need to purchase ingredients to cook a meal after receiving daily wages. Pricing strategies should account for these tendencies by incorporating them into pricing structure and carefully communicating the relationship between costs and benefits to consumers. Costs and benefits beyond the near term, or benefits that may outweigh costs, need to be communicated carefully. This should be done in a manner that is respectful of the value judgments of consumers, but also educational in encouraging the formation of new types of value judgments.

Marketing Communications

Individual characteristics of subsistence consumers also have important implications for marketing communications. Chief among these is the lack of informational resources that results from the economic resource constraints faced by these individuals. This is especially important for products that offer unique benefits, since it is critical that firms communicate their value proposition effectively. For example, Hindustan Lever Limited's (HLL) campaign to promote hand-washing has seen the company go to extraordinary lengths to explain the need for hand washing by encouraging consumers to visualize the problem of germs (Prahalad 2005). In this case, the "get" component was communicated in a manner that accommodated the distinctive cognitive style of subsistence consumers, notably concrete and pictographic thinking.

Market-level aspects of the 1-to-1 interactional marketplace are also extremely important when developing strategies for marketing communications. For one thing, the social nature of these environments suggests that subsistence consumers may be particularly receptive to the use of spokespersons or characters to personify the brand, because individuals who are accustomed to dealing with people rather than abstract information may process such information more readily. In addition, marketers are likely to draw substantial advantage from using cultural knowledge, such as popular folklore, since this provides a rich repository of shared meaning that the marketer can draw upon without needing to explain. Particularly germane here are marketing communications that can build on the heavy influence of word-of-mouth in a 1-to-1 interactional context. Such marketing communications include relying on peer-to-peer contact to spread information. Given the central role of social networks in the 1-to-1 marketplace, such techniques may be especially effective in subsistence settings. Rather than creating ads for mass communication, for instance, subsistence marketers may find it more effective to create branded content that can be circulated orally (such as jokes, jingles, or vernacular phrases).

As has been widely acknowledged, the effectiveness of word-of-mouth marketing depends heavily on the firm's ability to identify and influence the right people—that is, the opinion leaders or "market mavens" (Feick and Price 1987). To be able to exert such influence, a person—for example, the owner of a retail store or the leader of a self-help group—must possess both the respect of others and a sufficient number of social connections to allow the influence of his/her opinion to spread. Marketers who seek to partner with these individuals must thus be sufficiently embedded in the community that they are not only able to identify them, but build a sound and trusting reputation with them, emphasizing the importance of market research approaches discussed earlier.

In addition, the power of social networks in subsistence markets can be harnessed more directly via efforts to incorporate local individuals into the firm's sales network. The social relationships possessed by these individuals can facilitate trial and adoption of products as well as gathering high-quality consumer feedback that would be difficult to obtain through other means. A good example is HLL's distribution system in rural India—the Shakti program. By working with women in villages who function as resellers for their health and hygiene products and communicate with rural customers, the firm credibly communicates its value proposition. Although the main innovation of this strategy is at the level of distribution, it is also a highly effective communication vehicle. HLL has recognized this in a formal sense by creating two distinct roles within the Shakti program—Shakti Amma for the physical distribution of products and for one-to-one communication, and Shakti Vani for broader marketing communication. Key to the long-term effectiveness of such promotional systems is to safeguard the social capital that makes the local representative a partner in the first place. At the most basic level, this comes from ensuring that products are high quality and affordable, such that the individual's role as a vendor is seen to add value to her relationships, rather than detract from them. Relatedly, firms also need to reinforce the notion that it is indeed a partnership, rather than a conventional employer-employee relationship, by including subsistence consumers as genuine stakeholders when designing their marketing goals and strategies.

Perhaps most importantly, effective marketing communications in subsistence contexts requires "out-of-the-box" thinking. Rather than using one-size-fits-all top-down approaches, our findings emphasize the need for marketers to work from the ground up and look for ways to customize their approaches for what are invariably widely dispersed fragmented markets. For example, village fairs, advertisements on vehicles, and other locally suited media outlets are often extremely useful. Moreover, the nature of these communications must accommodate the constraints imposed by low literacy as well as the differences in local language across various subsistence markets. Marketing communications must also expand beyond informational to educational approaches, and take on the challenge of conveying product benefits to a low-literate audience.

Marketing Channels

In developed markets, the norm is to make products available to end-consumers by moving them through formal, centralized distribution channels. In subsistence markets, delivery to market is usually accomplished in a less formal manner, with small merchants obtaining their products from a diverse set of wholesalers, large retailers, and manufacturer representatives. This represents both a challenge for firms, as well as an opportunity to create value through innovation in go-to-market strategies. For example, as Prahalad (2005) points out, consumers in many subsistence contexts—urban and rural—are often forced to pay a large premium to local intermediaries for services such as money loans. This is the result of a system in which doing so is often the only way to obtain a particular product or service, and has the effect of putting intermediaries in a position of unusual power that can lead to unscrupulous practices. An interesting implication, according to Prahalad, is that firms adopting certain types of direct distribution models have an opportunity to alleviate this "poverty penalty." In India, for instance, ICICI bank now offers rural consumers direct access to financial services through microfinancing institutions and self-help groups, demonstrating this potential to innovate through marketing channels. In Bangladesh, too, one of the key ingredients of Nobel Prize-winning Grameen Bank's microcredit programs is the facilitation of direct access for subsistence consumers to credit and loans. ITC's *e-choupal* represents an approach where the supply chain has been streamlined to enable direct interaction between farmers and the company (Prahalad 2005).

Interestingly, the direct-distribution model that this implies does not always need to be specifically designed to overcome the predicament caused by intermediaries. In many instances, the 1-to-1 interactional marketplace discussed earlier creates an environment where small, local retailers or service providers enjoy the trust and patronage of local customers. In these instances, a direct-distribution model can benefit significantly by securing the cooperation of local individuals rather than bypassing them. As illustrated with the HLL example, individuals from specific communities can work as resellers, giving the company access to previously neglected markets. This is also evident in the distribution of cellular phone services through local entrepreneurial women, a phenomenon increasingly employed by firms in subsistence markets around the world (e.g., Grameen Telecom in Bangladesh, Roshan in Afghanistan). As with marketing communications, approaches to distribution need to incorporate a willingness to work from the ground up (Dawar and Chattopadhyay 2002) and customize approaches, rather than adopt a one-size-fits-all approach.

As noted earlier, one of the key characteristics of the 1-to-1 interactional marketplace is the willingness of vendors to extend credit and adjust terms of trade when consumers find themselves in times of need—two practices that create a form of customer lock-in that is not easily disregarded. In similar fashion, retailers form relationships with suppliers, creating mutual obligations that influence the future actions of both parties. This can be built upon by firms operating in such markets. By adopting pricing and distribution practices that make it easier for retailers to extend credit, adjust prices, and vary product offerings to accommodate the changing circumstances of their customers, manufacturers are likely to be more successful themselves. Part of the solution lies in offering products whose final stage of manufacture occurs at the retail level, allowing customization of products. Local production also has potential advantages in terms of improving livelihood opportunities, lowering transportation costs, and potentially lessening negative impact on the environment.

Another way that firms can align their distribution systems to the needs of subsistence markets is through the use of information and communication technologies (ICTs) that leverage the strengths of the 1-to-1 interactional marketplace. A good example is the Inter-City Marketing Network, an initiative of the Chennai-based Foundation of Occupational Development (FOOD). This program provided mobile phones to some 100 community-based women's organizations as a means of encouraging the creation of social networks between artisans/ skilled workers and individuals who could provide sales and promotion for their products in neighboring markets. While created to encourage the small-scale manufacture and marketing of locally manufactured products, the program is a good example of a system that helps subsistence communities identify and respond to commercial opportunities, using their social relations as a productive asset. Similar approaches could be used for a broad range of products and services.

Marketing Structure

As we have suggested throughout this chapter, a critical difference between developed and subsistence markets is the extent to which 1-to-1 interactions and interpersonal relationships play a role in facilitating economic exchange. This suggests that marketing activities in a firm must be organized in a manner that is mindful of the relational aspect of subsistence markets. One possible solution is to decentralize and externalize a firm's marketing activity in order to utilize social capital available in subsistence markets. Decentralized marketing entails shifting responsibility and power to boundary-spanning employees who are close to the customers and can thus respond more nimbly to their needs and feedback. This is critical in subsistence markets, where social capital endows local individuals with superior access to knowledge about customer needs, preferences, and ability to pay. Externalized marketing goes one step further, and sees the formation of marketing partnerships with local entities that are external to the firm—empowering these local partners to make marketing decisions independently on the firm's behalf. This "external" locus of marketing activity is critical from a social capital perspective because the rich social capital that facilitates effective marketing exchanges in subsistence markets is often available only within a specific "radius of trust" (Fukuyama 2001)—that is, among a given community's members who know each other and are somewhat interdependent. In fact, a firm's attempts to internalize this asset by hiring community individuals as employees would likely fail because it would undermine the social credibility of the individual in his/her community, thereby nullifying the benefits of the social capital.

Decentralizing and externalizing marketing activities in subsistence contexts holds the promise of several benefits for firms. First, it systematically increases the firm's access to detailed and nuanced knowledge about the customers and communities it aims to serve. Such market knowledge allows firms to be highly responsive to subsistence market needs, and helps them to offer tailored products and services. Externalization, in particular, makes the marketing system highly flexible and adaptable to changing local market conditions. Second, when these principles are pursued at a basic level, such that even the design and manufacture of products and services is decentralized and externalized, local marketing partners benefit from engaging in these value-adding activities and profit from them. This new stream of income creates wealth in the community, which in turn makes it more attractive as a market for the firm.

A final benefit of decentralizing and externalizing the marketing organization is that it facilitates a symbiotic relationship between the firm and subsistence consumers. This stands in stark contrast to the unidirectional or independent relationships prevalent in traditional markets. This symbiotic potential can be most clearly seen in the forms of social capital that each party contributes to the marketing relationship. Close-knit subsistence communities can provide firms with access to a unique network of trusted relationships formed as a result of dense, strong links between people within the community—bonding social capital (Iyer, Kitson, and Toh 2005). In turn, firms can bring to bear their significant skills of coordination and communication to facilitate relationships between disparate communities—bridging social capital. The form of social capital contributed by each entity is important to the other. For example, while strong bonds within a group are valuable from the firm's perspective—for successful product diffusion within the community, for instance—they may actually hinder the ability of group members to trust and work effectively with members of other groups (Fukuyama 2001). Seen from a macro level, this has been argued to hinder economic growth (Olson 1982). However, firms with experience interacting with several disparate local communities can facilitate sharing of information and technology across communities, enable the flow of new ideas for innovation, and even reduce conflict between communities. All of this can contribute to economic growth by encouraging the formation of business relationships that cross normal social and community boundaries.

Marketing Culture

The importance of a firm's marketing culture to its business performance has been well-documented (e.g., Deshpande and Webster 1989). Marketing culture refers to the unwritten policies and guidelines that provide employees with behavioral norms, and more generally to the manner in which marketing activities are executed (Webster 1995).

As a starting point, we discuss marketing culture at a broad level by considering it in terms of how subsistence contexts are viewed by marketing managers. Regarding such contexts as mere variations on traditional markets can easily lead to certain counterproductive tendencies, such as believing that solutions for such markets can and should be found by the firm or "exported" from non-subsistence contexts. A better approach is to treat subsistence environments not just as markets, but as individuals and communities from which to learn. To conduct effective market research and design successful products, firms need to embrace this perspective and learn lessons that may be applicable even in non-subsistence environments. Indeed, marketers who are amenable to this learning perspective can facilitate the process of transferring knowledge of innovative practices back to non-subsistence contexts—a process labeled "innovation blowback" in the international business literature (Hagel and Brown 2005). The Villageherbs brand of herbal remedies and products offers a case in point. Launched by Gram Mooligai, an entrepreneurial venture in South India, this line of products was developed using the traditional medicine and knowledge of rural subsistence communities, and is now being successfully marketed to urban, nonsubsistence markets as well.

There is also considerable innovation in subsistence markets, at both the entrepreneurial and consumer level, related to a basic need to survive. Such insights arising from "doing more with less" arise from ingenuity in surviving under extreme resource constraints, using available products in innovative ways that cannot be easily anticipated by market researchers not exposed to life in these conditions.

Well-intentioned efforts to conduct research and create solutions for subsistence contexts can also be hindered by subtle assumptions of "knowing what the poor need." An example is the dominant logic of product functionality mentioned earlier, which can obscure the reality that subsistence consumers may value very different features from those imagined by outsiders—product aesthetics, for example. It is instructive to note, for instance, that some of the world's finest art, handicrafts, and ornamentation are made by individuals living in subsistence conditions—a testament to their traditionally honed skills and appreciation of aesthetics. An approach that is open to learning from buyers and sellers in subsistence can lead to many advantages including opportunities to co-create successful product designs.

Whether one examines these issues from the perspective of an educator, researcher, or practitioner, it is important to approach them with an open mind and a clean slate. Preconceived notions that there is "nothing new here" or that subsistence markets are merely a special case of things already understood are particularly unproductive, especially in light of the failure of past efforts to successfully engage subsistence markets. If anything, the opposite mind-frame is preferable, with a healthy dose of skepticism about what is new following data analysis, rather than data collection. It is difficult for literate researchers and practitioners to recall the experience of being low-literate. It is similarly challenging, and perhaps impossible, to imagine what extreme poverty and living near subsistence mean for relatively resource-rich individuals.

What all this calls for is recognition that these extreme conditions may well challenge conventional notions of theory and practice. For example, when we asked a woman in rural India if she planned her purchases and decided how to spend her income, she replied, "Why should I plan?" "Why should I plan when I don't know where my next source of income is coming from?" What at first seemed like an irrational attitude toward financial management became eminently sensible when viewed from the perspective of an individual whose life must be lived moment to moment. Examples of such "rational irrationality" abound in subsistence contexts. For instance, even when consumers have enough money to buy wholesale and stock up at prices much lower than retail, many do not do so. Explanations exist, but make sense only when understood in the context of the life of the subsistence consumer. For one thing, buying in retail quantities preserves the household's money, and thus its flexibility, since one all-important option during a crisis is to forgo consumption. For another, consumers see advantages to buying from their usual retail store, even if prices are higher, because this builds goodwill with an individual who can offer them credit during the next crisis. We asked one woman who patronized a retail store whether she checks prices. She said no, and suggested that we consider how the retail owner would feel if she were to do so, after all the credit he has provided in times of need.

Conclusion

Alleviating poverty is one of the great challenges of our time, for reasons that range from the ethical to the practical. It has long been suggested that business has a role to play in this regard, and that individuals living in poverty may even constitute an opportunity of profit for firms that possess the ingenuity and resolve to serve them as consumers. To date, the challenge has been one of finding ways to transform this potential into practical reality. In this chapter, we have strived to take an important step in this process by presenting key insights into the nature of subsistence marketplaces, and using this as a basis for innovative approaches in marketing strategy, marketing structure, and marketing culture. Using unique market-level and individual characteristics in subsistence contexts, our discussion covers issues in market research, new product development, and other marketing mix elements, as well as broader issues relating to marketing structure and marketing culture. Our findings emphasize the need to view individuals living in subsistence marketplaces as both producers and consumers and using an understanding of buyer and seller behavior to design appropriate marketing strategies. Due to space constraints, we briefly mentioned but did not elaborate on issues of sustainability in terms of conserving natural resources and minimizing negative impact on the environment. However the ecological impact of elements of marketing such as product design, distribution and disposal, and the need to conserve natural resources needs to be front and center as well, in marketing for subsistence marketplaces.

We believe that the approaches proposed here, grounded as they are in subsistence marketplace research experience, provide a promising starting point for firms seeking to meaningfully engage these markets to create both business and social value. By adopting a mindset that strives to attain a deep understanding of these environments, and using this as a basis for practical marketing innovation, we believe that firms can make significant progress in improving both the efficiency and the effectiveness of their business practices, allowing them to realize meaningful improvements in their performance and in general.

Note

1. In a sense, the inherent uncertainty and unpredictability of subsistence settings poses a similar product development challenge as that posed by the market turbulence that characterizes high-technology environments in developed markets. As such, useful parallels can be drawn between the two contexts even though the nature and root cause of the uncertainty is fundamentally different—arising from a lack of stable infrastructure in the former case, and rapidly evolving products and needs in the latter.

References

Dahl, Darren W. and Page Moreau. 2002. The Influence and Value of Analogical Thinking During New Product Ideation. *Journal of Marketing Research* 39: 47–60.

Dawar, N. and A. Chattopadhyay. 2002. Rethinking Marketing Programs for Emerging Markets. *Long Range Planning* 35(5): 457–474.

Day, George S., Barton A. Weitz, and Robin C. Wensley. 1990. *The Interface of Marketing and Strategy.* Greenwich, CT: JAI Press.

Deshpande, Rohit and Frederick E. Webster, Jr. 1989. Organizational Culture and Marketing: Defining the Research Agenda. *Journal of Marketing* 53(1): 3–15.

Feick, Lawrence F. and Linda L. Price. 1987. The Market Maven: A Diffuser of Marketplace Information. *Journal of Marketing* 51(1): 83–97.

Frenzen, Jonathan K. and Harry L. Davis. 1990. Purchasing Behavior in Embedded Markets. *Journal of Consumer Research* 17(1): 1–12.

Fukuyama, Francis. 2001. Social Capital, Civil Society and Development. *Third World Quarterly* 22(1): 7–20.

Hagel, John III and John Seely Brown. 2005. Productive Friction: How Difficult Business Partnerships Can Accelerate Innovation. *Harvard Business Review* 83(2), February: 82–91.

Iyer, Sriya, Michael Kitson, and Bernard Toh. 2005. Social Capital, Economic Growth and Regional Development. *Regional Studies* 39, November: 1015–1040.

Kotler, Philip.1999. *Kotler on Marketing: How to Create, Win, and Dominate Markets.* New York: Free Press.

London, Ted and Stuart L. Hart. 2004. Reinventing Strategies for Emerging Markets: Beyond the Transnational Model. *Journal of International Business Studies* 35(5): 350–370.

Malhotra, Naresh K. 2001. Cross-Cultural Marketing Research in the Twenty-First Century. *International Marketing Review* 18(3): 230–234.

Monroe, Kent B. 2002. *Pricing: Making Profitable Decisions.* New York: McGraw Hill.

Olson, Mancur. 1982. *The Rise and Decline of Nations.* New Haven: Yale University Press.

Portes, Alejandro. 1998. Social Capital: Its Origins and Applications in Modern Sociology. *Annual Review of Sociology* 24(1): 1–24.

Prahalad, C.K. 2005. *The Fortune at the Bottom of the Pyramid: Eradicating Poverty through Profits.* Upper Saddle River, NJ: Wharton School Publishing.

Ritchie, Robin and Srinivas Sridharan. 2007. Marketing in Subsistence Markets: Innovation through Decentralization and Externalization. In *Product and Market Development for Subsistence Marketplaces: Consumption and Entrepreneurship beyond Literacy and Resource Barriers,* ed. José Rosa and Madhu Viswanathan, 195–214. Advances in International Management, 20. Amsterdam: JAI Press.

Robert W. Veryzer, Jr. and J. Wesley Hutchinson. 1998. The Influence of Unity and Prototypicality on Aesthetic Responses to New Product Designs. *Journal of Consumer Research* 24(4): 374–394.

Sethi, Rajesh, Daniel C. Smith, and C. Whan Park. 2001. Cross Functional Product Development Teams, Creativity, and the Innovativeness of New Consumer Products. *Journal of Marketing Research* 38, February: 73–85.

Srinivasan V., William S. Lovejoy, and David Beach. 1997. Integrated Product Design for Marketability and Manufacturing *Journal of Marketing Research* 36, February: 154–163.

Viswanathan, Madhubalan. 2007. Understanding Product and Market Interactions in Subsistence Marketplaces: A Study in South India. In *Product and Market Development for Subsistence Marketplaces*, ed. Rosa and Viswanathan, 21–57.

Viswanathan, Madhubalan, S. Gajendiran, and R. Venkatesan. 2008. *Enabling Consumer and Entrepreneurial Literacy in Subsistence Marketplaces: A Research-Based Approach to Educational Programs.* New York: Springer.

Viswanathan, Madhubalan and José Antonio Rosa. 2007. Product and Market Development for Subsistence Marketplaces: Consumption and Entrepreneurship Beyond Literacy and Resource Barriers. In *Product and Market Development for Subsistence Marketplaces*, ed. Rosa and Viswanathan, 1–17.

Viswanathan, Madhubalan, José Antonio Rosa, and James Harris. 2005. Decision-Making and Coping by Functionally Illiterate Consumers and Some Implications for Marketing Management. *Journal of Marketing* 69(1): 15–31.

Webster, Cynthia. 1995. Marketing Culture and Marketing Effectiveness in Service Firms. *Journal of Services Marketing* 9(2): 6–21.

Wind, Jerry and Vijay Mahajan. 1997. Issues and Opportunities in New Product Development: An Introduction to the Special Issue. *Journal of Marketing Research* 34(1): 1–12.

Zeithaml, Valarie A. 1988. Consumer Perceptions of Price, Quality, and Value: A Means-End Model and Synthesis of Evidence. *Journal of Marketing* 52(3): 2–22.

List of Contributors

Alam Aguilar-Platas is a Mexican student at HEC Montreal who is part of a bursary program for advancing education between the government of Canada and the Mexican Secretary of Exterior Relations in Mexico. In 2001, he participated in a research with the Miami North-South Center/ITESM collaborative project called: "The Impact of Free Trade on Small Size Business: The Case of Nafta in Mexico." From 2003 to 2005, he worked as a commercial advisor for Bridgestone Mexico. Today he is writing his Master in Science Administration thesis on Social Entrepreneurship.

Wolfgang Amann is a faculty member at the University of St.Gallen, Switzerland, and Executive Director of the MBA program. After earning his PhD in St.Gallen, he taught at Henley Management College in Henley/UK and IMD in Lausanne/Switzerland. He also held visiting academic positions at the Wharton School of the University of Pennsylvania, the Indian Institute of Management (IIM) in Bangalore, and Hosei University in Tokyo/Japan. Wolfgang's primary expertise relate to successful internationalization and sustainability strategies. For more than a decade he was a consultant to a number of leading multinationals on a variety of issues.

Alain Berranger is an Executive-in-residence at Schulich School of Business at York University, Toronto, Ontario, Canada. His career has been invested in international development as a private sector executive and a consultant for international development agencies. He was Honorary Consul for Sao Tome and Principe in Canada from 1985 to 2000. He has worked in 31 different African countries, as well led numerous missions to Asia and Latin America. From 1996 to 2006, Mr. Berranger was Director, Partnerships and Business Development for the International Development Research Centre (IDRC). He is listed in Who's Who in Canada since 2000. He now acts as a Senior Advisor to the Global Knowledge Partnership, the Micronutrient Initiative and is a Consultant to the UNDP for the evaluation of Equator Ventures.

Albert Bruno is the William T. Cleary Professor at Santa Clara University and cofounder of the Global Social Benefit Incubator

(GSBI), where he currently serves as academic dean of GSBI. He earned an MBA and PhD at Purdue University. He has an international reputation as a consultant and seminar leader and has lectured and consulted for a variety of U.S. and international organizations. He has published over 50 research articles and book chapters. His book, *The Market Value Process: Bridging Customer and Shareholder Value*, was published in 1996. At Santa Clara, he currently teaches New Venture Creation and Financially Effective Marketing Strategies.

Lisa Jones Christensen is currently an Assistant Professor of Entrepreneurship at the Kenan-Flagler Business School at the University of North Carolina at Chapel Hill. Her teaching includes core courses in the MBA curriculum entitled "Sustainable Development" as well as an elective course entitled "Innovation and Entrepreneurship in Developing Economies." Lisa earned her undergraduate degree from the University of California at Berkeley; and her MBA and an MA degree in International Development from Brigham Young University. She earned a PhD in Organizational Behavior from the University of North Carolina at Chapel Hill. Lisa's research focuses on sustainable enterprise, commitment to change, and on the relationship between microfinance and sustainable business. She has consulted with various Fortune 500 companies on their strategies for emerging markets, and has worked with the microfinance organization FINCA doing postdisaster microcredit training and capacity-building in Honduras.

Mine Eder received her PhD at the University of Virginia. She now works at the Department of Political Science and International Relations, Bogazici University, Turkey where she teaches courses on political economy of development, political economy of Turkey, along with international relations theory and IPE. She is the coauthor of a book entitled *Political Economy of Regional Cooperation in the Middle East* (Routledge, 1998) and has written extensively on various aspects of Turkey's political economy.

Patrick Guerra is cofounder of the Global Social Benefit Incubator, and Executive Entrepreneur-in-residence, at the Center for Science, Technology, and Society at Santa Clara University. He has served in senior management, information technology, manufacturing, distribution, product management, and business development roles with Hewlett-Packard, Advanced Micro Devices, PSB, Ariba, and

SpinCircuit, where he was president and CEO. Pat holds a Bachelor of Science Degree in Economics and an MBA in Operations Management and Information Systems from Santa Clara University.

Laura P. Hartman is Associate Vice President for Academic Affairs and Professor of Business Ethics at DePaul University and as Research Director of DePaul's Institute for Business and Professional Ethics. Also invited professor at INSEAD (France), HEC (France), the Université Paul Cezanne Aix Marseille III, and the Grenoble Graduate School of Business, among other European universities.

Jan Hack Katz is a PhD from the Massachusetts Institute of Technology and is a Senior Lecturer of International Marketing and Management at Cornell's School of Hotel Administration. In addition to her work in the United States, Jan Katz has taught international marketing at Universidad de los Andes (Colombia), ESAN (Peru), and also to managers in Argentina. She has written and presented papers in the areas of international corporate strategy and international organizational behavior.

Scott Kelley is currently a Visiting Assistant Professor teaching business ethics in the Religious Studies department at DePaul University. He finished a PhD in Theological Ethics from Loyola University Chicago in 2005. Prior to that, he taught English in Tokyo, Japan and was a volunteer in Pohnpei, Micronesia with Jesuit Volunteers International.

Shiban Khan leads the research initiative on "Access to Medicines in India" at IMD, Switzerland. She is completing her PhD in the University of St. Gallen. Her dissertation topic is corporate social responsibility in India. In addition, she is an expert on integrating sustainability in higher education and has previously been the Executive Director of Oikos International.

Shelby McIntyre is a Professor of Marketing at Santa Clara University and a fellow at the university's Center for Science, Technology, and Society. He is also a collaborator in the Global Social Benefit Incubator at Santa Clara. He has focused for many years on the retail sector and retailing practices and takes a particular interest in the marketing, distribution, and retailing needs of social mission ventures. He recently attended the 2006 summer conference at the University of Chicago on "Product and Market Development for Subsistence Markets." Professor McIntyre holds an engineering degree from

Stanford University, an MBA from Stanford's Graduate School of Business, and a PhD in Marketing from Stanford.

Özlem Öz received her PhD at the London School of Economics and Political Science (LSE). She now works at the Department of Management, Bogazici University, Turkey, where she teaches courses on strategy, organization theory, international business, and Turkish business environment. She is the author of several articles and the books titled *The Competitive Advantage of Nations: The Case of Turkey* (Ashgate, 1999) and *Clusters and Competitive Advantage: The Turkish Experience* (Palgrave MacMillan, 2004). Her research interests include the locational attributes of competitiveness, strategic planning in not-for-profit organizations and local economic development.

Emmanuel Raufflet is Associate Professor of Management at HEC (Hautes Études Commerciales) Montreal, Quebec, Canada. His research concerns the changing relations between organizations and their social and natural environment. He has conducted research on forest management in Mexico (Las paradojas del manejo forestal: el caso de Tlalmanalco, Plaza y Valdes-UAM Editores: Mexico, 2005). A French and Canadian national, he has lived in Spain, Brazil, and Mexico. He received the NACRA Emerson Award for Best Case in Business Ethics in 2005, the Best Case Award at the Fifth Dark Side of Business Case Competition in 2006, and the Prix de Pédagogie for assistant professor at HEC Montréal in 2006. Raufflet also coedited International Business and the Dilemmas of Development (Palgrave-MacMillan 2004).

Robin Ritchie is Assistant Professor of Marketing at the Richard Ivey School of Business. He earned a BA in Political Science at the University of Calgary, along with an MSc in International Business and a PhD in Marketing from the University of British Columbia. His research examines consumer suspicion of marketers and its influence on interpretation of advertising claims. He also studies the role of trust in consumer behavior, the effects of advertising executional cues on consumer information processing, and the nature of competition in the nonprofit sector. His current research examines marketing approaches to subsistence markets.

James L. Ritchie-Dunham, PhD, is chief strategist of the Institute for Strategic Clarity, associate of the Psychology Department at Harvard University, and managing partner of Growing Edge Partners. His work within and across business, civil society, and government sectors, as a researcher, consultant, and board member, bridges the rigorous characterization of social systems and the rigorous character-ization of the individual and collective intentional mental models of those social systems, creating greater individual and collective strate-gic clarity. He was previously a visiting scholar in Organizational Studies at MIT, a professor of systems sciences at the ITAM, and an engineer at Conoco. His PhD is in the Decision Sciences from UT Austin.

Srinivas Sridharan is an Assistant Professor of Marketing at the Richard Ivey School of Business. He has a PhD in Marketing from the Kelley School of Business, Indiana University, USA. Prior to entering the academic field in business management, Professor Sridharan worked as an engineer in India. He has a BE (Honors) in Mechanical Engineering and an MSc (Honors) in Physics from Birla Institute of Technology and Science, Pilani, India. His research explores the "internally oriented" activities of sales forces, that is, those directed toward the organization. His other research interests include multi-level theorizing and modeling of organizational phenomena; and exploring the role of marketing in alleviating poverty through the study of marketing approaches in subsistence markets.

Charles Wankel is Associate Professor of Management at St. John's University, New York. He received his doctorate from New York University. Dr. Wankel has authored and edited many books including the best-selling *Management*, 3rd ed. (Prentice-Hall, 1986), *Rethinking Management Education for the 21st Century* (IAP, 2002), *Educating Managers with Tomorrow's Technologies* (IAP, 2003), *the Cutting-Edge of International Management Education* (IAP, 2004), *Educating Managers through Real World Projects* (IAP, 2005), *New Visions of Graduate Management Education* (IAP, 2006), and the forthcoming *University and Corporate Innovations in Life-Long Learning* (IAP, 2007), *Handbook of 21st Century Management* (SAGE, 2008), and *Being and Becoming a Management Education Scholar* (IAP, 2008). He is the leading founder and director of scholarly virtual communities for management professors, currently directing eight with thousands of participants in more than seventy nations. He has taught in Lithuania at the Kaunas University of Technology (Fulbright Fellowship) and the University of Vilnius, (United Nations Development Program and Soros Foundation funding). Invited lectures include 2005 Distinguished Speaker at the E-ducation without Border Conference, Abu Dhabi and 2004 Keynote speaker at the Nippon Academy of Management, Tokyo. Corporate management development program development clients include McDonald's Corporation's Hamburger University and

IBM Learning Services. Pro bono consulting assignments include reengineering and total quality management programs for the Lithuanian National Postal Service. Email: wankelc@stjohns.edu

Madhu Viswanathan is Associate Professor of Marketing at the University of Illinois, Urbana-Champaign, where he has been on the faculty since receiving a PhD in Business Administration from the University of Minnesota in 1990 and a BTech in Mechanical Engineering from the Indian Institute of Technology, Madras. He focuses on two programs of research; measurement and research methodology, and literacy, poverty, and marketplace behaviors. His work in measurement includes a book entitled *Measurement Error and Research Design* (Sage, 2005). His research on literacy, poverty, and marketplace behaviors examines low-literate consumer behavior in the United States and low-literate buyer and seller behavior in subsistence marketplaces. Publications stemming from this research include a forthcoming book, *Enabling Consumer and Entrepreneurial Literacy in Subsistence Marketplaces: Research-Based Education Across Literacy and Resource Barriers* (Springer, 2008). His research on literacy, poverty, and marketplace behaviors is applied through the Marketplace Literacy Project (www.marketplaceliteracy.org). This organization has developed and conducts entrepreneurial and consumer literacy training programs for low-literate, low-income adults in India with plans to expand to other developing contexts as well as an e-educational platform.

Patricia H. Werhane is the Wicklander Chair of Business Ethics in the Philosophy Department and director of the Institute for Business and Professional Ethics at DePaul University with joint appointment as the Peter and Adeline Ruffin Professor of Business Ethics and Senior Fellow at of the Olsson Center for Applied Ethics in the Darden School at the University of Virginia.

Nilay M.Yajnik, PhD, has worked for several years in the IT Industry across functions such as Learning Services and Program Management. He has also been teaching for several years at the NMIMS University in Mumbai, India, where he is currently Professor of Information Systems. His research and teaching interests include the Digital Divide, Information Systems and issues in the ICT Industry. He is on the Executive Boards of several IT and Management forums of India.

Index

Breinigsville, PA USA
08 March 2010
233764BV00001B/2/P

9 780230 104044